"O ma Carmen"

"O ma Carmen"

Bizet's Fateful Gypsy in Portrayals from 1875 to the Present

VICTORIA ETNIER VILLAMIL

McFarland & Company, Inc., Publishers
Jefferson, North Carolina

LIBRARY OF CONGRESS CATALOGUING-IN-PUBLICATION DATA

Names: Villamil, Victoria Etnier, author.
Title: O ma Carmen : Bizet's fateful gypsy in portrayals from 1875 to the present / Victoria Etnier Villamil.
Description: Jefferson, North Carolina : McFarland & Company, 2017 | Includes bibliographical references and index.
Identifiers: LCCN 2017020793 | ISBN 9781476663241 (softcover : acid free paper) ∞
Subjects: LCSH: Bizet, Georges, 1838–1875. Carmen. | Romanies in opera.
Classification: LCC ML410.B62 V57 2017 | DDC 782.1—dc23
LC record available at https://lccn.loc.gov/2017020793

BRITISH LIBRARY CATALOGUING DATA ARE AVAILABLE

ISBN (print) 978-1-4766-6324-1
ISBN (ebook) 978-1-4766-2924-7

© 2017 Victoria Etnier Villamil. All rights reserved

No part of this book may be reproduced or transmitted in any form or by any means, electronic or mechanical, including photocopying or recording, or by any information storage and retrieval system, without permission in writing from the publisher.

Front cover: promotional photograph of Emma Calvé as Carmen

Printed in the United States of America

McFarland & Company, Inc., Publishers
  Box 611, Jefferson, North Carolina 28640
    www.mcfarlandpub.com

For Chafo

Table of Contents

Acknowledgments	ix
Introduction	1
1. "What Is It?"	9
2. Breaking Away	21
3. North, South, East, West	31
4. Home Again	41
5. Emma Calvé and the New Realism	56
6. More Than the Singing	66
7. Farrar, Film and Psychology	78
8. In the Time of Dictators	87
9. American Idyll	102
10. Sea Change	116
11. 100 and Counting	133
12. Game Change	148
Appendix A. Alphabetical Listing of Singers Mentioned in the Text	165
Appendix B. Chronology of Premieres and Significant Performances	172
Appendix C. Discography	177

Appendix D. Videography	185
Chapter Notes	188
Bibliography	201
Index	209

Acknowledgments

Though authors tend to take the Internet for granted now, I cannot proceed with these acknowledgments without first and foremost recognizing its importance to this project. To be able to access libraries, archives, newspapers and periodicals; to be able to obtain countless hard-to-find recordings and photographs; to be able to find, query, and correspond with so many individuals with knowledge of my subject, all from my home, has, quite simply, made it possible.

That said, however, I want to thank the following for their invaluable contributions: Csilla Petho who so thoroughly, expertly, and indefatigably unearthed masses of clippings for me from Parisian sources on decades of Carmens who performed the role in that city; Michael Lorenz who did similar research on *Carmen's* early years in Vienna; Joseph Stremlin and Houston Maples who provided the materials on Obukhova and Maksakova, respectively; and Karen V. Kukil, reference archivist of the Sophia Smith collection which houses the de Lussan archives for the papers she provided regarding Zélie de Lussan's performance for Queen Victoria.

Thanks too to my translators: Alison Jourdet (French), H. George Christ (German), Ella Barova (Russian), and Winnifred Hallwachs, who did yeoman work in translating from Swedish the story of Olfine Moe and the first performance of *Carmen* in Sweden.

And to the readers of my manuscript, thank you for the advice, comments, criticisms, and corrections as well as for the encouragement with which you always backed them up. That the buck stops on my desk, and that I alone am responsible for any mistake of fact, goes without saying. But they include Sybil Baldwin, Elizabeth and Clinton Elliot, John Guarnaccia, Rose Hirschorn, Joseph Norris, and notably Joe Pearce, whose encyclopedic brain and spirited but always meticulous reading saved me from countless errors. As to Harold Bruder, my gratitude knows no bounds. He not only read everything, much of it more than once, and gave me his full support, but his extensive knowledge of the subject, discerning eye, quiet wisdom, and solid good sense were as lifelines throughout the project's many twists and turns.

Many thanks to my son Andres Villamil, who was so patient in helping with permissions, photographs, and all sorts of technical computer matters; to Michael and Janine Zaikowski for preparing the photographs; and to Ellen Brennan for her invaluable work on the index.

And finally to my husband, to whom I dedicate this book. It is true that, as I tell in my Preface, when early in my singing career I was cast as Carmen, he, a Latin, questioned how I, a reserved New Englander, could possibly know how to portray a tempestuous Spanish Gypsy. But lest that anecdote give the wrong impression, I add here the caveat that it was a one of a kind event in our long marriage, for, with that one exception—and he did come around—my husband has supported me in every endeavor from my singing career to my writing. My mother liked to say that it's a matter of luck whom you marry, to which I say I was really lucky.

Introduction

"As an artist, Carmen challenged everything I had. What can I say? She possessed me."—Risë Stevens[1]

I sang Carmen once. My Latin husband called it serious miscasting; how, after all, could I, a rather reserved Yankee from the state of Maine, possibly know how to portray a tempestuous Spanish Gypsy? But not unlike the spitfire herself cautioning, "When someone defies me to do a thing, it is soon done,"[2] I had taken up his gauntlet, accepted the engagement, and set to work. I studied flamenco and the castanets; I analyzed every word, every dynamic marking, every dotted sixteenth; I took copious notes; and I read and reread the Mérimée story from which the opera was adapted, hoping (against hope, as I would learn) to uncover the elusive one's secret and thereby *my* Carmen. Because, as Geraldine Farrar, one of the greats in the role—and, I might add, herself a New Englander—once explained it: "Each one of us probably sees something that the others have not seen—or thinks she does—and that 'something' is *her individual Carmen*.... Carmen has, seemingly, as many variants as there are stage folk ready to express their varying ideas of her."[3]

It is then these "variants" as filtered through and expressed by the "stage folk" of different nationalities and different times that make up the chapters in this life of an operatic portrayal. It is about how their portrayals evolved and changed—musically, stylistically, vocally, dramatically, and, above all, interpretively—from generation to generation and country to country; it is about how historic events, cultural drifts and societal upheavals as well as changing vocal styles and performance practices impacted their portrayals; and ultimately, it is about the individual singers themselves: their personalities, temperaments, physical and vocal makeups, minds and sensibilities, and, always, their personal connection with the inscrutable Gypsy. For be she libertine or libertarian, gamine or siren, *femme fatale* or *bon vivant*, fatalist or nihilist, extrovert or introvert, victim or victimizer, heroine or anti-heroine, Carmen is from everywhere and from nowhere, from all time and from no time. And there's the rub: "She is an anthology of womankind no one interpreter can ever define or exhaust."[4] And if "the psychology of *Carmen* is the psychology of Life," as the Gypsy's literary creator Prosper Mérimée purportedly said, "then every 'expression' of his variable heroine will be a new expression of Life. So why should the procession of Carmens ever end?"[5]

* * *

Readers will inevitably—and understandably—complain that I have neglected one or other of their favorites. To be sure, I hated leaving anyone out, especially as part of the fun for me was making discoveries, both of the singers I knew nothing about and those best described as "anomalies." Who would have thought, for instance, that Kiri Te Kanawa and Beverly Sills actually performed Carmen (and I don't mean Micaëla, though they did that too); that Renata Scotto pondered a try; that Marian Anderson declined an offer; that Kathleen Ferrier sang the role in concert then vowed never again; and that Ewa Podles, Stephanie Blythe, Alice Coote, Diane Soviero, Susan Graham, Rose Bampton, Marjorie Lawrence, Maria Cebotari, Anja Silja, Lillian Nordica, Adelina Patti, Ernestine Schumann-Heink and Lorraine Hunt-Lieberson all gave her a try. And then, of course, there is everyone's dream Carmen: like Cecilia Bartoli, a popular choice for today; Teresa Stratas, my choice, who Risë Stevens has said was hers as well[6]; or Pauline Viardot, who, had the opera been written earlier, Saint-Saëns believed might have bested even Célestine Galli-Marié, the role's creator.[7]

But parameters had to be established since an all-inclusive approach would not only have been impossible but could only have ended in a laundry list of Carmens, thereby destroying the narrative and, with it, the book's intention. Therefore, the singers who make up these chapters—drawn from a list that began with approximately 200 but expanded virtually every month with reports of new ones—are either those whose portrayals are of historical significance; those whose celebrity and stature in the role could not be overlooked; those who brought something unique to it; or those whose portrayals best represent their time and place.

The book, however, does not consider in any depth either the careers or the lives of these singers other than where they might apply to the story. Neither does the book attempt to analyze Carmen as a cultural icon, nor consider the role as featured in any of the other genres from ballet to Hip Hopera; nor does it discuss the opera per se, nor even give a synopsis of its plot. All this has been done many times over and can be readily accessed.

* * *

But how best to learn about their portrayals? Though first generation Carmens preceded the invention of recording, the period produced a vast amount of important, well-considered, sometimes lengthy critical writing on which to draw. Indeed, *Carmen* expert Lesley Wright has assembled around 100 reviews of the premiere alone while, in addition to reviews, accounts abound in contemporary memoirs and autobiographies. What is more, photography having been invented just in time to capture images of even the earliest portrayers, we have photographs with which to study the singer's costumes, hairdos, accessories, poses, postures, expressions, and attitudes. I have a wonderful collection, largely thanks to private collectors, and Carmens have covered my walls, providing information and inspiration, throughout the writing.

To the writings and images we next add recordings which—the gramophone (as we know it) having been invented in 1887—were beginning to be made around the turn of the century; first an occasional aria, but then, in 1908, the first complete recording. And in addition to innumerable recordings (see the discography), beginning in the mid–20th century, come precious videos of all kinds, including many of live performances. Though I often refer to such videos, many were privately made and, if not found on YouTube, are available from such valuable sources as Premiere Opera and House of Opera, but I only include the commercial ones in my videography. Finally, like manna from heaven, the amazing Internet appears, providing access not only to all kinds of print resources (reviews, articles, blogs, news) but also to everything from videos and recordings on YouTube to streamings of whole operas from practically anywhere in the world. Of course, none can equal being in the theater itself, but, though I have seen many a Carmen in person, without these resources I would not have dared attempt such a chronicle.

* * *

But from where does the singer—or more recently the director—get her ideas and ultimately her interpretation? Should they—as some believe—come only from what she sees in the score? Or does she read the Mérimée novella from which the opera was adapted—a short work, comprising four sections (87 pages in total), with Carmen herself appearing in only two. It's a difficult decision because differences between opera and novella abound. And, actually, though Carmen is certainly central to the story—the catalyst for it—in some ways she is not the main character. Rather the main character is, first, the amateur French archaeologist, who narrates, and, second, José, who, while waiting to be executed for her murder, tells the narrator how Carmen brought about his downfall. What we know about her, therefore, comes only from the two men's experiences with her, both individually and as they overlap. And though the story revolves around Carmen, because it is entirely from their points of view we learn only about her doings and words, and, with the exception of the Card Aria, very little about her innermost feelings.

At any rate, there being far too many differences to list them all, a few examples for anyone who has not read the Mérimée should give the idea. The Mérimée, for instance, has a great deal more than the Bizet about the often violent activities of the smugglers and Carmen's importance to the business. ("On our expeditions she acted as a spy for our group, and there was never a better one.")[8] There is the additional character of Carmen's husband, the ugly Garcia the One-Eyed, and there is Garcia's murder by José, who we learn is actually José Navarro, a notorious bandit who killed a man before becoming a soldier. On the other hand there is no innocent, all-good Micaëla, created for the opera as foil to the "evil" of Carmen, primarily to appease the Opéra-Comique's usual bourgeois audience; nor are there Mercedes and Frasquita, Carmen's devoted friends, a wonderful construct of the opera by which to glimpse Carmen's affection for her people; nor is there Escamillo, just the suggestion of him in the character of Lucas, a picador. It is, however, when José sees Lucas give Carmen a rosette from the bull that he determines to kill her if she will not start life over with him in the New World. And it is here that we get perhaps the most astounding difference, for José does not murder Carmen outside the bullring, as in the opera. Rather, he waits back at her house, and on her return, demands she accompany him to the country. "First me, then you. I knew it had to be so," she tells him as she mounts his horse and silently rides with him through the night, knowing he will kill her because it is her destiny. When they arrive, José pleads with her. But the scene in the Mérimée is not nearly as confrontational as in the opera. Indeed, even when he gives her a chance to escape, Carmen does not take it. She no longer loves him, and again, as in the opera, she tells José, "Everything is over between us. As my *rom*, you have the right to kill your *romi*. But Carmen will always be free. *Calli* she was born, *Calli* she will die."⁹ And so José kills her with a knife that had belonged to Garcia; then remembering she had always wanted to be buried in a wood, he digs a hole and buries her with her ring and a little cross before riding to Cordoba to give himself up.

Such plot differences aside, the character of Carmen as created by Mérimée, though she fairly bursts from his pages and is considerably more disturbing than she is in the opera, will almost certainly haunt and, at the same time, confuse the singer who reads the story. That she is an outright seductress—often only for the purpose of ensnaring a man because she needs a favor—is indisputable, but the outright sexy Carmen, which singers work so hard to show, can hardly be found in the Mérimée. Rather, especially in the beginning, it is the fun-loving, mischievous, mercurial free spirit that, in addition to the "strange, wild beauty"[10] of a Gypsy outsider, makes her so attractive to men. In the novella there are 19 references to Carmen laughing, from "laughing fit to burst"[11] to "When that girl laughed there was no talking sensibly."[12] But images describing her eroticism amount to little more than "pulling her mantilla open to show her shoulders" and "swaying her hips like a filly from the Cordova stud farm."[13] As in the opera, the darker, more troubled Carmen only comes to the fore after she realizes her mistake in getting involved with José. Though she nurses José to health when he is badly wounded because it is her duty, the more she tires of him the meaner she becomes. There is no Card Scene, however. Rather, it is all about sorcery and magic in the Mérimée. As José tells the narrator, "Engrossed in her magic, ... she would sing one of those magic songs."[14] Cards, in fact, appear only when she tells the narrator his fortune (and uses the occasion to steal his gold watch), and it is not from cards that she sees it written that he will kill her but from such omens as coffee grounds; the priest she had just met at her door when she first saw José; a hare crossing between his horse's legs. What both Mérimée and Bizet deliver in full measure, however, is Carmen's insistence on and passion for freedom. Using almost exactly the same words as in the novella, she tells José at the end of the opera: *"Jamais Carmen ne cédera! Libre elle est née et libre elle mourra."* (Never will Carmen give in. Free she was born and free she will die.)

Other descriptions and references in the novella to help fill out her person for the singer might be the constant references to Carmen as Devil, witch, and sorceress; her passion for eating ("She ate sweets like a child")[15]; her extreme volatility and temper ("Her eyes grew bloodshot, her expression terrifying, her features contorted, and she stomped her foot ... then, seating herself cross-legged in a corner of the room, she selected an orange, peeled it, and began to eat it")[16]; and, finally, those inexplicable little somethings which make her so impossibly endearing ("And she clicked her castanets as she always did when she wanted to banish some disturbing idea").[17]

This then is just a suggestion of what a singer gets when—rightly or wrongly—she reads the Mérimée. Just how much she should take from it is the question. Some read it over and over looking for clues to her character and insights for their interpretations, while others refuse to consider it in the belief that only the work of Bizet and the librettists as we know it in the score counts. Nonetheless, the Mérimée story is a powerful piece of literature, short though it may be, and one can only applaud the opera's creators for their skill in adapting it, especially in light of the particular theater, audience, and period for which they wrote.

* * *

That said, though of no particular help for singers, the reader might also find the following two curiosities about Carmen of some interest. We do not know when Bizet first encountered the Mérimée story, but we do know that well before he began work on the opera, there was one Céleste Vénard, whom he met on a train in 1865, when the composer was 27 and she 41; that Bizet "came under her spell and was fascinated by the wildly romantic La Mogador,"[18] as she was known. To be sure, La Mogador was clearly an interesting lady with a background that included dancer, equestrian, author, theater manager, mistress of many important men, and singer in a café, where among the songs she sang were some by the Spanish composer Yradier, including one said to have been the basis for the Habanera. It is unlikely they had a romantic relationship and there is no proof that she was a secondary inspiration for Carmen. But the way she described herself in her *Mémoires* certainly sounds very much like our Gypsy. "Moderation is no part of my nature.... I feel with a passion that devours me.... I have always been capricious and proud. No one, among women whose tendency it is to say 'yes,' derives more pleasure than I do from saying 'no.' So the men to whom I have given the most are those who asked least of me."[19]

A curiosity of another kind, though coming well after Bizet's death, was a link to a possible real Carmen in the person of a young singer by the name of Mintz Nadushka who had made her operatic debut in the role of Carmen (no date or place given) and claimed to be the great-granddaughter of that very same Carmen. Nadushka's story first appeared in the Parisian press in 1907 and was soon picked up by newspapers around the world. As she told it, Carmen, her great-grandmother, was a Gypsy by the name of Ar Mintz whose tribe lived by smuggling outside of Gibraltar. After her first husband was killed in a fight with customs officers she met José, a handsome brigadier, who, smitten by her, helped her escape when she was arrested for smuggling and then deserted for her. But, said Nadushka, when Ar Mintz lost interest in him, José, "mad with rage and discomfiture, killed her."

Ar Mintz (our Carmen), however, left a daughter—no name, nor father's name provided—and this daughter married a famous Gypsy singer, Dyarko, with whom she had a daughter, Thiecla. Thiecla in turn married an English artilleryman stationed at Gibraltar, and that is where Mintz Nadushka, Carmen's great-granddaughter, was born. Nadushka studied singing with her grandfather Dyarko and made her debut as Bizet's Carmen at the age of 20. But because, she said, *gitanos* believed it was sacrilege for one of their own to appear on the stage, they attempted to poison her two years later in London, thereby ending her career. And here, though we know she later married a French journalist, the tale essentially goes cold.[20]

* * *

Though the matter of interpretation always comes first in any discussion of Carmen, the matter of voice type and color is not far behind and thus appears regularly throughout the book. "Carmen?" exhorted Risë Stevens. "Oh anyone can *sing* it."[21] To be sure, some might even say all the role requires is for the singer to be a woman. But because so much of her part is written for middle voice with only brief extensions up and down, it lies, as Lorraine Hunt-Lieberson has said, "in the no-man's land of lots of voices."[22] And any singer without a solid middle will, therefore, not only find it exhausting but also—though Bizet kept the orchestration fairly light—have difficulty being heard over the orchestra in the more dramatic passages. Furthermore, each of the four acts requires her character to change dramatically and, as a consequence, vocally—probably one reason listeners sometimes have trouble choosing a favorite, since the singer who is right for one act can be wrong for another. In any case, from the full-out lyricism of the opening to the deep emotion of the Card Scene to the quasi declamatory drama of the end, as Bizet responds to his chameleon of a heroine, so, too, the singer must respond in kind.

As we will see in the first chapter, the Opéra-Comique, where *Carmen* premiered in 1875, was known for presenting light opera in a relatively small house. Audiences would not have expected a big voice, and Galli-

Marié who created Carmen there primarily sang light middle-voiced, even soprano, roles. Moreover, even before Galli-Marié, it was a soprano in the person of Marie Roze whom Bizet, at the director's urging, first approached to create the role. Thus, as will become clear throughout this book, sopranos outnumbered mezzos in the role for decades and the notion that Bizet wrote it with a mezzo voice of the voluptuous kind in mind is not altogether true. The turnabout only really began when Italians—a land rich in "voluptuous" mezzos—took to the role earlier in the 20th century with the result that today's audiences, especially in big houses, have come to believe that no one but a mezzo with a big, round voice can provide the sensuality they have come to expect. If such voices don't suit Carmen's youthful shenanigans in her first acts (and can even sound matronly), it's a trade-off they seem willing to take. After all, there are two more acts to go, they could argue. The tide may turn back one of these days, but, for now, lush mezzo voices in the role far outnumber lyric mezzos or sopranos of any kind, and one has only to read customer reviews of Carmens on CDs and DVDs to know it is the preferred voice.

* * *

I have always wanted to write a biography but feared I would get bored living with just the one person for so long. But given Carmen's myriad guises and infinite ways allowing for every kind of look, voice, and interpretation, I have been enthralled writing the life of this bewitching operatic heroine (one time anti-heroine) as she passed through time and place. What is more, the opera is that great; the drama that thrilling; and, as José knew and I quickly learned. "You couldn't get bored with that girl."[23]

Chapter 1

"What Is It?"

> I am, yes, fascinated by Carmen! What richness of expression, what dramatic possibilities; I no longer sleep!—Célestine Galli-Marié, letter, September 7, 1874[1]

She was born March 3, 1875, on the stage of the Salle Favart in Paris, France, in the person of one Marie-Célestine-Laurence Galli-Marié. "Your little marmoset of a director writes to ask if I wish to create Carmen. What is it?"[2] the busy mezzo, on tour in September of 1873, had written her friend the tenor Paul Lhérie,[3] inadvertently addressing the envelope to Camille du Locle—himself the "little marmoset." But the popular director of the Opéra-Comique had his priorities straight. He would keep the spunky star and, on eyeing her own little pet monkey peeking out of her muff at the first rehearsal, merely quip, "You're certainly fond of marmosets, aren't you?"[4]

It is curious, though, that Galli-Marié had never heard of Carmen. True, the Gypsy had received little notice when she first appeared in an 1845 literary magazine as the eponymous protagonist of a new novella by Prosper Mérimée.[5] Yet in the three decades since, her notoriety had grown considerably, or at least to the point that du Locle was having second thoughts about allowing such a questionable character into his state-subsidized opera company. Though he and his colleague Alfred de Leuven had commissioned young Georges Bizet to write an opera for the Opéra-Comique, it was to have been on the kind of light-hearted subject the company's bourgeois clientele expected from it—something like the composer's recent *Djamileh*, only, they hoped, more successful. And yet, as it had also been his "dream to revitalize the repertory," when Bizet suddenly proposed the Mérimée story, du Locle had cautiously agreed, as had the librettists assigned to the project, Henri Meilhac and Ludovic Halévy, leaving only the older and more conservative de Leuven to oppose the idea. And oppose it he did. "Mérimée's Carmen? Isn't she killed by her lover?... And that background of thieves, gypsies, cigar-makers! At the Opéra-Comique, a family theater! The theater where marriages are arranged.... You will frighten off our audience.... It's impossible."

But Halévy, sent to try to calm the director, promised that he and Meilhac had been writing light opera librettos for more than a decade and knew just what to do. They would soften the story, he promised. They would add "a character in the tradition of opéra comique —a young, innocent girl, very pure [Micaëla]" and turn Carmen's Gypsy friends into comical characters. As for the final scene, "the death of Carmen would be glossed over ... with a parade, a ballet, a joyful fanfare." But, De Leuven protested, murder on the stage of the Opéra-Comique was simply out of the question, and said Halévy, whose recollections these are, his subsequent resignation was probably "because he felt a terror and horror of introducing so revolutionary an opera as *Carmen*."[6]

* * *

Much has been written about the night the inscrutable siren first stepped onto the gas-lit stage and into history following five months of stormy rehearsals. In addition to du Locle's growing concerns, both orchestra and chorus had vehemently objected to the difficulty of the music. What is more, despite Charles Ponchard's generally old-school stage direction, the chorus had threatened to strike over being asked to act—even fight and smoke—which was "something unprecedented at the Opéra-Comique, [where] members ... were accustomed to singing their ensembles standimg still in neat lines."[7]

Nevertheless, everyone agreed that the performance began well enough. The audience, which included not only the customary families— if fewer than usual because du Locle, fearing scandal, had discouraged them—but also composers, performers, critics, and publishers, who, while prepared for scandal, came well-disposed toward Bizet, who was regarded as a promising composer. They responded favorably to Carmen's first aria (the *Habanera*), the duet between Micaëla and Don José, and the first act finale; and they applauded the entr'acte so enthusiastically that the orchestra had to repeat it. And for a while things even looked good for the second act. The opening *Chanson Bohémienne* and its accompanying dance were well received, as was the Toreador's aria.[8] And the merry, fast-moving quintet that followed was enthusiastically received, in part because Meilhac, with his particular "gift ... for humorous characterization,"[9] had, as promised, turned Carmen's smuggler friends into quasi-comic characters.

In other words, all appeared to be going well and in keeping with the conventions of the house. But with José's arrival at Lilas Pastia's—Lhérie having gotten seriously off-pitch in José's unaccompanied off-stage song[10]—the mood in the hall, like the story on stage, had darkened. The feeling was that Carmen's dance for José bordered on depravity. To see a singer dancing was disturbing enough in 1875, but to see her dancing exotically, and after breaking a plate to serve as castanets, was outrageous, and José's following, seemingly formless, aria, which Lhérie sang poorly, only accelerated the downslide. In the third act Micaëla's aria alone enjoyed some success. But, thereafter, the spoken dialogue, a requirement of every Opéra-Comique production, curiously vanished and what had begun as a light opera evolved into a full-scale lyric drama. "As Bizet, from this point onward, got further and further away from the traditional manner of *opéra-comique*," Halévy explained, "the public was surprised, disconcerted, puzzled."[11] When the final curtain fell just after midnight it was to a half-empty house and only a few loyal friends backstage to attempt congratulations.[12]

* * *

In the introduction to her *Carmen, Dossier de Presse Parisienne* (1875), which includes 35 reviews, the eminent Bizet scholar Lesley Wright informs us that "among the more than 750 periodicals published in Paris in 1875 ... virtually all the major daily papers plus the illustrated press, music periodicals ... magazines and newspapers oriented toward art, music and/or literature, and even fashion magazines, covered [the premiere] with reviews of varying length and depth."[13] By today's standards—even with the Internet—this is an astonishing number for a single city and clearly a powerful force capable of making or breaking a new work, and in the days immediately following the premiere the city's music critics were for the most part of one censorious mind. Only after taking the time to see more than one performance and reconsider did a few begin to write more positively.

It had been less than a year since their colleagues in the art world had attacked some young upstart painters as iconoclasts in a group exhibit that rocked Paris. Now, a similar fear of the new compelled them to declare Bizet's latest too complicated, too imitative of the dreaded Wagner, and—like the paintings of the new Impressionists, as the painters had come to be known—too formless and obtuse. What is more, making much of the fact that it had been performed at the Opéra-Comique, the plot was too brutal, the protagonists too real, and, above all, the heroine altogether too obscene, immoral, and abhorrent.

Mérimée was not at fault, they said. "Certain types of character that are intriguing in a book are less appealing on the stage, where they take on a realistic nature that shock even less timorous spirits," the more positive Victorin Joncières wrote. "The two heroes of Mérimée's novella, a lost woman and a soldier who has deserted, cannot be transported to the stage with impunity."[14] Blame, therefore, had to go to those who, in adapting the immoral tale for the stage, had failed to sanitize it enough to be acceptable viewing for the unsuspecting bourgeoisie.

One tries to imagine how Bizet's heroine actually appeared to those first audiences. As Winton Dean has written in his biography of the composer: "Hitherto the heroines of nineteenth-century opera—and still more of *opéra-comique*—had belonged, almost to a woman, to the spotless soprano school.... They tended to suffer rather than act. Despite (or because of) their scrupulous moral rectitude they were the football of men and fortune."[15] But Carmen was neither spotless nor passive. On the contrary, she was "a savage ... sensual, foul-mouthed, brazen, believing in neither God nor devil ... a veritable gutter prostitute," said one critic.[16] Or, as the dean of Parisian music critics, Oscar Comettant, spewed:

> Carmen should be gagged, a stop put to the unbridled twisting of her hips; she should be fastened into a straightjacket after being cooled off by a jug of water poured over her head.... This distinguished artist [Galli-Marié] could have corrected what was shocking and antipathetic in the character of this heartless, faithless, lawless gypsy. She has, on the contrary, exaggerated Carmen's vices by a realism that would at best be bearable in an operetta in a small theater. At the Opéra-Comique, a subsidized theater, a decent theater if ever there was one, Mlle Carmen should temper her passions.[17]

* * *

So who was this singer, this "distinguished artist" who refused to "temper her passions"? Born in Paris in 1840, Célestine Galli-Marié, as she was known professionally, was the daughter of Claude-Marié-Mécène Marié de l'Isle (1811–1879), a tenor (later a baritone) chiefly remembered as the creator of Tonio, a role famous for the nine high Cs he sings in a single aria in Donizetti's *La Fille du Régiment*. Her three sisters also sang professionally, and all studied with their father. In 1859, the same year as her marriage to the sculptor Antonio Galli, the young mezzo-soprano had made her stage debut in Strasbourg and then set off to build her reputation in the provinces of Italy and France. Widowed in 1861, in 1862 she was singing Balfe's eponymous *Bohemian Girl* in Rouen when Émile Perrin heard her and engaged her for the Opéra-Comique, where, at the time, he was director. Her debut there as Serpina in Pergolesi's *La Serva Padrona* was a triumph and Galli-Marié was soon not only singing leading roles but also creating them. To be sure, her touching impersonation of Mignon, a child of nobility abducted by Gypsies, in the 1866 premiere of Ambroise Thomas's opera of that name certainly would have ensured her place in history even had she not created an actual Gypsy nine years later. For, as one critic pronounced, "*Mignon is* Galli-Marié; no other artist should sing it."[18] And for some time, in France, few did.[19]

Since Bizet, as a young man, had been hired to reduce the Thomas score for its publisher Heugel, he would almost certainly have seen Galli-Marié as Mignon and probably in other parts as well, for her repertoire was large and she performed often. We know, too, that even though she had declined owing to other commitments, he had wanted

Célestine Galli-Marié, Carmen's creator, a rare image from the time of the premiere.

the popular mezzo to create the title role in his *Djamileh* in 1871. Thus, it is not surprising that when discussions about casting Carmen got underway in September of 1873 Bizet, after initially deferring to his colleagues, again proposed Galli-Marié.

That the librettists wanted Zulma Bouffar, the popular Algerian-born operetta soprano Offenbach had discovered singing in a café in Cologne, as Carmen proved only a rumor, quashed by Meilhac himself when he told a journalist that "it was out of the question for Zulma to be stabbed."[20] More serious was du Locle's proposal of pretty Marie Roze, another Opéra-Comique star. But Bizet avoided their choice by personally visiting the young soprano in her apartment and describing the role in such a way as to prompt her to write him afterwards: "I am entirely of your opinion. The tragic end of *Carmen* had made me presuppose dramatic action that would modify the very scabrous side of this character; the explanations you were kind enough to make to me at the outset of our interview having showed me the character was to be scrupulously respected, I understood immediately that the role would not suit me, or, more accurately, that I would not be suited to it."[21]

With Roze then out of the way, Bizet could insist on Galli-Marié, who, after listening to him play the score for her, assured him by letter of her commitment to his music. But if the mezzo was an artist of the highest order, she was also a professional for whom singing was a living and, accordingly, she could be uncompromising when it came to the business side of her art. As Bizet held his breath, the complexity of her negotiations with du Locle regarding fees and scheduling drove the director almost mad throughout the fall of 1873. But on December 18 she succumbed, writing du Locle: "Yes, *cher Monsieur*, I accept—2500 per month—four months—October 1874, November, December, January—12 times a month—to create the *Carmen* of Messrs. Bizet, Meilhac, and Halévy—Is that it? Are you satisfied?... My best wishes to M. Bizet. (I am sure that he will dine well tonight.)"[22]

The following summer, while Bizet worked on the orchestration at Bougival, his country getaway near Versailles, Galli-Marié, worn-out from performing, found time for a little vacation near Bordeaux. To his offer to bring her the entire opera, she protested, "Monsieur, I wish only to work on the difficult passages in my role and not on the role as a whole, which I shall read at sight on October 1, the day my contract starts."[23] And so, as promised, on October 2, Galli-Marié sight-read through her part with Bizet at the piano and the next day met with the other principals. Thereafter, from early November on, she attended the almost daily rehearsals.

* * *

The writer Henry Malherbe has proposed in his book, *Carmen*, that the composer and his leading lady had a love affair during rehearsals. His information, he wrote, came from Paul Lhérie (Don José), who told him that virtually everyone in the cast believed it. But most authorities dispute this. It is true that Bizet's recent marriage was already in trouble, for Geneviève Halévy, daughter of Bizet's former teacher, the composer Fromental Halévy, and niece of the librettist Ludovic Halévy, has been described as a disturbed woman and difficult wife.[24] But there is no evidence that Galli-Marié was ever unfaithful to the composer Émile Paladilhe with whom she had a long-standing romantic relationship after the death of her husband. Rather, indisputable and obvious to all was Galli-Marié's devotion and loyalty to Bizet. Indeed, her support during the composer's battles with both du Locle and Charles Ponchard was pivotal in maintaining the integrity of his opera. She and Lhérie even threatened to quit when management tried to press Bizet into toning down the ending to avoid scandal. As Mina Curtiss, Bizet's first important English language biographer wrote: "Throughout the embattled rehearsals of *Carmen*, it was not the composer's wife who sustained him either as a man or as an artist. It was Galli-Marié, the woman of the theater, who became the embodiment of his creation by her own gifts, her faith in his talent, her fierce loyalty to his conception of the interpretation of her role, and her willingness to make sacrifices for it rather than compromise."[25]

* * *

As free-spirited, independent, shrewd, and passionate as the Gypsy herself, Galli-Marié, even if she lacked her long black hair, great dark eyes, and copper complexion, must have felt a kinship with Mérimée's creation. Moreover, at 35 years of age at the time of the premiere, she still had the body and verve. "[Galli-Marié] is small and graceful, moves like a cat, has an impish, pert face, and her whole personality seems unruly and mischievous,"[26] a critic had said of her debut as Serpina. Compare that to "agile as young goat.... A monkey could not have competed with her for capers, grimaces, and mischievousness,"[27] which is how Mérimée described his Gypsy.

And Bizet was not the first to imagine Galli-Marié in the part. As early as 1864, in fact, in a letter to Victorien Sardou asking the famous playwright to provide a libretto for an opera he was planning based on the same Mérimée story, the composer Victor Massé had mentioned engaging the mezzo for the title role. In a city bloated with operetta (Malherbe tells us that in 1875 alone no less than 30 operettas were premiered in Paris)[28] what this composer, best known for light music, might have done with the Carmen story can only be imagined. In any event, the Massé version never came to fruition and Galli-Marié was probably never even approached since, as we know from her note to Lhérie, she claimed to be ignorant of the character.

In the early decades of photography people who sat for portraits did not smile. And so images of Galli-Marié, whether as Carmen or as any of her operatic impersonations, show her looking intense, even forbidding; to such a degree, in fact, that one can hardly imagine her Gypsy laughing as much and as easily as in Mérimée's characterization. But if no review comments on this aspect of the mezzo's portrayal, it should be noted that the famous soprano Félia Litvinne, who saw her in the role, described her as an accomplished comedienne.[29] And Théodore de Banville, one of the few critics to praise the opera from the outset, wrote that the kind of humor and lightness she chose for Carmen was that of "a young woman who, by dint of elegance and intrigue, could have persuaded fish in the pond to frolic with her on the grass."[30]

But what Galli-Marié so powerfully does exude in photographs is the gravitas and *duende*—a Spanish word denoting a combination of soulfulness, mystery, and ultimately what Unamuno called a "tragic sense of life"—that many feel distinguish the greatest Carmens. Such was certainly among the qualities that so moved Peter Tchaikovsky, who saw her in the part several times and, as reported by his brother, said that Galli-Marié's Carmen, "while retaining all the vitality of her type, was at the same time shrouded in a certain indescribable magic web of burning, unbridled passion and mystic fatalism."[31] Again, compare "a strange, wild beauty, a face that was disconcerting at first, but unforgettable ... her expression, at once voluptuous and fierce,"[32] which was Mérimée's Gypsy with that of Galli-Marié, which one critic described as "fascinating by reason of her animal beauty and in the exposure of her animal instincts."[33]

* * *

How did Galli-Marié more precisely act the role? We can certainly assume that in the year 1875 she neither hiked her skirt up nor spread her legs in the way we've come to expect from Carmens today. According to the *livret de mise-en-scène* for the premiere we know she entered from the back "with some flowers in her bodice and a cassia flower in her mouth" surrounded by six tenors who were instructed not to block the audience's view, and that she sang the *Habanera* from in front of the prompter's box. Following the *Habanera*, the *Livret* continues: "Everybody's gaze follows Carmen. She stops for an instant in front of Don José, hesitates, then goes to the side of the factory, stops, and returns resolutely to Don José" and asks what he is doing. "Then, after his answer, she throws her flower between his eyes, and leaves quickly, laughing."[34]

In point of fact, while much of this scene follows the novella, we also know that Galli-Marié, who always prepared extensively for a new role, looked to the Mérimée wherever possible. In Karen Henson's excellent chapter describing Galli-Marié as exemplifying a new era in opera performance in that she was concerned more with the drama of a role—verbally and physically—than the beautiful singing of it, the author suggests that the mezzo "was enacting Mérimée directly, speaking his heroines's words and acting out her gestures."[35] And even some critics, far more familiar with the Mérimée than critics are today, recognized that the novelist's recounting of José's first sighting of Carmen, "swaying her hips like some filly out of the Córdoba stud ... fist on her hip, brazen like the true Gypsy she was,"[36] was clearly inspiration for the singer in her search for the right body language. "Can you imagine," the illustrious critic Henri Blaze De Bury writes, "the *Habanera* ... having the same effect without this pantomine, which accompanies it. The music is strange, monotonous, of a lazy, dragging rhythm, as if imbued with that feeling of exhaustion particular to the thundery regions of the tropics!... Bizet has very expertly drawn inspiration from this, and Mme Galli-Marié has poetically translated its languor *(morbidesse)*."[37]

But one wishes for more details, especially because, as the great British critic Herman Klein—"struck by the unexaggerated strength and convincing individuality of this remarkable creation" when he saw it in 1886—believed, the decade's "best known Carmens ... based their rendering[s] either directly or indirectly" on Galli-Marié's interpretation.[38] For not only did the dynamic little singer intervene in the staging and costuming of all her roles but, most significantly, she was also the only singer to study Carmen with the composer himself, giving everything she did a veracity no one else could claim.[39] What is more, she performed the role some 300 times over the next decade, making a strong impression and, thankfully, inspiring some who saw her to leave their recollections.

That Klein recalled that when Galli-Marié danced for José in act two, "she only sings an occasional bar or so, leaving it to the orchestra to sustain the melody" is curious in that the orchestra does not play melody at this point.[40] Certainly Klein could be mistaken; he probably didn't have a score and certainly didn't have a recording. But, then again, Galli-Marié may have asked that orchestral support be added for her. She was 46 when Klein saw her, and at that age and after so many performances, to be relieved of singing while dancing would have helped her get through one of the most exhausting moments in the opera.

From Blanche Arral, a later exponent of the role who saw her, we also know that Galli-Marié "sang the *Habanera* very slowly, almost like a menace, and this was in fine contrast to the *Séguidilla*, which comes not long after and is all that exists of seductive gaiety."[41] Assuming this is accurate—and Klein confirms it—the slow tempo clearly strengthens the argument that Galli-Marié's much reported rejections of Bizet's first 12 attempts at an opening aria for Carmen were by no means the whims of a prima donna demanding a display piece to show off her voice, as some have inferred, but rather the conscience of an artist seeking to establish character from the outset.[42] And, truly, it is this quality that set Galli-

Marié apart, as Blaze de Bury understood, when, in his review of the premiere, he directed the audience to "watch Galli-Marié's acting, which is skilled, truthful, always simple; no screams, no melodrama, movements that are almost imperceptible but deeply meaningful, fine details of gesture and physiognomy that betray all the ennui and agitation of the character."[43]

* * *

As to what her voice may have been like, though described by one reviewer as "full, fresh ... piquant and mellow,"[44] the more common observation was that its quality was high and clear but unexceptional. Writing to Pauline Viardot of Galli-Marié's Opéra-Comique debut in 1862, Hector Berlioz described her with "a certain dramatic intelligence and a voice less shrill than all the tit birds that cheeped and hopped about the planks of our second theater [Opéra-Comique]."[45] And even Tchaikovsky, who so admired her acting, dismissed her "vocal equipment [as] far from first class."[46]

But more to the point, as the celebrated teacher and fierce critic Mathilde Marchesi said, "she sang in perfect artistic style, her performance all the more admirable that she had not a large voice at her command."[47] Saint-Saëns noted that "in spite of her unequal voice and mediocre beauty ... she possessed that which is not easy to define, that which is above all, and gives life to a character; and she had diction and rhythm, these great qualities so seldom found."[48] And if "her voice was short and of no particular beauty," as Arral wrote, "her manner of using it was invariably fascinating."[49]

But just how "short" her range was is unclear. Carmen requires a great deal of physical stamina, but, as it rarely goes very high or low, vocally it is not especially difficult for any singer with a solid middle voice. It was typical of the era for sopranos and mezzos to cross into each other's territories, assuming each other's roles with ease and regularity. Galli-Marié sang not only many of the light middle-voiced *dugazon* parts— Mignon being the most famous—but some soprano parts as well, including the demanding soprano role of Marguerite in Gounod's *Faust*.[50] And we know from a letter she wrote du Locle early in 1874 that she wanted to use more of her high voice as Carmen. "Tell M. Bizet to use the tessitura of Marguerite for that part of my role not already done. His Mignon tessitura is too commonplace and rather bothers me."[51]

But the point must be made that if all of this explains the role's elastic vocal profile, it also suggests that, whether Bizet wrote the part expressly for Galli-Marié's mezzo or not, she did not sing it with the sumptuous sound modern audiences have come to associate with it. Had she done so, sopranos would probably not have appropriated it quite so quickly for themselves. Right from the start Galli-Marié's relatively high, light mezzo opened the door wide for them, and, though it is rare to hear a soprano as Carmen today, for decades they far outnumbered mezzos in the role. It was, in fact, not until the mid–20th century that, coupled with a major shift in how Carmen was perceived, mezzos reclaimed it.

* * *

Galli-Marié's costumes were designed by the famous painter and designer George Clairin, who had traveled in Spain with the painter Henri Regnault, whose sketches of the Gypsies and bullfighters had inspired Bizet. To be sure, despite du Locle's many reservations about *Carmen*, the director is said to have "produced it with scrupulous care," and made "a serious attempt to provide the singers with costumes ... which had historical accuracy."[52]

Photographs and other illustrations show Galli-Marié always in a bolero and her skirts, including the scene in the mountains, always a few inches above the ankle. Blanche Arral recalled that she "dressed the part in the style of the early nineteenth century and did not make the mistake of covering herself with a queen's ransom of jewels and satins."[53] Klein confirms this: "In the way of jewelry she contents herself with a pair of large gold earrings, a simple necklace of oriental beads and a brooch made of large Burmese crystal."[54] In all likelihood she honored as best she could the instructions in the librettists' score that her first act costume and entrance be as José describes so specifically in the story.[55] "She was wearing a very short red skirt, beneath which you could see her white silk stockings with holes in them, and dainty red morocco-leather shoes fastened with flame-coloured ribbons. Her mantilla was parted so as to reveal her shoulders and a big bunch of acacia flowers, which she had in the front of her blouse. She had another acacia bloom in one corner of her mouth."[56]

* * *

Returning to the narrative: on May 28, depressed by the reception for his opera and still trying to recover from an attack of quinsy he had suffered in late March, Bizet left Paris for his country house in Bougival. Chronologies vary slightly at this point, but it is certain that soon after arriving there he went for a swim in the stream near his home, still icy after the winter, and that "on May 30 he suffered a violent and incapacitating attack of rheumatism accompanied by a high fever, great pain and depression,"[57] which was followed by a severe heart attack on the night of June 1. We know too that on June 2, though he improved enough during the day to be visited by his young son, Jacques, he suffered a second heart attack around 11 o'clock that night and lapsed into an unconsciousness from which he never recovered.

And, finally, we know that that same night at the Salle Favaart *Carmen* was being performed for the 33rd time; that on her arrival at the theater Galli-Marié, though unaware of events in Bougival, seemed to be "in a state of indescribable hyper-excitement and enervation"[58]; that she had nonetheless gone ahead and performed without a problem; but that, as she read the cards in the third act—Tarot cards in which she, like Carmen, passionately believed: "Her heart beat as though it would break and she seemed to feel a threatening chill in the air. She mustered enough self-control to finish the scene, and then fainted in the wings. After she had been revived, other members of the cast tried to calm and reassure her ... but she insisted that it was not for herself she feared."[59]

* * *

The next day, June 3, on learning of Halévy's telegram informing the company of the death of the 36-year-old composer, Galli-Marié developed a fever and cancelled that night's performance. On June 5, she was spotted looking "utterly crushed"[60] as she sat beside her Micaëla, Marguerite Chapuy, among the four thousand mourners attending Bizet's funeral in the Church of la Trinité; yet that night, while backstage everyone wept, Galli-Marié went onstage to sing Carmen as scheduled. And, finally, after again cancelling twice, on June 13, she summoned the strength for just one more to close out the season.

Chapter 2

Breaking Away

A new era of operatic art dawned.—Minnie Hauk[1]

In the mid–19th century, Paris was so widely considered the capital of the music world that any new work its critics deemed a failure, especially one by a native, was likely to be soon forgotten. It is true that *Carmen* had enjoyed a nice run of modestly attended performances and even an occasional supportive review. But with no further performances planned, Bizet's masterpiece too might well have fallen into oblivion had not an agent in search of new material for the Vienna Court Opera heard the opera that May and, finding the composer in Bougival, signed it for a premiere in the Prussian capital that very fall. Bizet would die in a matter of days, but at least (we can console ourselves) in the knowledge his Gypsy still had life.

For *Carmen* to succeed in Vienna, however, there would have to be changes to the score. For the Viennese, though more willing than most to give modern works a chance, were addicted to the "grand" in their opera, and would probably not have accepted it in its *opéra comique* form. Bizet had agreed to make the necessary changes,[2] but with his sudden, untimely death it was now left to the company's new director, Fritz Jauner, to implement them himself. The two most important: the addition of the composer's own *L'Arlésienne Suite* to serve as the music for grand opera's obligatory ballet, and the commissioning of Bizet's friend Ernest Guiraud to compose sung recitatives as replacements for the original spoken dialogue.[3] And then, to further ensure success, Jauner cast favorite singers in leading roles: Georg Müller, renowned for his high C#, as Don José, and the pretty, ever popular Bertha Ehnn as the Gypsy.

A leading member of the company since her debut as Gounod's Marguerite in 1868, the Hungarian-born Ehnn was indeed a favorite in a city where everyone from shop girls to princesses treated opera singers as celebrities. Said to possess a lovely, warm soprano, Ehnn's extensive vocal compass and repertoire, which ranged from Mozart's Pamina and Wagner's Sieglinde to the Galli-Marié specialty of Mignon and even the contralto role of Leonora in Donizetti's *La Favorita*,[4] made it perfectly logical for her to sing a role with a middle tessitura like Carmen's. What is more, she was considered a good actress, called "brilliant" even in the *Taming of the Shrew* by Hermann Goetz—success as a "shrew," perhaps inspiring Jauner to envision her as Bizet's headstrong troublemaker.

Carmen, however, is far more than an ill-tempered, scolding woman (as "shrews" are defined) and reviews of the premiere on October 23, 1875, suggest the role was "just too deep" for the soprano, who missed "the sinful nature of this demonic woman."[5] Even so, the opera itself, in its German translation, enjoyed a modest success, and, with Ehnn continuing in the title role, was performed with some regularity at the Court Opera for the next four years.

* * *

But just as Vienna was enjoying its dressed-up grand *Carmen*, back in Paris at the Opéra-Comique, the opera, in its original garb, was beginning a series of farewells to the city of its birth. On the strength of its reception in Vienna, the Théâtre de la Monnaie had offered Galli-Marié 800 francs to create the Gypsy for Brussels that winter, but the ever loyal mezzo had told du Locle she would accept half that amount from him if only he would mount the opera again for her in Paris.

And so, after reading a poem about Bizet by Louis Gallet as part of a memorial concert for the composer, from November to February Galli-Marié sang Carmen at the Opéra-Comique some 13 times more for a final total of some 48 performances. In Paris, the role had been exclusively hers, but now she had to find stages for it elsewhere. The city would not see *Carmen* again for eight years—a loss that, as we shall see, was soon the music capital's shame. For, having proved itself in Vienna, barely a month would go by that some other city did not want it for itself.

Next up: La Monnaie, one of the smallest houses on the continent but one with a distinguished history, which, unable to obtain the services of Galli-Marié, now assigned the Gypsy to her third impersonator.

A virtual unknown as compared to her grandfather and father,[6] both prestigious basses, Maria Dérivis had nonetheless appeared in leading soprano roles in many of the major houses of Europe. Though little is known of her Carmen—Gaudier dismissing it as merely "*quelconque*" (mediocre)—Halévy's comment that "she saved the piece by a very naive interpretation"[7] is important. For if its failure to excite may partially explain why the opera soon slipped out of the Monnaie repertoire,[8] its failure to create controversy, like Ehnn's in Vienna, probably helped save the opera at a time it was still on tenuous ground. Anything too provocative might well have spelled *Carmen*'s end, especially with the Paris premiere still so fresh in everybody's mind. But, as it happened, Brussels had only to wait three years for its return, and, at that time, to see its place in the repertoire secured—this, in large part, thanks to the talents of one determined American soprano with the improbable name of Minnie Hauk.

* * *

Given the New World's reputation for enterprise, it is not surprising that it was a Yankee who first saw what Carmen could do for a career if the singer took full advantage of its unprecedented dramatic possibilities. Because America had come late to opera and so lacked its centuries-old traditions, its singers knew they must employ every available means to make a place for themselves in a profession in which they were still anomalies. As fearless as she was talented, Hauk had managed to make her way out of the American plains, where she had grown up, and back to her native New York City for a highly successful—especially for a 14-year-old—operatic debut as Amina in *La Sonnambula* at the prestigious Academy of Music in 1866, and from there to the stages of the world's music capitals. As it did with most of her peers, the *bel canto* repertoire, then in its heyday, constituted the greater part of the nearly one hundred roles Hauk would sing over her career. But cognizant of a kind of real-life dramatic expression making its way into contemporary opera, Hauk saw its potential for her own talents. Despising the old-fashioned singers who stood "nailed to the boards … every high note … accompanied by the raising of their right arms,"[9] she believed a great artist should know how to blend acting and singing. And imagining herself just such an artist, on hearing of the new Bizet opera, she seized on it, declaring in her memoirs (as would so many of her successors): "I had made up my mind to sing Carmen."[10]

Unfortunately, Hauk does not give us much background for her fixation. *Carmen* was still very new. What's more, she never saw anyone else perform it until after she retired, or so she wrote. We know, however, that around the time of the Paris and Vienna premieres of *Carmen*, she was in Berlin, where, honored with the title of Royal Prussian Chamber Singer, she starred in roles as diverse as Wagner's Elsa and Donizetti's eponymous

Fille du Regiment. But, as she tells it, when she asked to create Carmen for Berlin, the director, adamant the opera would not succeed there, had refused her. And so, not one to be denied, the Yankee with the flashing black eyes and upturned nose left for Brussels. La Monnaie was not as prestigious as Berlin, nor was the money as good, but the company had offered her a contract, and, on the condition they cast her as the Gypsy, she had signed it.

Severely criticized for her French pronunciation after her Brussels debut as Marguerite in 1878, Hauk reapplied herself to the language in preparation for her Carmen later that spring, and of that role debut she would proudly recollect: "There was no further reference to my French pronunciation; nothing but unstinted praise for my singing, my acting, my costumes.... Felix Fétis, the critic of the *Indépendence Belge*, said that I had created the prototype of Carmencita."[11] And as Carmencita she would in fact be known for the rest of her adventurous career. For on hearing of her success in Brussels, the British impresario James Henry Mapleson determined it was Minnie Hauk who must introduce the opera to London.

* * *

Though in *The Golden Age of Opera* Herman Klein recalled that at the time few people on the British side of the Channel had even heard of *Carmen*, the London to which Mapleson brought the Bizet in 1878 had in recent years become a major operatic center. In addition to any number of smaller companies, including some that toured, the city boasted the Italian Royal, which performed at Covent Garden under the direction of Frederick Gye, and Mapleson's own Her Majesty's Opera, which that year performed at Drury Lane—its regular home at the Haymarket being out of commission due to fire.

In accepting Mapleson's offer, Hauk had stipulated that he cast the Italian tenor Italo Campanini, the American soprano Alwina Valleria, and the Italian baritone Giuseppe del Puente in the other leading roles. Famous singers themselves, all had initially refused on the basis their roles were too small, but with little time to spare the impresario—"as wily and wide-awake a strategist in his profession as, perhaps, there has never been before"[12]—had somehow convinced them otherwise. There was to be no "footlight-singing facing the audience" however; for, as Hauk recalled, "we hoped to present to the Londoners for the first time in English operatic history, a performance in which acting and scenic effects would go hand in hand with singing."[13]

Minnie Hauk, the first American Carmen (photograph by Sarony).

Herman Klein, who attended the premiere on June 22, 1878, in the company of the world-famous voice teacher, Manuel Garcia, himself both a Spaniard and a friend of Mérimée, years later described the historic premiere in detail. While noting the audience's disappointment that Campanini's and Valleria's entrances were so modest as to go almost unnoticed, he continued:

> Everyone was waiting to see Minnie Hauk, the Carmen. Nothing intrigues like the unknown, and I confess that, of the many dozens of Carmens I have seen since that night, I have not awaited one with the same palpitating thrill of excitement and expectation, nor felt a fuller sense of satisfaction when at last the gipsy appeared, strutting forward with hand on hip and flower in mouth. I heard Garcia whisper "She looks the character well!" I felt how right he was when he noisily clapped his hands after her piquant "Habanera"; … The voice itself was not remarkable for sweetness or sympathetic charm, though strong and full enough in the medium register; but somehow its rather thin, penetrating timbre sounded just right in a character whose music called for the expression of heartless sensuality, caprice, cruelty, and fatalistic defiance. We felt all this, and more, as the opera proceeded and the gipsy's ardent and impulsive (yet repulsive) nature continued to unfold itself.[14]

* * *

To be sure, Minnie Hauk was not known for any personal or vocal warmth and, as better suited for Victorian audiences, she almost certainly played more to the Gypsy's coquetry than her sexuality. Actually, she was known to be quite prudish, at one point (by her own admission) even earning the sobriquet 'the American icicle,' which must have made for a curious Carmen by today's standards. On the other hand, she did share with Mérimée's minx an endearing volatility. The conductor Luigi Arditi's description of the prima donna's "little fiery outbursts of temper … resembling April showers [that] disappear as quickly as they came, leaving her smiling countenance sunny and more radiant than ever,"[15] could have come straight out of the novella.

In any case, Londoners embraced the intrepid Gypsy, so persuasively introduced by the fetching American, and, with the gates thus opened, many a Victorian nightingale now thought about appropriating the role for herself. It seemed, as Hauk herself believed, truly "the beginning of a new era of operatic art."[16]

* * *

Certainly, other than that it offers few chances to flaunt her instrument, there was no reason for any of these singers to be put off by the role of Carmen from a vocal standpoint. Strictly and exhaustively trained from an early age, so strong was their vocal foundation that 19th-century opera singers regularly made debuts before they were 20 and were, moreover, capable of singing everything from the bel canto disciplines of Rossini, Bellini and Donizetti to—by the end of the century—the most dramatic utterances of Meyerbeer, Verdi, and even Wagner, displaying a staggering vocal versatility. On stage almost constantly, Carmen is physically and emotionally demanding, thereby requiring the singer to pace herself carefully. But the generally soft dynamic markings for all her arias, the relatively narrow range, and the middle-voice tessitura—a problem only for one weak in that department—otherwise keep vocal challenges to a minimum. High notes are few and easily accessed and low notes, though sometimes a worry for today's singers with fears of carrying their chest registers too high, were as nothing to 19th-century singers, who used chest voice with abandon. The outstanding vocal question then was only: was this first generation of Carmens ready for the kind of new stylistic, expressive, and dramatic challenges the role presented?

Some had sung Verdi's Violetta, a role that calls for a wide vocal palette, especially when dealing with the complicated emotions of her death scene, and Gounod's Marguerite, another scorned woman, who, however, must hold her powerful emotions in check. But the role of Carmen demands a more reckless kind of impassioned expression and, to that end, a somewhat new vocal approach. For despite the more conventional vocalization of her early scenes, as the character evolves and the tragedy grows, so must the intensity of the delivery so that by the final confrontation with her rejected lover many Carmens are ready to throw vocal caution to the wind. Indeed, while José's passionate pleas to win her back remain generally melodic, calling for a fully intoned legato, Carmen's defiant retorts are terse, fragmented, and declamatory. (The pair, in fact, neither have a traditional love duet nor sing in unison anywhere in the opera.) Later, when this kind of veristic expression—as this type of operatic writing came to be known—was in full flower, singers in the heat of the drama occasionally took it upon themselves to speak (or shout) words the composer had written to be sung, as, for example, the *"tiens"* Carmen spits out when she throws away the ring; or they might mix singing and speaking as in *"Frappez-moi donc, ou laisse moi passer."* But with such early examples of true verismo as *Cavalleria Rusticana* and *Pagliacci* still almost two decades in the future, the Gypsy's first portrayers probably never even considered such devices.

* * *

With few photographs and no films or recordings to help us, we rely on the era's plethora of important writers on music to tell us how the first half-generation of Carmens sang, looked, acted, and interpreted the wench. But because they lived at the same time and therefore lacked the perspective, they were not in a place to tell us how daunting the notion of publicly performing a protagonist of such questionable repute must have seemed to these first impersonators. Victims of a double standard, the female singers of the 19th century were both adulated by society for their glamour and talent as opera stars and, in the same breath, condemned by it for their exhibitionism. If they sinned by going on the stage in the first place, one can only imagine what it was for them to present themselves on it as an unapologetic champion of the liberated woman who smokes, brags, seduces, corrupts, and, furthermore, as a Gypsy at a time when Gypsies were considered anti–Christian, immoral, and essentially evil and taboo. But if the role of Carmen flew in the face of Victorian morality, her allure was such that the temptation to impersonate her was simply too great for some of the period's most famous songbirds—no matter how unsuited.

"Yes, *Carmen*," was the retort from Adelina Patti—arguably the most famous of the foolhardy—to her disbelieving friend, the critic Klein. "I have been longing to sing it for years and I am going to do so at last…. *J'aime tout ce qui est Carmen!* You will see me dance; you will hear how I play the castanets. I have never longed for anything so impatiently in my life."[17] And so, after transposing the pesky low parts to a higher key—in addition to the soprano options Guiraud added after Bizet's death—and adding some ornamentation to please her fans, the "greatest living mistress of the art of bel canto"[18] tried out her impersonation some four times for packed houses in London and New York—only to fall short. She sang well enough; some reviews even pointed to passages that were rendered with beautiful tone. But if her small, pure, high soprano was at too great a disadvantage, more to the point: "Her personality … was never fitted for the embodiment of a commonplace woman of the people…. Her rare gift of 'pantomime,' soon to develop to remarkable heights," said Klein, "stood her in good stead; but nothing could metamorphose the *grande cantatrice* into a *Carmen*."[19]

Then there was Zélia Trebelli, who, having introduced the *Habanera* to London in a concert, pleaded with Mapleson to mount the entire opera for her. Mapleson, of course, passed over her and chose Hauk. But Trebelli did get a measure of comeuppance five years later when, though 45 years old and a bit portly, and offering a portrayal best described as "intelligent and inoffensive, but nothing more,"[20] she created Carmen for the Metropolitan Opera during its inaugural season. In that the Parisian-born Trebelli was much loved for both her sweet persona and pure contralto—ideal for oratorio, a genre much favored by the British—"no more luscious rendering of the [Bizet] music could have been imagined." But, simply put, "she was not the right type for the wayward gypsy, and dramatically her impersonation proved a disappointment."²¹ And whereas George Bernard Shaw praised Trebelli as the most musical of all the Carmens of his time, he also noted her total absence of interest in the new naturalistic movement of acting. To be sure, the celebrated playwright and critic was almost certainly referring to the French soprano Emma Calvé, whose portrayal of the Gypsy as "a disorderly, lascivious, good-for-nothing factory girl,"²² he had initially blasted for its tasteless and excessive histrionics. But he might also have had Pauline Lucca of a half-generation

Adelina Patti, determined to sing Carmen no matter how wrong for her temperament (from the studio of Elliot & Fry).

earlier in mind. For, a pioneer when it came to realism in operatic acting, the soprano had shunned the charms of Hauk and rendered the Gypsy with a fierce mien..

Only a year younger than Galli-Marié and of a similar artistic disposition, in 1879 Lucca had replaced Bertha Ehnn as Carmen in her native Vienna, and all but turned the opera into a box-office sensation with her lifelike acting. Whereas Ehnn, as one critic said, had offered a "poetic" impersonation, Lucca had "portrayed her right away as the demonic lady who sold love by the hour."²³ "Lucca was piquant and she was 'sexy' (long before the word was invented)," the Viennese critic and historian Marcel Prawy noted a century later. "Her natural and uninhibited vivacity foreshadowed the later verismo."²⁴

Absent a photograph of Lucca as Carmen, one has only to look at any of those of her in her younger years or at the painting by Gustav Wertheimer to imagine her in the role. Small in stature, Lucca was renowned for her large, sultry eyes with their long black lashes. Furthermore, when playing herself as opera diva she was reputed to be as "capricious and unreliable as the Carmen she impersonated with so much vivacity."[25] And while her voice was "full, warm-blooded, and beautiful like the maiden herself," as the formidable soprano Lilli Lehmann testified,[26] it was "her ability to blend her singing and acting so intimately, that one did not consciously think of either, but enjoyed her impersonations as if they were scenes from life," that was, as Henry Finck believed, her greatest strength.[27]

Already in her late thirties when she first sang the part in Vienna, it did not take long for Lucca's Carmen to be touted in all the capitals, and by the time she returned to London after a decade's absence—plumper but still beautiful at the age of 43—the public was "agog" with anticipation to see her in the role. As Klein remembered it: "The 27th of May (1882) was a great night at the opera. [Lucca's] originality of treatment and her extraordinary powers of characterization had been expended upon a new role which was at all points suited to the bent of her genius."[28] "In working out her conception of the part," furthered the critic for the *Daily Telegraph*: "Mme. Lucca does not shrink from realism for the purpose of making things pleasant. Taking the broadest view of Mérimée's conception, she makes Carmen a very tigress, with cruel claws ready to dart forth and rend and tear on the smallest provocation. The slightest brush the wrong way turns our fascinating gypsy into a fiend. Mme. Lucca takes care that this shall be seen, almost as soon as she comes on the stage, in the furtive vindictive glance, and in the hard, set expression that falls like a cloud of night upon the whilom smiling face."[29]

Yes, the *Times* objected to "some effects of realism—including [the] inarticulate cries"[30] she interpolated in the last act but, albeit in fits and starts, realism on the stage was gaining ground. "Carmen is very remote from the old style operatic marionette," Krehbiel would write regarding Patti's attempt. "To present Mérimée's singularly fascinating though wicked creation, even in the modified form in which she appears in the French opera, calls for subtle acting and expressive singing—dramatic singing in the modern sense."[31]

CHAPTER 3

North, South, East, West

> But Bizet has his reward. Genius is immortal ... and it is no light honor that within four years of its introduction to the Parisian world crowds have assembled night after night to listen to the music of "Carmen" at the antipodes.—*Sydney Morning Herald*[1]

It is in effect a truism that people who live in the North yearn for the South. "Long live the sun and love!" Bizet himself had written from Rome, where he was spending two years as the recipient of the Rome prize.[2] To be sure, to escape the gloom of long Northern winters, those with the means, even today, travel great distances to bask in the light and warmth of the meridian sun, while those without make do with the books and paintings and music that evoke it. Not surprising then that the spring of 1878 found the citizens of frigid Russia and Sweden among the earliest to welcome the fiery Iberian.

"Here was sparkling full-blooded life," Gustaf Fröding, a future novelist, recalled of *Carmen*'s first performances in Stockholm:

> The sun burns hot on the Andalusian coast. The Mediterranean spreads wide with a thousand sails upon it. The life of the people is out on the beaches. Bare arms and legs. Dance, laughter, fervent talk. Dark warm eyes, merry, dreamy or impassioned. Wait, here comes Carmen. Yes, there she is, Mérimée's gypsy woman, wild girl, panther in woman form. Her blood is hot, she is supple like nothing else in this world, her skin blazes of warm colors, her eyes have a thousand capricious nuances, of which no one would speak of chastity and feminine shyness, for none of the Ten Commandments has she heard or ever felt in her heart.

* * *

Young Olfine Moe created the "wild girl" for her homeland. That her soprano voice was a little weak the critics ascribed to her pregnancy—some seven months. Nevertheless, having wisely adopted a position of "less is more," her dramatics they found praiseworthy—as did Fröding:

"Just now her eyes are sparking menace.... 'Be on guard—yes, beware.' It recurs unceasingly, and each time there is a new tone in passion's song. For Carmen is a vivid creature of her own kind, though she cannot think, and is without a conscience. And all of that I heard and saw in Moe's song alone ... for Fru Moe did not perform a single gesture to paint the mood. All lay in the song."

That Moe performed the "creature" only five more times before childbirth called was a disappointment to at least one critic, who complained her replacement, the mezzo Dina Niehoff, presented only the engaging side of Carmen whereas Moe had succeeded in presenting both the demonic and the engaging. Nonetheless, Moe, who, like Galli-Marié and Ehnn, was also known for her Mignon and Marguerite, returned later to sing the Gypsy some two dozen times for the Royal Theater as well as to create the role for the Christiania Theater, and to perform scenes from the Bizet in hotels in Sweden and abroad. All contributed mightily to the opera's successful early reception, and, in fact, annals show that from the time of its premiere (22 March 1878) through 2003 *Carmen* was one of the Royal Theater's most popular works, garnering some 1426 performances in that one theater alone.[3]

What is more, among Sweden's large output of internationally famous opera and concert singers, we find many a notable native Carmen, including Olive Fremstad, Sigrid Arnoldson, Kerstin Thorborg, Karin Branzell, Gertrud Wettergren, Kerstin Meyer and most recently, Anne Sofie von Otter. "Temperamentally we Swedes definitely have a streak of melancholy," von Otter once told an interviewer, "and because of the climate, the seasons, there's a lot of longing for the summer, the light nights, the sun."[4] Indeed, portrayals by singers from Northern and colder climates, more often than not informed the siren with a darker cast than she generally receives from Southerners. Her blood might be hot, but Carmen was, after all, a child of the cold mountains; moreover, a Gypsy, cunning and quick, who lived as much by her wits as her sex appeal, and an "other" who knew dark things the rest of us can only imagine. Did, in fact, the Carmen of the North understand something that the Carmen of the South could not? But returning to her chronicle.

* * *

In the words of Boris Schwarz: "Next to the Italians, the Russians are probably the world's most opera-loving and opera-conscious people. Long before there was a 'Russian' opera, there was opera in Russia."[5] And, by that, the noted Russian-born scholar meant opera as imported from

Mariya Slavina, the first Russian Carmen, 1885.

abroad, primarily from Italy. For in the 19th century Russia was still such a remote land that, much like America, it depended on European companies to supply its cosmopolitan centers with what was still a wholly European genre. Accordingly, then, it was an Italian company singing in Italian that in the winter of 1878 first performed *Carmen* for Russians in a theater known as the Bolshoi Stone in St. Petersburg. Perhaps it was the fault of a too decorous Bertha Ehnn—the same Austrian soprano who had created the role for Vienna—that the opera apparently made little impression at this time. But seven years later, on September 30, 1885, when it was led by St. Petersburg native Mariya Slavina at the Mariinsky Theater, it caught fire.

The "majestic"[6] Slavina had been for decades a beloved star of the Mariinsky. Described by her compatriot soprano Félia Litvinne as a "superb" mezzo-soprano[7] and by the baritone Sergei Levik as a "wonderful singer-actress,"[8] she was renowned for her Dalila, Ortrud, Amneris, and, later, as the creator of the Countess in *Pique Dame*. In the first year she sang the Gypsy a dozen times (spelled occasionally by the soprano Emiliya Pavlovskaya) and thereafter virtually owned the role at the prestigious theater, ultimately recording some 70 performances, some even after the arrival in 1896 of the popular Mei-Figner, whom we meet in a later chapter.

Other Middle European capitals embraced the Gypsy early as well: Budapest, even before Stockholm and St. Petersburg, in 1876; and Prague, Hamburg, Geneva, and Berlin in 1880. Berlin, as we remember, had refused to mount the opera for Minnie Hauk in 1877 in the belief that its audience would not accept it. But that was then. Thereafter, first with Emilia Tagliana, a pretty Italian coloratura soprano, in the title role, and then—with far greater effect—with the compelling Pauline Lucca, the Bizet would become such a favorite with Berliners that prior to the outbreak of World War I, the city would record more performances of the Bizet than any other opera—more even than any by Mozart or Wagner.

* * *

Australia first heard *Carmen* in 1879, compliments of the Rose Hersee Opera, a touring English troupe, during its visit to Melbourne. From the outset, critics raved, marveling at Bizet's score, especially its evocation of Spain, and noting that though "there is nothing refined or polite about the story ... there is that kind of reality in it which is excuse enough for the absorbed attention with which the audience watches its progress."[9] Hersee herself sang the title role. A veteran of the road, the comely soprano had toured in America and helped found the Carl Rosa Company in England. "Madame Hersee made a most effective Carmen," said one critic, "now piquantly mutinous, now archly persuasive, and now the restless termagant, but never outstepping the limits of discretion."[10] Said another: "Madame Hersee plays the role of the fickle fair one with appropriate hard-heartedness and fascination, and sang the music in her usual charming style."[11] As the performance was in English, with the *Habanera* and *Seguidilla* translated as "Love's a Willful Boy" and "This Night in Fair Seville City" respectively, one gets a pretty good idea of how "quaint" the performance must have been—most likely accounting for some of the opera's success. In any case, the indefatigable Hersee performed the role every night for three weeks; then, as the Australian winter progressed, took it upon herself to introduce it yet further Down Under.

* * *

In Southern Europe, *Carmen* found fertile ground in Italy after its 1879 premiere in Italian at the Teatro Bellini in Naples with Galli-Marié undoubtedly bringing the kind of fervor to the role Italians would have appreciated. Performing in Genoa in 1882, she even suffered a knife wound from her overzealous José—only the first of many such injuries Carmens would sustain over the generations. The Bizet scholar Winton Dean has written: "The influence of *Carmen* was much greater in Italy, where its realism was exploited at the expense of its artistry."[12] But if it is unlikely Galli-Marié sacrificed artistry at any turn, word of her performances in Italy very likely emboldened others, for, following the Naples premiere, the country embraced the new opera from abroad. So that when the lowlife characters, raw stories, violence and passion of *Cavalleria Rusticana* in 1890 and *Pagliacci* in 1892 established Italy as the birthplace of verismo opera, the country was primed.

* * *

In 1880 the *New York Times* reported that *Carmen* had "been translated into nearly all European languages and performed in every country but that of the native country of the gypsy girl."[13] Leave it, then, to the opera's greatest advocate, Galli-Marié, to rectify that curious omission the very next year. In a fascinating article, "Confronting Carmen Beyond the Pyrenees," we learn from Elizabeth Kertesz and Michael Christoforidis that when Barcelonas's Teatro Lirico engaged the mezzo to sing four roles in 1881, she may have insisted that *Carmen* be one of them. For it seems the Bizet received only a few perfunctory performances at the end of the season about which little was written. That one critic complimented Galli-Marié "on her characteristic and dramatic execution of a role difficult for an artist who had not been born in Spain"[14] might have been appreciated elsewhere in Spain but not by the Catalans, who considered themselves (then, as now) virtually a separate country. In any event, the Barcelona performance came and went relatively unnoticed, and for the next six years Spain all but forgot about *Carmen*.

But when the Gypsy finally reappeared in 1887, this time it was in her native Andalusia, and there the matter of Spanishness suddenly became one of singular urgency. Despite the best efforts of the Teatro Real, the city's principal opera house, the Teatro de la Zarzuela had managed to receive the rights to create the work—or, more accurately, adapt it—for Madrid. To turn *Carmen* into the popular *zarzuela* genre for which the theater was known, they engaged the writer Rafael María Liern to translate the libretto with its dialogue into the vernacular, and, at the same time, remedy what they perceived its French creators glaring misconceptions about Spain and its customs.[15] In as much as the Gypsy herself was concerned, "Liern created quite a different and uniquely Spanish effect by writing for Carmen in the first person and removing overt references to the gypsies from the text," Kertesz and Christoforidis explained. Carmen reflects on how she feels when singing and dancing, activities to which she was born, and which wipe away all her tiredness and pain. For a Spanish audience "these lyrics ... perform a hispanicising function, authenticating Carmen as both Andalusian and *aflamencada* [flamenco-like]."[16] In any case, though critics attending the premiere at the Teatro de la Zarzuela on Nov. 2, 1887, were mixed as to the company's efforts to turn *Carmen* into a zarzuela, Bizet's music was enough to overcome not only the poor singing by Eulalia Gonzalez in the title role, but the blatant butchering of the libretto.

And so it was left to Madrid's Teatro Real to unveil the true *Carmen*, and this they did in traditional grand opera style on March 14, 1888. Happy to forget about the controversy as to its foreign elements—though discussion away from the theater was ongoing—the Madrileños delighted in the lavish production and its excellent cast, led by the superb mezzo Giuseppina Pasqua. The Italian, renowned for having created Mistress Quickly in Verdi's *Falstaff* at La Scala,[17] had been a star of the Teatro Real for many seasons. In any case, *Carmen* soon became a repertory work in much of Spain, but over the decades the country itself would produce only a precious few natives in the title role. We meet them in later chapters; precious not just because they are so rare, but because, in imbuing their portrayals with qualities unique to the culture, they reveal yet more of her infinite ways.

* * *

The Teatro Real performed *Carmen* in Italian because the company was Italian. But the matter of what language *Carmen*, or any opera, was performed in the 19th century was complicated. Even today, one can never be sure what language management will decide on. But, generally speaking, until the Second World War, most companies performed opera in the language of the audience—Hungarian in Hungary, Swedish in Sweden and so forth.

The exceptions were the English-speaking countries, where many operas, some even written in English by native composers, were translated into Italian, in part because they still considered Italian to be the language of opera. The British, in fact, did not hear *Carmen* in French until 1886 when Galli-Marié sang the original at the Haymarket as a guest with a French company, and Covent Garden audiences had to wait until 1894 when Zélie de Lussan led the cast. At the Metropolitan Opera in New York, Trebelli and Hauk sang Carmen in Italian and Lilli Lehmann in German. It was not until 1893 that, thanks to Emma Calvé's insistence, Met audiences finally got to hear a French language *Carmen*.

The English touring companies, however, did perform in the vernacular. One of the best was the Carl Rosa Opera Company, which first took *Carmen* on the road in 1879 with two rival English stars of light opera, the lyric mezzo Selina Dolaro and the soprano Emily Soldene, alternating in the title role. "I had a natural turn for the tragic," Soldene recalled, "and my acquired taste and experience in comic opera enabled me to give many little touches which had not been thought of before." (Oh, to know what they might have been.) But while both would take their separate versions to the New World, it was Minnie Hauk who got to create the seductress—in Italian as she had in London—for her native land.

With London's endorsement of the new Bizet, the astute Henry Mapleson, alert to America's growing fascination with opera and opera stars, had, in September of 1878, rushed his *Carmen* production along with its star, Minnie Hauk, to Dublin, where it was both loudly protested and loudly cheered; and from there across the ocean for a premiere in New York City the following month. Though the city had as yet neither a Metropolitan nor Manhattan Opera Company, opera at its Academy of Music flourished as impresarios vied to present a steady stream of international stars to eager New Yorkers.

Word of Hauk's triumphs as Carmen abroad had preceded her; but on seeing the opera for themselves, New York critics struggled to reconcile the artist with the un–Christian character she was depicting. For while they thought her impersonation—red flower between her teeth and all—"very clever ... full of character; conceived well from instinct; equally well wrought by art," they viewed the protagonist as "a vulgar gypsy girl, and a young girl in whom we can take no interest."[18] Two weeks later, an editorial for the same *New York Times* took the matter further, as it described the "strange fascination [the] despicable character exerts, especially on women who have never seen anything like her," speculating that the opera's success must, therefore, be the result of the "mental and moral tone of the period."[19]

In any case—Hauk having run interference—in no time America was awash with portrayers of the "despicable character," including stars of various touring companies, who introduced her in towns and cities across the sprawling young country. Among them, not only some we have already met in Europe, such as Lucca, Soldane, and Dérivis, but also the American Clara Louise Kellogg, the Russian Anna de Belocca, and the very French Marie Roze, who, since turning down Bizet's offer to create the role apparently had had a change of heart.

* * *

It would be nice to know just what made Roze decide to reverse herself and take on the role she had told Bizet was too "scabrous" for her. But seeing how popular the *fille du Satan* had become, she now met her challenge with gusto, first in England and then throughout America, even on the West Coast, where she created the role for Max Strakosch's touring company as early as 1879. The opera had been written for her, she liked to say—prior commitments having kept her from singing the premiere. To be sure, that tall tale aside, Roze—usually described as a light soprano, though she sang everything from Verdi's Aida to Wagner's Ortrud—was not one to have missed out, even if the role did, in fact, prove too scabrous. "The gentlest mannered gypsy that was ever stabbed by a jealous lover," her rival, the Connecticut-born Kellogg, remembered, "—a handsome Carmen but too sweet and good for anything."[20]

As for Kellogg, though, the soprano would make her own false claims: correct in that she was the first American woman to make a major career in opera abroad, but wrong in that she did not create Carmen for America, as she wrote in her autobiography, even if she almost did. For, in truth, only three days after Hauk introduced Carmen to America in New York,

3. North, South, East, West 39

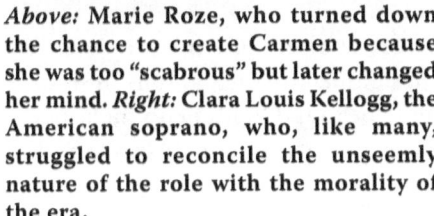

Above: Marie Roze, who turned down the chance to create Carmen because she was too "scabrous" but later changed her mind. *Right:* Clara Louis Kellogg, the American soprano, who, like many, struggled to reconcile the unseemly nature of the role with the morality of the era.

Kellogg created her in Philadelphia. What is more, having taken her portrayal to Toronto in March 1879, she could probably rightfully claim to have created the Gypsy in Canada.

But despite her criticisms of Roze, Kellogg too struggled to reconcile the "scabrous" nature of the protagonist with the morality of the epoch. As one critic judged: "The leading part, taken by Miss Kellogg was simply Miss Kellogg as she always is in comedy, but more than usually vulgarized. She overdoes the whole business of the low, reckless, insolent heroine of the story, and makes of her a person not worthy of the sympathy and tender interest that the opera heroine normally inspires."[21]

On the other hand, Anna de Belocca seems to have avoided the problem by simply keeping anything that could be seen as "scabrous" in check. For the handsome Russian contralto of aristocratic birth, who had been singing in America since 1876, was, plain and simply, "a very lady-like

Carmen, graceful and earnest," according to the *New York Times*, and "much gentler in her manners than [Hauk, who] in America still remains without a peer in the character."[22]

Indeed, Minnie Hauk had become the era's prototype of Bizet's creation. No other singer had been more successful at tempering the brutality and sexuality that so shocked Victorian era audiences while still providing the deviltry and sensuality that beguiled them. Hauk's Carmen teased but did not offend. And if this sounds like she was evading the sexuality inherent in the part, she must be forgiven. She certainly didn't "invent" the role, as she claimed,[23] but it was she who truly popularized it. In an age of picture postcard portrayals, the naked realism that Galli-Marié and later Lucca brought to the role, if probably minimal by today's standards, was still viewed with caution.

In her memoirs, Kellogg protested what she perceived as the era's "unwritten law against realism in emotion," a law which may have worked for some roles but not for such a "too terribly human" character as Carmen. With audiences seemingly ready to make the leap, however, she felt certain the problem would soon be nothing more than a matter of *"autres temps, autres moeurs!"*[24]

No matter: while Kellogg looked for answers, Carmen, now established in North America, continued her globe-trotting, and in 1881, only six years after the premiere in Paris, could be found lighting up such southern metropolises as New Orleans,[25] Mexico City, Buenos Aires, and Rio de Janeiro.

Chapter 4

Home Again

"Finally! Carmen has come back to us!"—Leon Kerst, November 1893[1]

But while *Carmen* progressed rapidly and triumphantly across countries and even continents,[2] back in the city of its birth Bizet's magnificent score went unheard for seven years. Shocking as this was, there were reasons—complicated ones. For the opera had to contend not only with its detractors but also with the daunting contractual obligations the city imposed on its two publicly funded theaters, one of which was the Favart's Opéra-Comique, where *Carmen* had premiered.

Key among these were the stipulations that each of the two theaters (the other being the Théâtre-Lyrique) produce only the genre of opera the city assigned it, and that any opera it did produce not be performed in any of the city's other numerous theaters. Thus, *Carmen*, when in Paris, could only be heard at the Salle Favart, the city's designated theater for opéra comique (light opera). Its successful transformation to grand opera in Vienna and other cities counted as nothing in Paris. Consequently, when Camille du Locle withdrew the Bizet from the Comique's repertoire after its final performance in February 1876, he was, in essence, ending its chances for performance in Paris unless it was revived by the Opéra-Comique itself. But when, with the company on the verge of collapse, du Locle retired soon after, his replacement Leon Carvalho, formerly a director of the Théâtre-Lyrique, had no interest in reviving an opera that he himself had not liked and considered inappropriate for the "family" theater he had been appointed to rescue.

All the same, despite these obstacles, in the early 1880s a groundswell for *Carmen*'s return began to build, no doubt spurred on by reports of its successes abroad. From Barcelona, where she had premiered the work in August 1881, Galli-Marié wrote Bizet's widow: "I am very happy to tell you that we have had another great success, this time in Carmen's own country.... I shall be playing Carmen at Dieppe the eighteenth of this month—Dieppe is very near Paris!"³

The Gypsy's faithful creator, whose fervent wish it was to be the one to bring the *sorcière* home, had, in fact, never ceased lobbying for the opera's return, and by 1882, many of the Parisian press, obviously chagrined by reports of its triumphs elsewhere, were ready to put their original criticisms aside and join her. At the same time, having taken to heart what these same critics had originally written of her role in its failure, Galli-Marié, for her part, had worked to temper the inflammatory aspects of that initial portrayal. The "new manner I have adopted, which seems to me less harsh than the first,"⁴ she believed would be enough to placate Halévy and Meilhac. But the librettists remained implacable: Galli-Marié, they said, had played Mérimée's Carmen and not theirs and was to blame for the opera's failure. So when Carvalho finally agreed to revive the opera, he did not turn to the mezzo to lead it, but, instead, engaged a soprano he believed would be safe.

Yet when on April 21, 1883, the Favart's curtain finally rose again on the square in Seville, it was almost as if the director's personal dislike of the Bizet had gotten the better of his usually excellent judgment. Not only were the scenery and costumes shabby and the performers shockingly under-rehearsed, but he had sanitized the entire production to such a point that the original was barely recognizable. And in that vein, he had cast as the charismatic seductress a singer who, despite having once attempted the Gypsy in Lyons, could hardly have been more wrong for the part and was totally out of her depth.⁵

* * *

A coloratura soprano, Adèle Isaac had made her Opéra-Comique debut as Marie in *La Fille du Régiment* in 1873, and in 1881 created both Olympia and Antonia in *Les Contes d'Hoffmann* for the company. Immensely popular and still young—a full 14 years younger than Galli-Marié—though her music as Carmen was transposed up to compensate for the weakness in her lower range, her singing was highly regarded. But there was no compensating for her quaint acting style, genteel look, and absence of temperament. What greeted Paris after its long wait, then, was "an expurgated Carmen, a cool Carmen," who "sang correctly, but [without] the fire and deviltry of Galli-Marié."⁶ No rose between the teeth à la Galli-Marié; rather, Isaac "wears a flower modestly on her bodice and throws it with such modest grace one would believe one is seeing a young

4. Home Again

girl at a charity auction."[7] "She seems to say: The requirements of my art compel me to show myself to you in the costume of a shameless hussy; but believe me it means nothing. You can come to my home. I have a spic-and-span sitting room, and, on my mantelpiece, are little knick-knacks, neatly arranged. My family is honorable, and I frequent only the homes of well-bred, bourgeois, peaceful folks, not at all [those of] gypsies or smugglers."[8]

Nonetheless, Bizet's masterpiece, it seems, was foolproof; for the revival would be well-attended for some 17 performances before the critics' outpouring of anger against the disgraceful production left Carvalho no choice but to try again the following fall with singers who were well-rehearsed, with music, sets, and costumes restored to the original, and with the title role returned to its creator.

As such, even Halévy had to finally acknowledge that "the triumph of Bizet was absolute, complete."[9] And so too the triumph of Galli-Marié, who, despite whatever modifications she may have made, critics agreed, "did not hold back on the interpretation she had developed during some 350 performances of this role around Europe."[10] Said one: "As an actress Mme. Galli-Marié has come back to us more accomplished perhaps than before. She rendered the passionate, bizarre, dynamic, cruel portrait of this girl of the streets with a power and an ease that compel admiration."[11]

Indeed, those who had crucified her portrayal in 1875 now heaped praise on the reinstated—albeit plumper—creator.[12] "Mme Galli-Marié is the personification of Carmen as Mérimée conceived her," declared Commetant—the very same who, as we remember after the premiere, had demanded her Gypsy be "fastened into a straitjacket,

Celestine Galli-Marié, at the time of her return to Paris for the revival of Carmen (drawing by Henri Meyer, cover engraving of *Le Journal illustré*, May 18, 1884).

after being cooled off by a jug of water poured over her head." And, as an explanation for his about-face: "This incarnation at first seemed shocking to the decent audience of the Opéra-Comique, which today accepts it without reservation. Carmen, the most hair-raising strumpet of Moorish blood gained her naturalization papers at the bourgeois, prudish Salle Favart."[13]

* * *

Her triumphant return behind her, Galli-Marié sang Carmen some 63 more times at the Comique, then departed to fulfill prior commitments, leaving it to Marie Castagné, just out of the conservatoire, to put her own stamp on the "hair-raising strumpet," and, thereafter, to any number of the other young, primarily native, singers who made up Carvalho's roster. Other than a few performances at the end of the season Galli-Marié herself was not heard again in the role until December 11, 1890, when she came out of retirement for one final performance, a gala to raise funds for a monument to Bizet. Surrounded by a cast of giants—Jean de Reszke, Jean Lassalle, and Nellie Melba—it was a brave gesture for the former star, now aged 50. "Poor Gallé-Marie [sic], the original Carmen, looked still herself, but her voice is entirely gone," the *New York Times* reported in a communiqué to America. "She was visibly fatigued long before the end of the performance."[14]

* * *

In the more than eight decades between the premiere and its official entrance into the repertoire of the Opéra de Paris in 1959,[15] the Salle Favart would mount so many performances of *Carmen* that it began noting just what number performance each was in its programs. Milestone numbers received special mention: the 100th performance on December 22, 1883, led by Galli-Marié; the 1000th on December 23, 1904, by Emma Calvé; the 2000th on June 29, 1930, by Lucy Perelli; the 2,500th on June 1, 1947, by Solange Michel.

Carvalho himself—his lapse of judgment a thing of the past—not wanting to slow the momentum, presented his vastly improved production continuously throughout the remainder of his tenure with a great variety of excellent Carmens, among them: the Swedish soprano Sigrid Arnoldson (a former Micaëla), the charming Parisian-born lyric mezzo Charlotte Wyns, and the rapidly rising Emma Calvé in her first performances of the role that would seal her considerable renown. At the same time he successfully fought to rid the company of many of the city's restrictions, thereby opening up new opportunities for it. But in 1887, blamed for a tragic fire at the theater, which killed many, he was jailed for six months and forced to resign. Reinstated in 1891, he went on to serve the Opéra-Comique till his death in 1897.

Albert Carré was Carvalho's even more progressive successor. Fortunate to have inherited a company that was prosperous and mostly free of the city's regulations thanks to his predecessor, the new director made the most of these gifts and took the Opéra-Comique triumphantly into the 20th century. Spoken dialogue no longer a requirement, he weeded the lighter-weight operas from the repertoire, and in their place presented not only the latest in verismo from Italy but also such provocative new works as Charpentier's *Louise* and Debussy's *Pelléas et Mélisande*. And he revisited *Carmen*, a staple in the repertoire but burdened by the conventional notions of what opera at the Opéra-Comique should look like. For the grand opening of the rebuilt Salle Favart in December 1898[16] he scheduled a new production and—though he must have known the risk he was taking—cast one of the most eccentric, flamboyant, vocally questionable artists of the era in the title role.

* * *

Georgette Leblanc had attempted her first Carmen—probably the first to wear a blonde wig for the role—at Brussels' La Monnaie three years before. At the time she was in the first throes of a long and turbulent relationship with the famous poet and playwright Maurice Maeterlinck, which almost certainly affected her approach. "It was a strange Carmen that my mood was incarnating," she recalled in her memoirs. "Fanatical, burning.... I worked in a delirium."[17] Or, as one critic saw it,

> in a tavern where gipsy women meet soldiers, [Leblanc] evoked the apparition of a woman of Mantegna or Boticelli, degraded, vile, who gives the idea of a shameless creature that has not lost entirely the gracefulness of her original rank. She is sensual, impudent, voluptuous, gross, but in her white diction, in her blithe walk, you divine her desire of evoking something else.... Carmen is, according to Leblanc, a hybrid, monstrous creature. You look upon her with eager curiosity and infinite sadness.... She is one of the most emotional interpreters of our period.[18]

With that incarnation a thing of the past, however, for Carré, with whom she claimed to share "the same ardor for uprooting old prejudices," the diva was now quite willing to give up her "fantastical gypsy" and in its stead bring "a realism hitherto unknown" to the role.[19] And so, with Maeterlinck and Carré in tow, she headed to Spain to learn just exactly what that would be. Though the trio found no sign of "Mérimée's cigar

Georgette Leblanc, who claimed to have brought a "realism hitherto unknown" to the role (photograph by Paul Boyer).

girl" in Seville, in Granada they met "Carmen herself, the real gypsy," who, according to Carré's memoirs, they brought back to teach the dancers.[20] In the end, "Our Carmen caused an upheaval," Leblanc recalled. "My costumes, my gestures, my walk, the authentic atmosphere of the ensemble disconcerted lovers of routine and enchanted everyone else. The essential thing was the impulse that was generated. A new tradition was born."[21]

Maybe, maybe not. In casting Leblanc, Carré had invited trouble and got it. We know from his memoirs that in addition to her inadequate singing, her characterization was so extravagant as to border on caricature. Her performance had clearly crossed the line. Though pleased with the new production, the soprano had to go.[22]

No matter: there was no dearth of notable new sirens to assay the Gypsy for Carré, whose enlightened tenure would extend—except for a break during the war—until 1925. Among them: Jeanne Marié de l'Isle, Blanche Arral, Zélie de Lussan, Marie Delna, Claire Friché, Maria Gay, Alice Raveau, Marguerite Sylva, Marguerite Merentié, Lucienne Breval, Genevieve Vix, Mary Garden, Marthe Chenal, Ninon Vallin, and Clotilde Bressler-Gianoli. Even *La belle* Otero was given a chance, though it is not clear why. But as the beautiful courtesan and sometime music-hall actress was obsessed with the idea, Carré probably thought her notoriety too good for his box office to pass up.

* * *

While some of these new interpreters would take their portrayals around the world, most, especially those who were French, typically stayed home performing at the Comique or in the French provinces. Steeped in the company's best traditions (Carré having weeded out most of the bad) and isolated from the "grand" version, though now accepted everywhere else, these singers knew just how to reconcile the "scabrous" in Carmen's character with the refinement, charm, and emotional restraint of the French style and elegance of Bizet's music. In this they were helped by the smaller size of the theater and simplicity of the productions, including the smaller orchestra and the plain, sometimes even drab, costumes we see in many of their photographs. Yes, the company had a budget, but its avoidance of anything very colorful was more a matter of its style. As none other than Fedora Barbieri, a popular mid–20th century Italian Carmen, once told an interviewer: "The French colors of Carmen are not so bright, not so torrid.... The French spirit and language of Bizet and Mérimée give more subtle hues to the drama."[23] In any case, a performance at the Opéra-

Comique was the one place an operagoer could hear a *Carmen* true to its origins—unlike, for that matter, any other in the world.

* * *

It is all but extinct now—this French school of singing. Indeed, national schools and styles have become so globalized, leaving distinctions between them so blurred, as to be all but unidentifiable as such anymore. Even today's celebrated French soprano Natalie Dessay, whom one would think might have protected every last vestige possible of the Gallic school, on the contrary, applauds its gradual shift to the Italian school, which she believes provides greater warmth and fullness to the high register.[24]

And so we depend on old recordings to hear that certain something only the French school once provided. Of course, as the industry was still in its infancy when they were made, our ears have to make allowances for their foibles and limitations. But while without these recordings we would know only what we read, with them we can hear for ourselves how singers born into or trained in such a distinctive vocal style delivered its unique characteristics.

* * *

Like most national vocal styles—and perhaps more than most—French singing until after the Second World War stemmed from the specific nature of the language itself, which insisted on a high and forward placement of the voice and resulted in a firm, focused, narrow sound. Moreover, as it was part of the Gallic singer's makeup to reach the tone through the word, language contributes mightily to his or her elegant phrasing and natural way with tempo rubato. One has only to hear how effortlessly the artists in any recording from the Opéra-Comique alternate between dialogue and singing to appreciate the correspondence. "Lyric sound is finest when it is most akin to speech," said the composer Charles Gounod, himself a former tenor. "Purely vocal sound, however beautiful, needs to be varied by words, which alone give expression, dramatic feeling, warmth and life. Pure diction is the first law of song."[25]

Thus, for the French singer, as for her listeners, the intelligibility of the text was everything. Words were not demons that must be tamed and molded into the column of sound as in other schools; rather they were the spring-board to an ideal placement of the voice. As a result, Gallic voices were recognized by their brightness, purity, float, and clarity; but never volume or richness.

On the other hand, because the character and contours of the language require a greater involvement of teeth, lips, and nose than do other languages, a certain amount of resonance is unavoidably cut off—and this greatly affected how Carmen sounded in that time and place. One rarely hears from a singer trained in the French school the juicy, plush sound generally associated with the role of Carmen today. There are exceptions, naturally, but even when one listens to such a gigantic contralto as that of Jeanne Gerville-Réache one is struck more by the laser intensity of the voice than by its opulence—though "opulent" it certainly was as well.

At any rate, because the Salle Favart was relatively small, seating only a little over 1200, singers could deliver the text easily and with greater attention to verbal clarity and nuance than their colleagues in houses where amplitude of voice took priority over style, explaining much about Bizet's writing for voice. "When I opened the score," Lorraine Hunt-Lieberson, a one-time Carmen, told an interviewer, "the first thing I noticed is that all the arias are marked piano and pianissimo ... [*Carmen*] is French lyric writing with lots of intimate singing."[26] But because such intimate singing was not easily exported to big houses or to countries where audiences were used to the more rounded vocalism that came from a conventional Italian training, French lyric singing gradually fell into disuse. Anna Arnaud, who sang Carmen often in France and, as a replacement for an ill Olive Fremstad, in one performance at the Metropolitan Opera in 1905,[27] was clear as to the consequences when she told an interviewer: "In France the interpretation of Carmen is different from that one seen here [in America]. The presentation of the part is light. The Metropolitan in New York is too large 'a frame' for this opera, and in assigning the part to artists accustomed to sing grand opera, a heavy character which is not in accord with the music nor with the subject, results."[28]

* * *

Fortunately, multiple recordings of exemplary singing of French music by French and French-trained singers are available and *Carmen* is well represented. True to every aspect of French style, these are all straightforward, even spare, readings in sharp contrast to the inflated ones we hear on recordings from the second half of the 20th century on, and from them we get a glimpse as to how our heroine might once have presented herself.

In 1905 an interesting article by one Gabriel Bernard, titled "Carmens et Carmen," appeared in *La Revue Théâtrale*, which included interviews with several of the earliest Carmens. Among them we find 60-year-old Galli-Marié recalling how she had played the role 1200 times; how important the Mérimée was to her; how she was accidentally cut by José in Genoa and still had the scar, and how management at the Opéra-Comique had originally wanted José and Carmen to marry at the end. But he also speaks with two singers closely connected to Carmen's creator, affording history a direct line to the premiere.

It has been said that Galli-Marié considered the now forgotten Cécile Ketten to be her "faithful successor" in the role[29]; but Ketten's remarks here are slight; and, alas, she left no recordings. On the other hand, Jeanne Marié de L'Isle, who was not only Galli-Marié's niece but also coached the role with her aunt, tells us quite a bit about the original collaboration both by way of her recordings and, though she is naturally speaking for herself, in her remarks to Bernard. For example:

> Here is how I imagine her and how I would like to portray her. She is 18 years old, *proud*, proud like every animal of breeding, refined and elegant, proud by the very strength of the beautiful proportion of her figure ... morally proud like every primitive being that education has not made more tractable. Completely instinctual, she knows only her desire and the fulfillment of this desire, whatever the price and whatever the consequences.
>
> To be in love; it is this desire that guides her to the exclusion of all other feelings.... Carmen, as she has been created by the authors, knows what she *does* and what she *wants*.
>
> Very superstitious and fatalistic, and believing one does not escape one's destiny, she goes to her death bravely, without fighting very long against it, certain that what is written must transpire. She very sincerely believes herself a sorceress, which gives her a sense of great superiority, whence comes her provocative, attractive charm. She is not coquettish but rather fascinates by the sheer will that her *desire* ignites in her.
>
> Once the artist has studied the novella, the libretto and the score, and once she has understood and felt them separately, she melds them together and tries to extract from these three creations a synthesis, a Carmen who is the fourth creation, an archetypal Carmen, the "lyric" Carmen.
>
> I have worked hard to respect Bizet's music religiously, by singing it without altering either the rhythm or the tempo, and by observing all the stylistic nuances, hoping thereby to achieve the ideal as the composer conceived it.[30]

Marié de l'Isle had first sung Mercedes to Leblanc's Carmen but soon replaced the controversial soprano in the title role. The recordings she made in 1905,[31] the year of Bernard's interview and the year her aunt died, are not only documents of invaluable historical interest, but also show her as a superb singer in her own right.

She sings Carmen lightly in a crisp, lyric mezzo, totally free of show or mannerisms, and, as she insists to Bernard, with total fidelity to the score—all of which point to Galli-Marié's coaching. This was a time—the turn of the 19th century—when singers had no compunction about changing

4. Home Again

the score to suit themselves and, as exemplified by Leblanc, when temperament and personality were in high gear—even at the Opéra-Comique. But for Galli-Marié's niece only French style at its purest would do.[32]

* * *

In 1911 Pathé initiated a series of nine complete opera recordings, including the first ever of *Carmen* in French—an earlier version having been made in 1908 in German, about which more later. One could not ask for a better send off. Marguerite Merentié, who had come over from the Opéra de Paris to make her Opéra-Comique debut as Carmen in 1909 leads the cast. A dramatic soprano, who had sung roles ranging from Aida to Sieglinde, Merentié's voice is perhaps more full-bodied and ripe than many of the French Gypsies, but her richly nuanced delivery is clean and direct. No artifice here, just Carmen—comfortable in all her guises—being Carmen.

Jeanne Marié de L'Isle, who studied Carmen with her aunt, Galli-Marié, the role's creator (photograph from Reutlinger studio).

Other complete or near complete recordings in the Opéra-Comique tradition, though none with as much of the original dialogue as in the Pathé, offer Carmens by Germaine Cernay, Ninon Vallin (in extended excerpts), Raymonde Visconti (slightly abridged), Solange Michel, Suzanne Brohly, Suzanne Juyol, and Lucy Perelli.

Juyol was actually a last-minute replacement for Martha Mödl, because the recording—only the second complete *Carmen* on LP—was being made in France and there were objections to using a German singer so soon after the war (1951). The producer John Culshaw has described the French soprano as "a large, jolly lady" whose specialties were Brünnhilde and Isolde.[33] Not surprisingly, then, her singing is loud and aggressive. By comparison, the mezzo Lucy Perelli's voice in a recording from 1927 makes for easier listening, except that her characterization is almost too cool and casual, even for the Opéra-Comique, where she nonetheless sang the role often.

Others from the above list, however, show just what it is that people admire about French singing and the Opéra-Comique performance style. The beautiful Germaine Cernay sang with the Opéra-Comique, though never Carmen, from 1927 till her untimely death, at age 43, in 1943. A lyric mezzo, Cernay's repertoire was wide ranging. She was renowned for her Bach, but other of her recordings include a vivid Santuzza in *Cavalleria Rusticana*. *Carmen*, her last, was actually made from a broadcast from Marseilles the year before her death. That she took on the promiscuous Gypsy at this time seems a little strange in that her great wish had been to become a nun and she was believed to be about to enter a convent. In any case, under the French composer and conductor D. E. Inghelbrecht, who once wrote a book about how *not* to interpret *Carmen*, *Faust* and *Pelléas*,[34] Cernay is scrupulous in observing every marking, while rendering a firm, somewhat understated, but nonetheless detailed and highly personal reading. Her blunt delivery of the card aria is especially affecting as it is only for a moment that we hear Carmen betray her anguish and vulnerability in front of the card's prophecy before ending the aria shaken but steady. Similarly, in the final duet she divulges only glimpses of fear; she will not lose control no matter how pressed.

One of the most recorded artists of her time and a favorite in her native land, Ninon Vallin is—excepting Conchita Supervía whom we meet later—arguably as far removed from the typical idea of Carmen as any on disc. In fact, the sunny lyric soprano had made her Opéra-Comique debut as Micaëla to the Carmen of Marthe Chenal in 1912 and continued to sing the village maiden. But it is as the Gypsy herself, a role she purportedly studied with Calvé, that she is better known. Author and opera enthusiast Vincent Sheean, who saw *Carmen* at the Opéra-Comique when the company was at an all-time low owing in large part to the city's inadequate funding, said that Vallin's portrayal lifted everyone else to a higher plane and was all in all the best he ever heard at the Comique.[35]

One of the few French singers to have an international career, Vallin retained her French manner whether at La Scala, in South America where

4. Home Again

she was especially popular, or in the U.S., where she was not. Whereas, prior to the First World War, French singers at the Opéra-Comique tended to like their isolation, it was different afterwards when those who wanted to work "had to compete internationally and homogenize their sound and manner."[36] But Vallin remained Vallin, to the point that in 1934 San Franciscans, lacking an understanding of the restraint and nuance inherent in the French style, found Vallin's light, elegant Carmen too "cool, intimate and straight-laced."[37] In other words, her portrayal in no way resembled the sultry seductress that Americans—especially those in a city reared in Italian opera, as was San Francisco—had come to expect from the Gypsy.

But on her recordings how compelling and seductive is her portrayal as she sculpts the words at every turn of the music to meet Carmen's every meaning, every inference. How what might seem just a straightforward sprightly *Seguidilla* actually abounds in telling details, all aimed at making her plan to have José meet her at Lillas Pastia's impossible for him to resist.

Ninon Vallin, an exquisite exponent of the French style.

Unfortunately there is no complete recording of Vallin's Carmen, but the recorded excerpts are extensive—and irresistible.

Making her way up from the chorus to small roles and in 1946 to Mignon and other leads at the Favart, Solange Michel, though a guest artist with many important houses in London and on the continent, was never considered an international star. But she sang over 500 Carmens in her career—primarily at the Opéra-Comique—and in 1950 made a complete recording of the role that to this day holds a place of honor in the *Carmen* catalog for many connoisseurs. Under the baton of André Cluytans, who gives a superb representation of the authentic Comique style, her easy-going, vibrant mezzo with its soprano overtones is ideal; and her delivery—excepting some clumsiness with ornaments—crisp, assured, and free of any affect. Her Carmen is the chameleon Mériméé describes; a woman always of the moment—laughing, teasing, infuriating, ranting; raw emotion—albeit blunt and poised—only rising to the surface in the Card Scene.

* * *

Owing, then, to recordings, reviews, and reminiscences we have some idea of how Carmen might have been performed in Bizet's time and place. Looking again at Bernard's interviews with the

Solange Michel, arguably the best recorded Carmen in the authentic Opéra-Comique style (photograph from the Harcourt studio).

early Comique singers, it seems that most thought of Carmen as capricious, passionate, honest, whimsical, fatalistic; and they resisted any suggestion that she was unlikable, that she could be mean or evil, or that she could be a whore or prostitute. "Very female, very captivating, but *never a prostitute*," the soprano Mathilde Tarquini d'Or insisted, "because her character would lose its interest and its most endearing side."[38]

One thing, however, is curiously missing in the Bernard interviews. Whereas singers of other nationalities ascribe great importance to her determination to be free at any cost—*"Libre elle est née, et libre elle mourra,"* as she declares in defiance of José's threats—it seems that *"la libertad"* was of little consequence to these early French Carmens, for none of them mention it. Was it just a coincidence? Or did they think being free was just a "Gypsy" thing, unrelated to their own situation, and thus of lesser significance? After all, French women came late to the feminist movement, and did not even receive the right to vote until 1944, far later than almost any other western country. Nevertheless, in keeping with both the time-honored practices of the company and the conservative nature of the French in general, those who sang Carmen with the Opéra-Comique never lost sight of the sophistication of Bizet's score and tended towards restrained, even cool, impersonations, free of melodrama, and, consequently, quite different from what operagoers saw elsewhere.

* * *

Exceptions there were, of course. For, as Marie Castagné had told Bernard in 1905, "things called audacious 15 years ago have become very easily accepted by audiences now."[39] Georgette Leblanc's excess and unruliness certainly come to mind. And in 1909 the Swiss soprano Lucienne Breval, a handsome, big woman best known for her Wagner, would unveil "a conception of Carmen never before seen" at the Comique, or so thought an American critic, who observed: "More gypsy than Spanish, she [Breval] communicates ... throughout the piece the tragic fatality of her passion."[40] In point of fact, the French so seldom referred to Carmen as a Gypsy that Breval went out of her way to explain that she simply saw her as a child of nature, neither good nor bad, neither French nor Spanish but rather a true *gitana*. "It was inevitable that a role that had become everybody's role would lose its authenticity and simplicity," she said, "[but] Carmen is a gypsy, nothing more." Thus, when José killed her, Breval did not take even one step back, but, stabbed in the chest, fell forward on her knees—a moment that apparently astounded those who saw it.[41] Breval, who had spent months living among the Gypsies in Spain, even commissioned the Spanish painter Zuloaga to design her costumes and paint two portraits of her in them, looking, said a critic, like "a Goya heroine come to life."[42]

Among others who refused to conform to the acting and staging traditions seen at the Salle Favart we find Bressler-Gianoli, Maria Gay, Mary Garden, and, of course Emma Calvé, who, after despairing of the *traditions* she so hated, ended up unwittingly making some of her own. But while all performed Carmen at the Opéra-Comique at the turn of the century, these particular groundbreakers would go on to build international careers and are better placed in the next chapter, where we watch a new kind of Carmen emerge in conjunction with the rapidly changing mores of the coming century. "Look here, I'm me," women were beginning to say. And had they looked in the mirror, these spirited new artists might well have seen the defiant one as herself.

Chapter 5

Emma Calvé and the New Realism

> As a low woman of the people does she [Emma Calvé] effect her first entrance, garbed in the shabbiest of finery.... A woman with a heap of pasts.—*New York Herald*[1]

> She [Galli-Marié] was charged with immorality, but it is not likely she allowed herself as many gipsy liberties as some of her successors.—Carl van Vechten[2]

It was "undoubtedly the greatest and most elaborate theatrical representation ever given at Windsor," said the *Times*.[3] The queen had been intimating that she wanted to see Bizet's *Carmen* for herself, and on the evening of December 3, 1892, Augustus Harris and members of his Royal Opera Company had mounted it for her and her court.

Seated beside the venerable old monarch—albeit slightly below, as etiquette required—Queen Marie of Romania, noted that her grandmother, though "somewhat bewildered by the passionate story," followed the music and the plot "with keen interest" and clearly "enjoyed the excitement of being so deliciously shocked." The Gypsy was "not really very nice,"[4] she whispered at one point. But Queen Victoria was an ardent opera fan[5] and we know from her journal that she thought Zélie de Lussan "a most perfect Carmen, [who] sang delightfully ... and acted admirably, full of by-play, with coquetterie and impudence, and accompanied by grace so that it was never vulgar."[6] She had, in fact, specifically asked to see De Lussan as the spirited troublemaker, having been charmed by her recent performance of Donizetti's spunky *Fille du Regiment* at Balmoral. Furthermore, the soprano—American-born of French parentage—was already a favorite with Londoners in the role, this, being her 280th Carmen—or so she informed Her Majesty while being awarded a diamond and ruby brooch in gratitude.

5. Emma Calvé and the New Realism

In any event, the Queen could hardly have made a better choice, if for no other reason than that De Lussan's impersonation, like Hauk's and most others raised in the Victorian era, titillated without offending: a far cry from the Gypsy's newest impersonator, one Emma Calvé who at 34—older than De Lussan—would, only two weeks later in Paris, take the role "beyond the limits of good taste."[7] As it turned out, the two starkly different portrayals—one "deliciously" shocking, the other aggressively so—would continue in tandem throughout the explosive cultural and societal changes of the next two decades. For if Calvé's scandalously realistic impersonation mesmerized operagoers of the new *Belle Époque*, Victorianism was tenacious, and De Lussan's engaging representation, by virtue of its humor, grace, and vivacity, remained so popular she ultimately boasted over 1,000 performances with some 57 different Josés.

Give an extra nod to the Queen, though. Not only had she invited the errant Gypsy into her castle a first time, but she was soon asking to see her again—and this time in the guise of the provocative Calvé herself. Perhaps Her Majesty's mores were not as strict as believed, nor her castle walls as thick.

* * *

There is no overstating the impact Calvé's impersonation had on all who saw it. Simply put: it was one of the most brilliant in the history of operatic performance and, at the same time, one of the most revela-

Zélie De Lussan, Queen Victoria's choice to introduce Carmen to Windsor Castle (photograph from the studio of Falk).

tory. "We never had a Carmen before like it," said one American operagoer. "All the memories of Galli-Marié ... and Minnie Hauk ... disappeared with Mme. Calvé.... This Carmen is not a dressed up piece of mummery, but a living, breathing daughter of Seville, reckless in her love, savage in her hate, a demon in her revenge."[8]

Had *Carmen* never been written though, Emma Calvé would still be considered one of the greatest performing artists of the late 19th and early 20th centuries. She had problems early on. But once she was able to overcome some technical vocal difficulties and free herself of certain long held tenets of acting that still held sway over the operatic stage, she was on her way.

From the mountainous province of Aveyron in southern France, Calvé was clearly born with a remarkable voice, notable, particularly, for its haunting purity, infinite colors, and extensive range (from A below middle C to the F in Alt). In her prime her repertoire was vast and varied. With her wondrous legato and smooth scale she sang Mozart, including all three principal female parts in *Nozze di Figaro*; with her flexibility and easy top she excelled in such nightingale roles as Lucia, Ophélie, Amina, and Lakmé; and with power throughout the range, she reveled in the spinto roles she is said to have loved best: Wagner's Elsa and Gounod's Marguerite. Among the many roles she created we find the dramatic Anita in Massenet's *La Navaraise* and the lyric Suzel in Mascagni's *L'Amico Fritz*. And with her plummy middle and low voice she smoldered as Santuzza and Carmen, the roles for which she was fêted at the expense of all others.

Had she been born a half-generation earlier or even remained at the Opéra-Comique, where she first sang in 1890, Calvé's need to express herself fully would almost certainly have been thwarted by the pervading melodramatic acting style of the reigning queen of the stage, Sarah Bernhardt. Instead, as she makes abundantly clear in her autobiography, the impulse that informed Calvé's art is easily ascribed to Eleanora Duse, the riveting Italian actress she followed from engagement to engagement one summer in an effort to learn her secrets. Born, like Calvé herself, in 1858—some 14 years after the divine Bernhardt—Duse "sought to replace pictorial, declamatory, stereotypical acting with her own individual, modern style ... to show a physical, outward expression of the character's innermost thoughts and feelings ... [and] to portray women as sensual human beings."[9]

"Hers was the spark that set my fires alight," Calvé recalled in her autobiography. "Her art, simple, human, passionately sincere, was a revelation

5. Emma Calvé and the New Realism

to me. It broke down the false and conventional standards of lyric expression to which I had become accustomed."[10] From Duse, who herself later described Calvé's voice as "unique to the world, composed of all the colors of the rainbow, pure as mountain springs,"[11] the singer found all she needed to break the constraints that had held her back as an artist. And by way of one of Duse's greatest creations, Santuzza in Verga's play *Cavalleria Rusticana*, she found the ideal means by which to build on her newly acquired artistic freedoms when Pietro Mascagni composed an opera based on the play, and Calvé, in the footsteps of the role's operatic creator, Gemma Bellincioni, portrayed the troubled peasant girl, who had been rejected by her lover and excommunicated by the church. There were other triumphs in Italy, notably Ophélia in *Hamlet* at La Scala and Suzel in *L'Amico Fritz* in Rome. But it was as Santuzza and soon after Carmen, roles she could invest with the fervor of the new realism in acting, that she would win international stardom.

* * *

What was it about Calvé's Carmen then? Happily, a plethora of colorful and insightful pennings by some of the era's most esteemed writers on music give a good idea as to why for a decade and a half her impersonation remained the absolute. Born early enough to have seen virtually all her predecessors in the role, Herman Klein starts us off by putting it in context.

Emma Calve, probably the most famous of all Carmens (photograph from the studio of A. Dupont).

[Calvé's Carmen] had the calm, easy assurance, the calculated dominating power of Galli-Mariè's; it had the strong sensual suggestion and defiant resolution of Minnie Hauk's; it had the panther-like quality, the grace, the fatalism, the dangerous impudent coquetry of Pauline Luccas's; it had the sparkle and vim, the Spanish insouciance and piquancy of

Zélie de Lussan's. That is to say, it combined them each and all to some degree; and the wonder of the melange, added to exquisite singing, made Calvé's assumption from first to last superlative.[12]

Though better known (and noted earlier) for his initial scathing review of Calvé's Carmen, in which he accused her of desecrating her great talent,[13] G.B. Shaw later came to see her portrayal in a different light:

> Calvé, an artist of genius, divested Carmen of the last rag of romance and respectability: it is not possible to describe in decent language what a rapscallion she made of her. But the comedy she made of her audacities was irresistible. Her lewd grin at the officer after her arrest. The hitch of the dress by which she exhibited her ankle and defined the outline of her voluptuous figure for his inspection; her contemptuous lack of interest in Michaela's [sic] face followed by a jealous inspection of the exuberance of her hips.... All these strokes were ... so many instantaneous dramas in themselves, taking you every time into the heart of the character.... Calvé wasted no romantic flattery on her Carmen—allowed her no courage, nothing but rowdiness, no heart, no worth, no positive vice even beyond what her taste for coarse pleasure might lead her to; and she made her die with such frightful art that when the last flopping, reeling, disorganized movement had died out of her, you felt that there was nothing lying there but a lump of carrion. Here you had no monkey mimicry of this or that antic of a street girl, but great acting in all its qualities, interpretation, invention, selection, creation, and fine execution, with the true tragic-comic force behind it.[14]

Of her first performance of Carmen at the Met in 1893, the first in French for that company, Henry T. Finck exclaimed:

> Her impersonation is as vivid as the colors of a gypsy's garments. Sometimes it verges on coarseness, but it is the coarseness of realism.... She does not hesitate in a moment of excitement to leap the barriers of tonal beauty, to declaim, even to speak where song would seem artificial.... Her face, which would hardly be called beautiful when at rest, becomes so intensely fascinating in its constant emotional changes that one can hardly take the opera-glass from the eyes. Few roles present all the emotions, from mischievous flirtation, amorous dalliance, coaxing threatening, indifference, scorn, rage, and horror, as vividly as that of Carmen, and all of them are mirrored in Mme. Calvé's countenance and helped out with an endless variety of gestures.[15]

And if of the same performance W. H. Henderson famously wondered what the Metropolitan audience would think of Calvé's "unbridled passion" in the calmer light of morning,[16] on her return in the role in 1899, he had no doubts: "There was the sparkle of champagne in her comedy and the fire of absinthe in her tragedy. She swept the gamut of passion with a free hand, and made her audience vibrate like the chords of a big Eolian harp. And she sang with an exquisite art that does not get half the appreciation it deserves.... Calvé's finest dramatic instrument is her voice, which thrills and glows with wooing love or glittering like cold steel with anger as she wills. Her performance last night was that of genius."[17]

* * *

We know from her autobiography that Calvé attributed many of the details of her portrayal, such as the gestures and movements, to what she learned on a trip she took to Spain in preparation for her first performance at the Opéra-Comique. Being relatively large with long arms, she emphasized her arms and hands when she danced as she had seen the Spanish gypsies do. "The steps which had been danced with such grace and charm by Galli-Marié," who was "small and dainty," she said were not for her.[18] Nor were the costumes; and so, she introduced (so she claimed) the shawl, and discarded the boleros and skirts above the ankles, which, because they were worn by Galli-Marié, had become tradition at the Opéra-Comique. "Calvé's skirts were as long as the bedraggled streetwalker's," Frederic Dean recalled. "Her heels were worn down as if filed away by sharp contact with the city's pavements. She was a slattern in the first act, a trim little mountaineer in the third, and, in the last, a Queen reveling in the good things of the earth."[19]

In fact, though her Metropolitan debut in *Cavalleria Rusticana* had been a triumph, the drab skirt she wore as the peasant Santuzza in place of the silks and satins audiences expected from an opera star had made management wary as to what her Carmen costume might be. But Calvé had managed to keep her wardrobe a secret and when her Gypsy "first swagger[ed] onto the holy stage of the Metropolitan Opera House in a costume such as the chorus wore—a shabby shawl no different from the other workers ... the Golden Horseshoe nearly fell out of its boxes."[20]

It was, however, by way of the broader concepts of acting she had learned from Duse that Calvé brought Carmen into the 20th century. "Carmen is a complex woman, a mannerized woman, and it is her complexity and her mannerisms that I endeavor to portray by every possible means," she told an interviewer in 1907. Like Duse, she sought fluidity and spontaneity in her portrayals, which meant they were always changing. Moreover, contrary to what singers had previously been taught, as Shaw pointed out in his initial response to her Carmen, "she acted out of time the whole evening,"[21] which meant "her gestures were no longer tied to the music, but followed their own rhythmic logic according to the drama."[22] And like Duse, who sought to reveal "the immense gap between accepted ideas of woman and what a woman really was,"[23] Calvé succeeded in removing Carmen from the picturesque and irrelevant, and invest her with "the spirit of the eternal rebellion of all women,"[24] making of Carmen a woman with whom other women could relate.

But, somehow, the diva couldn't keep it up. She began to lose control of both herself and the role, allowing her once curvaceous figure to become too buxom and matronly for a seductress, and began to grow bored with her, amusing herself with an excess of tasteless characterization and stage business. Only a dozen years after her role debut in Paris, in 1904 the Metropolitan, where she had sung Carmen some 137 times, wanted no more. Her portrayal quite simply "went to artistic pieces," Henderson lamented. "The prima donna could not stand her enormous success. She became extravagant, whimsical, erratic, irresponsible."[25] Calvé's explanation was probably as accurate as it was unusual: "Unfortunately for me, no one dared utter a word of criticism; and, in consequence, I was carried away by my passion for realism. It became an obsession, and occasionally I overstepped the mark."[26]

And, sadly, this applied as well to her reading of the score. For while remaining true to the precepts of her vocal art, the freedoms she took musically became increasingly at odds with the written page. Not that it had not always been so. For even of her first Opéra-Comique performances in 1892, Arthur Pougin had complained: "What has happened to Bizet's adorable music? What has happened to the tempos, what has happened to the rhythms?... Not only are traditions broken, but so too is logic, even musical sense no longer exists."[27] But though recordings suggest she must have reined in some of the liberties after she took it to the international stage, conformity was not in Calvé's vocabulary; playing fast and loose with the score was as much part of her nature as it was part of the era's performance fashion.

Nevertheless, despite the disappointment in seeing such an inspired portrayal fall apart, Calvé's Gypsy had by that time become legend,[28] an impersonation against which all others would be measured for decades. What is more, she had turned the public's conception of operatic acting on its head, and thereby opened the door for a new line of distinctive and individualistic Carmens.

* * *

As it happened, on December 13, 1906—almost two years after Calvé's last performance at the Metropolitan—the Swiss soprano Clotilde Bressler-Gianoli unveiled a Gypsy at once so electrifying and real as to virtually keep Oscar Hammerstein's new Manhattan Opera Company in business in its bid to rival the Met. "A Remarkable Carmen at the Manhattan," declared the *New York Times*:

> [Bressler-Gianoli's] portrayal of Bizet's wayward heroine has at the outset no allurement through beauty or grace or personal charm; it is the allurement of sheer wickedness and all the wiles and treachery that wickedness suggests. She never emerges from the character of the common gypsy either in garb ... or in bearing. The essential commonness and sensuality of the creature are the dominant notes of the impersonation. Yet Mme. Bressler-Gianoli's suggestion of them is artistic. Her face is a continual mirror of the impulses that take shape in action, and the expression of that action, lithe, sinuous, impulsive is that of baleful Mediterranean passion and fire.[29]

To be sure, "Bressler-Gianoli's shabby, intense, earthy, and tempestuous" impersonation, so different from any of its predecessors, made Calvé's own seem—dare one say it—"a bit stagy and, worst of all, old-fashioned."[30] This is not to say that Calvé's highly veristic rendering was not good box-office anymore; Calvé, in fact, also sang the role for Hammerstein with some success. But just as Duse herself had begun to feel restricted by "the narrow confines of verismo," and sought roles which explored "a transformation of life, not an imitation"[31] such as she found in the modern dramas of Henrik Ibsen and Luigi Pirandello, in the same way, Bressler-Gianoli, looking beyond the "completely realistic portrayal of the [Carmen] character in all its outward manifestations ... lifted it from its tawdriness and vulgarity and immorality to a lofty tragedy of human life."[32]

Herself the mother of two, she likened the Gypsy's battles to those of a "tragic Peter Pan ... impulsive, thoughtless, headstrong—in a word young ... [but] a bigger figure than any of the colorless, neutral tinted other girls of the cigarette factory, who never stepped out of their small lives, and never, no never, inspired the genius of a Bizet."[33] And that "genius" she scrupulously respected, for, by all accounts Bressler-Gianoli sang the music as written, with no substitutions or transpositions. The voice itself was not exceptional in any way, but anyone would have had to agree with Algernon St. John Brenon of the *Telegraph*, who wrote: "I have never known anyone make so much of so little."[34]

And so, yet another totally individual Carmen had appeared—a Carmen impossible to compare with any other. Recalling all the famous Carmens she had seen, Blanche Marchesi once mused:

> As a child, I saw Pauline Lucca who was witty, passionate, funny, wild, beautiful, seductive, sympathetic and tragic. Then in Paris I saw Gally-Marié [sic] who first created the role. Her Carmen was haughty, strong, proud, tragic, and terribly fatal, and, as it seems, really Spanish. Calvé was a little more French, a little more

Clothilde Bressler-Gianoli, admired for her realistic portrayal.

5. Emma Calvé and the New Realism 65

of the boulevard than her forerunners, and in Spain the public was not at all flattered by her interpretation; but she was lively, human, and charming. I would compare the three Carmens as follows: Gally Marié [sic] a Velasquez; Lucca, a Chardin; Calvé a Toulouse-Lautrec.[35]

And now Bressler-Gianoli's uncommonly common depiction—the newest but not the last; for inexhaustible were the ways to render this elusive heroine.

Chapter 6

More Than the Singing

"A living paradox, a great singer with a little voice"—anonymous critic[1]

"The performance appears to me very exaggerated, but this is in fashion at present, and proves the possession of that gift of which we hear so much nowadays—temperament."—anonymous critic[2]

The early years of the 20th century found the opera world a veritable beehive of activity. If you were an opera lover it was wild and wonderful. And if you were a *Carmen* lover, you did not have to go far to indulge your passion. Indeed, ever since Emma Calvé sent its popularity into the stratosphere, no company wanted to go without the Bizet so great was its box-office appeal, while any number of singing-actresses—the term soon to enter the parlance—seized the opportunity to head the cast. Hammerstein's Manhattan Opera, for example, even with the departures of Bressler-Gianoli and Calvé at the end of the 1907–1908 season—Bressler-Gianoli back to Europe and an early death from appendicitis, Calvé into a quasi retirement—counted some five different impersonations (old and new) for New Yorkers to consider.

There was that of the French contralto Jeanne Gerville-Réache, already renowned for her portrayal of Saint-Saëns's Dalila, a role perfectly suited to her sumptuous sound and considerable personal beauty, as well as Gluck's Orfeo, the role of her Opéra-Comique debut in 1899, and Geneviève in *Pelléas et Mélisande*, which she created at the Comique and later recreated for its American premiere under Hammerstein. But while critics appreciated the careful attention she paid musical values, at least one criticized her Gypsy as being nothing more than a "common, heartless, dissolute woman without an elevating trait."[3] That said, her recordings of two of Carmen's arias are notable: an *Air des Cartes* of gripping power

6. More Than the Singing   67

and an utterly enchanting *Habanera*, which reminds us how at this early stage in the drama Carmen was quite simply an outrageous tease. To hear this overworked aria rendered with such nuance and humor is a treat.

Mariette Mazarin only sang a few Carmens for Hammerstein, a role she first sang at the Opéra-Comique, in part because her portrayal of Richard Strauss's Elektra, which she introduced to the United States at his Manhattan Opera—having visited a madhouse by way of preparation—overshadowed it. Indeed, wrote one critic, her Elektra was "one of the most powerful and repulsively fascinating impersonations ever witnessed on the operatic stage."[4] All the more reason, then, to regret the short shrift the city's critics gave her Carmen, a role in which, according to Van Vechten, who devoted an entire chapter to the undervalued Belgian soprano in his book on interpreters, "she appeared to be possessed by a certain *diablerie*, a power of evil, which distinguished her from other Carmens."[5]

And so, perhaps figuring that "evil" would not sell tickets, Hammerstein next looked to Lina Cavalieri. The Italian soprano was indisputably a lightweight by comparison, but she was, arguably, one of the most beautiful women in all opera, and even if her success sometimes seemed predicated more on looks than on any vocal gifts, the impresario must have surmised that she would draw audiences out of curiosity, if for no other reason. And, as expected, what they got was an interpretation as different from Mazarin's as night and day: "a young girl who was having a good time for the first time in her life ... a laughing Carmen, with a light heart and a light head, utterly lacking in repose."[6]

Then there was Maria Labia, who, having opened Hammerstein's New York season as Tosca, was awarded the honor of inaugurating his new Philadelphia Opera House as Carmen. But if the "pictorially" pleasing young soprano struck at least one critic as "disappointing dramatically ... lacking seduction, diablerie, wantonness,"[7] his words contradict the rest of what we know about her in the role. For the Venetian Labia—a granddaughter, daughter, and sister of singers—having spent most of her career in Europe, notably Germany,[8] had made her reputation primarily in such veristic roles as Tosca and Salome, and her Gypsy was a staple in her repertoire. Moreover, in a recording, in German, of her dance scene for José, we hear her as every bit the spitfire.

And in Hammerstein's final season, the Belgian soprano Marguerite Sylva performed the opera with spoken dialogue, as at the Opéra-Comique from whence she came, which may have affected the critic from the *New York Times* when he described her Carmen as "gaily and lightheartedly

Gallic rather than darkly and periodically Spanish in its essence."[9] Though probably best remembered for her work in films, Sylva nevertheless became one of the most popular Carmens of her generation, singing several hundred—but, like Calvé, with whom she was compared—seriously tiring of it.

* * *

If, however, compared to Calvé and Bressler-Gianoli, most of the Carmens at the Manhattan Opera were relatively mundane, at the rival Metropolitan, a Spaniard by the name of Maria Gay (pronounced Guy) was scandalizing audiences with an impersonation for which not even Calvé had prepared them. Since Calvé's departure, manager Heinrich Conried had been casting the celebrated Wagnerian Olive Fremstad as the Gypsy, a role in which the Swedish-born American had previously enjoyed considerable success in Germany. Certainly her lithe figure and expressive dramatic soprano with its sumptuous low notes should have made her well suited to the role. But the American public found her portrayal to be too much a "vulgar, passionate, ungoverned creature,"[10] who lacked any of the allure and spirit it had come to expect after years of Calvé. Never mind that the French diva "set a wrong standard for this generation of operagoers ... dazzl[ing] them with the appearance and manners of a Parisian cocotte rather than of a factory girl from the slums of Seville," Fremstad vented. "You can seethe with temper without throwing chairs about and pulling out human hair. Such behavior is not really seductive, and we have to remember that Carmen certainly was."[11]

In any event, when in 1908 Giulio Gatti-Casazza arrived to replace Conried as manager, it was only to discover that his predecessor had already signed Maria Gay, whose European reputation as the latest in be-all and end-all Carmens had preceded her. To be sure, the Spanish mezzo's *gitana* had been tearing up stages from the Monnaie in Brussels, where she first sang the role in 1905, to Paris, London, St. Petersburg, Florence, Warsaw, and Milan, where her hellcat portrayal opposite her husband-to-be, the tenor Giovanni Zenatello, caused a sensation. So great, in fact, was the unbridled fervor of her she-Devil that one tenor in Paris was said to have "brought her to earth with only the greatest difficulty" having had to chase her "round and round the stage quite madly."[12]

And now in her Met debut opposite Caruso and under Toscanini, who, having conducted her Carmen in Milan, claimed she made him hate the opera, "the roly-poly Maria Gay, of sparkling eye and flashing smile ... kicked and spat, till even the blasé New York dowagers were moved to raise their fans to shocked faces, to screen some of her more frank and realistic attempts at seduction."[13] Or so reported Geraldine Farrar, whose own first brush with the Bizet was as Micaëla the same night.

But in his remarkable memoirs, Sergei Levik, who, from 1908 to 1910, observed Gay's Carmen from both backstage at the Mariinsky Theater and the prompter's box in Kharkov, provides valuable insight as to what made the Spaniard's impersonation one of the most significant of the pre–World War I era. Though, admittedly, Levik, who had been a baritone, feared the effects of the vocal writing for verismo on bel canto, at the same time he credited the new verismo repertoire with initiating a vast improvement in acting, and in Gay he saw how singing and acting worked off of each other in a positive way. "The link between her acting and the timbre of her powerful and full-blooded voice with its deep contralto low notes was all important," he wrote. "Her clear enunciation and powerful theatrical temperament were completely subordinated to her artistic intellect, but some aspects of her singing were close to naturalism.... Anyone in the theater for the first time, without knowing the opera or the language in which Gay was singing, could sit with closed eyes and understand completely what she was singing about from the colouring of her voice."[14] Gay's recordings corroborate these findings: a *Habanera* and *Chanson Bohémienne* light and crisp, an *Air des Cartes* redolent with

Maria Gay, who shocked New York dowagers with her "frank and realistic attempts at seduction."

atmosphere and distress, and a death scene with Zenatello of spine-tingling intensity. "A fire-breathing volcano," Levik wrote, "everything about her said 'Admit it—I'm irresistible.'" Consider, for example,

> while listening to José's Flower Song, at first, she turned away as though she didn't want to hear but apparently perplexed by his sincerity she turned sharply in his direction, listening and looking attentively, while expressing her scorn by different gestures and grimaces. She blew her nose loudly and nonchalantly ate an orange, tossing the peel in his direction, but she was affected by his declaration which softened and altered her behavior.... Won over, she seated José at the table with a gesture of conciliation. She still pronounced the words "Non, tu ne m'aime pas" in an aggressive manner but the voice softened and with the words "La-bas la-bas dans la montagne" she abandoned her stage artifice and sang with simplicity. The voice was like a cello with an exceptionally singing tone. It is difficult to recall a Carmen whose singing had such passionate appeal.[15]

* * *

Prior to Gay, Levik tells us, Russian singers had two ways of interpreting Carmen. "One preserved the traditions of earlier performances, a rather Frenchified, affected coquette who in the last act goes to her death because of her feminine pride rather than an overwhelming passion. The other presented a slightly more exotic type, more passionate but still within the limits of operatic routine and rather affected."[16] It is difficult to know to whom he might have been referring in the first, but the latter likely included "the great singing actress Medea Ivanovna."[17]

Born and trained in Italy where her career began, Medea Mei (her maiden name) had married the Russian tenor Nicolai Figner and, in adopting his country, brought to it the vocal and performance traditions of her homeland. Originally a mezzo, Medea's beautifully sung and vigorous portrayal of Carmen was well known in Europe, and was so acclaimed in Russia after she introduced it to the Mariinsky in 1895 that it would serve as her farewell to that company in 1912. Her few recordings, including the duets with her husband singing José were made after she became a soprano. But despite the interpolated high notes and other liberties—notably, the tantalizing pauses (unwritten), which she so effectively employs in the *Habanera*—her interpretations are compelling.

She was not alone in playing fast and loose with the score however; other of the era's Russians who recorded the Bizet do much the same.[18] And if such freedoms seem reckless by today's standards, they were in keeping with a fervent search to bring new ideas to opera in Russia with the result, Levik noted, that in some of the more innovative theaters "talented and versatile singers replaced those who simply aimed to 'please the ears.'"[19]

To be sure, some of the ideas that developed in Russia in the early 20th century, particularly those that emanated from companies in the enlightened hands of Savva Mamontov and Konstantin Stanislavski, would prove an inspiration to opera theaters around the world. The ensemble-based Modern Art Theater—the very name conveying its purpose—had been active since 1898. Stanislavski, its founder, had himself once studied to be a singer, but it was his work as a director and teacher that evolved into the world famous Stanislavski method that is studied and practiced even today. A passionate believer in a naturalistic theater Stanislavski successfully challenged every tradition of the stage and in the 1920s opened a studio just for opera singers, the main purpose of which was to teach the performer how to arrive at total believability through naturalism.

Medea Mei-Figner, the Italian mezzo (later soprano) who married the Russian tenor Nicolai Figner, shown here with the pom poms often seen on the Russian costumes of the period (edition "Richard" St. Petersburg).

When, in 1935, on the brink of her momentous career, the contralto Marian Anderson was giving recitals in the Soviet Union and visited the Studio, Stanislavski asked to teach her Carmen. "No doubt the idea of a black Carmen intrigued him," Anderson's biographer Allan Keiler speculated. "He could develop the theme of Carmen as social outcast, as a woman scorned, as a figure barely tolerated in a social milieu to which she could not hope to belong."[20] Anderson did express interest, but she had never sung in opera, worried about the acting, and feared she "could not do the dancing a good Carmen must do."[21] And so the world can only wonder just what her racial origins and soul-stirring contralto might have brought to the role.

* * *

Recalling other, even more experimental, new theaters, Levik noted a *Carmen* by the Theater of Musical Drama using a new translation. Expressly made for the Carmen of Maria Veselovskaya, the director's wife, it allowed the characters to express themselves less poetically, more naturally, and transferred the action to the beginning of the 20th century with soldiers in khaki and Carmen in the dress of a "simple factory worker." Among the interesting details in Joseph Lapitsky's "very original" staging one in particular has Carmen, having watched José leave with Micaëla, climb to the very top of a cliff, and, in a powerful expression of her joy to be free again, pull the pins out of her hair allowing it to fall loosely.[22]

And at the same theater we find as well the "undersized" mezzo-soprano Maria Davidova, who "excelled as Carmen" despite neither voice nor looks of particular note. "Maria Davidova was one of those performers who … in her straightforward simplicity … compelled the audience to forget the most elementary requirements of appearance and voice…. Davidova spoke—she didn't speak, she sang—she didn't sing. She acted—she didn't act, but was so completely the femme fatale, doing only what she wanted to do at any given moment that her performance as Carmen was the success of the opera. At times it seemed that she wasn't part of the opera but that the whole opera adjusted itself to her."[23]

Yet another pioneering company, Savva Mamontov's Private Opera, founded in 1885, "revolutionized opera by introducing major innovations in acting, directing, and design, and became a crucible for the emerging modernist trends in stage aesthetics."[24] Much care was given costume and scenic design, casting, and preparing the singers in all aspects of their parts. While Mamontov, an older cousin of Stanislavsky, is primarily remembered as the impresario who launched Feodor Chaliapin, any number of other important singers grew up under his tutelage, including Tatyana Lyubatovich, whose signature role of Carmen was described as dramatically outstanding, though vocally routine.

* * *

To all intents and purposes, then, the day had come when a singer might be recognized more for how credibly she acted and interpreted a role than for how beautifully she intoned it. And this not only because of the new emphasis on direction, but also because of the new kinds of protagonists in operas that seemed to insist on it, thereby paving the way for a new kind of singer. For example, in Italy—former home of bel canto and now of verismo—Gemma Bellincioni was a sensation as the first Santuzza in *Cavalleria Rusticana*, her histrionics a major factor in the opera's instantaneous success. She represented "a new type of tragic opera singer," Max Graf wrote of her Nedda on *Pagliacci* in Vienna, who "completely captivated her audience by the nervous intensity of her expression."[25] And yet, criticisms of her actual voice abound. Of a performance of her Carmen in London, for example, we read:

> The actress's eloquent facial expression is often employed in taking the audience into her confidence and the play of the various passions is depicted with much force.... Her acting of the death scene was perhaps the best thing in a performance of incontestable power. Vocally, the execution of the music was sadly lacking in many essential qualities; not only has the artist's voice many and obvious shortcomings, but she appears to be quite incapable of treating a melodic phrase otherwise than as free declamation.... Scarcely ever was the real musical beauty of the part allowed to appear: the sacrifice thus made to dramatic effect was surely too great.[26]

To be sure, with a "'goaty' vibrato" off-putting to modern ears, Michael Aspinall in his notes for "The Creators of Verismo" (Marston) writes, she was already in trouble by the age of 31.[27] All the same, at least for a time, "Bellincioni's personality enabled her to triumph over a modest vocal endowment. Like Duse, to whom she was often compared, the separation between her real and stage personality was never very clear; she inhabited a theatrical limbo, half way between reality and the melodrama."[28]

* * *

Though not quite the hotbed of innovative production found in Russia, reform was also most definitely in the air at the Vienna Court Opera, where, since accepting the post in 1897, its new director Gustav Mahler, was determined to modernize a repertory mired in all the traditional practices, including those of the rotelike acting. *Carmen*, a favorite at the Court Opera, was also a favorite of Mahler's. But in Vienna the popular Marie Renard had all but owned the title role for years. "A real prima donna, for whom nothing mattered except her pianissimos, her trills, and her roulades, and who made little effort to fit in with an ensemble,"[29] Renard only "paid lip service to his [Mahler's] orders,"[30] which, as far as the new director was concerned, meant she was dispensable. Happily, though, the pretty soprano settled matters herself by retiring in 1900 to marry. Carmen had been the role of her debut in Vienna in 1887, so Mahler graciously allowed it to serve for her farewell. But soon after, as though relieving himself of the memory, he revised the Bizet, ridding the old production further of traditions, such as the Children's Chorus for which he now employed actual children and the quintet in the second act, which he now seated around a table instead of having them stand in a line at the front of the stage.

But no innovation was as revolutionary as his casting of the title role. In her debut in *Pagliacci* only days earlier, Marie Gutheil-Schoder had amazed the Viennese by actually lying on her back to sing her big aria. And now this rather unattractive soprano from Weimar, Germany was their Carmen. What to make of it? "It is inconceivable that the impulsive, willful, attractive coquette that Bizet has given us should be bony, lank, hoarse-voiced," one critic reported back to the United States.[31] But others applauded the moment for what it was. "The instinct of an inspired singer and the sensitivity of a conducting genius have rescued a neglected opera from the atrophy that threatened it."[32] Indeed, not since Pauline Lucca had Vienna seen a Carmen of such passion. Wrote Mahler himself: "Gutheil-Schoder is another example of the enigma of personality, which is the sum of all that one is. With her mediocre voice and its even disagreeable middle register, she might appear totally insignificant. Yet each sound she utters has 'soul' (*Seele*), each gesture and attitude is a revelation of the character she's playing. She understands its very essence and brings out all its traits as only a creative genius can do."[33]

Maria Gutheil-Schoder, whose "every gesture and attitude [was] a revelation of the character."

* * *

America never got to see Gutheil-Schoder, but it did see the soprano Mary Garden, of Scottish birth, whose impersonation of Carmen was, if not as admired, as individual and personal—as, for instance, a blue dress with white polka dots for her first entrance—as that of her German counterpart. Though similarly lacking an outstanding voice, Garden too was an uncompromising, daring, intuitive singing-actress of genius, who mesmerized in the French repertoire. Her portrayals of such titles roles as Charpentier's Louise, which sent her straight to the top on the night she came out of the audience to complete the performance for an indisposed colleague; Debussy's Mélisande, which she created in Paris and recreated in America for Hammerstein; Massenet's Thais, in which she made her American debut in 1907; the Juggler of Notre Dame, and more, opened the world of modern French opera to America. But if these were roles she had virtually an exclusive on, making comparisons impossible, Americans had seen an infinite number of Carmens, making comparisons inevitable.

So, what was said about Mary Garden's Gypsy? Above all, that it was an extremely complex portrayal, which changed—for the better, according to the author Carl Van Vechten—with the years. Of the era's many individualistic characterizations, hers was not as distinctive as it was indefinable, and this confounded the critics, who, while rarely agreeing on anything about it, repeatedly described it as different and interesting without ever quite explaining what made it so. Whereas Van Vechten, who attended several of her performances, saw in her portrayal "a study of a cold, brutal, mysterious gipsy who does not seek lovers, they come to her,"[34] we are contrarily told that in the first act she went almost compulsively after every man on stage. And while Reginald De Koven, having seen every important Carmen since Galli-Marié, wrote that Garden's "Carmen began by seeming hoydenish rather than seductive, subtly temperamental rather than sensuous, and unexpectedly restrained in the expression of mood and action," he furthered that "what this great actress meant ... to portray in finely graduated crescendo [was] an elemental feminine type; self-willed and uncontrolled, primitive in desire and the means to gratify it. A smoldering emotional fire to burst out finally into vivid and all consuming flame. And so," he concluded, he "found her impersonation novel, consistent through the varying moods ... and thus convincing."[35]

Garden—a tiny woman by all accounts—may well have been as self-centered, eccentric, publicity-seeking as any diva of her stature. But her art took priority over any personal concern. Carmen must appear as part of the ensemble, not as a personage apart, she insisted, and to this end she surrounded herself with the best possible colleagues. Ronald Davis alludes to this in his *Opera in Chicago*, and Van Vechten observed much the same, noting that she was at her best when the French tenor Lucien

Muratore became her José in later performances. An artist who plumbed the depths of every role in search of how she could serve it most effectively, she did as much for Carmen even though it was standard repertoire.

Unfortunately, her *Air des Cartes* recording is all we have of her Carmen. Nevertheless, it is a gripping example of her art, and in her autobiography, she lays out her interpretation.

> *Carmen doesn't read cards.* She shuffles the deck and she opens to death. When she sees that, she puts her cards together again. *And she stands.* Carmen doesn't sit and she doesn't put her mantilla on the floor and lie on it.
>
>   Then when Carmen says it is death for both of them, she sings to the audience not what is in the cards, but what is in her mind. It is a beautiful thing, that little bit of business. Finally when she gets through with that, she opens her cards again. She still sees death, and she closes them.
>
>   Now, instead of that, I have seen singers spread their things on the floor and put out their cards. But Carmen isn't reading her fortune.[36]

Mary Garden, whose off-putting portrayal confounded the critics.

Garden probably found the part of Carmen with its comfortable range easier to sing than others in her large repertoire, and, in fact, at least one chronology shows her singing it as late as 1935 when she would have been 61.[37] But at a time when most of the public still viewed Italian singing as the gold standard, when it came to the attributes they looked for in a voice, Garden's hardly measured up: more plain than sumptuous, straight than oval, steel than gold. "I know full well that I have not a great voice," she would say in retrospect. But then again, it "was never a thing apart. My voice, my acting, my whole personality were one."[38]

This kind of thinking was not new even before Bizet wrote *Carmen*. But the arrival of his enigmatic seductress had moved it to front and center stage. In writing for Don José, Micaëla, and Escamillo the composer had no trouble in obliging the public's first requirement of "voice." Carmen, however, was another matter. Bizet knew that the opera depended on the role of Carmen, which in turn depended on a sincere realization of her complexity. Galli-Marié had vocal limitations, but she was a fine dramatic artist with the ability to transcend them and create the portrayal of his imagination. And, in fact, in retrospect, in its countless reviews of the premiere, the critics barely noted the mezzo's actual singing of Carmen. Rather, it was, her acting of the role that drew inches of copy and caused the furor. So could acting truly trump singing? Over a quarter century later, an impressive handful of singers seemed to have pushed the question as far as it could possibly go.

Chapter 7

Farrar, Film and Psychology

> She [Calvé] told me that America wanted her to make a film of Carmen, but that she would not accept this sham world of the screen.
> —Colette[1]

> I adore to act.—Geraldine Farrar[2]

After Hammerstein's Manhattan Opera folded in 1910, Carmen was mostly absent from New York with the exception of an occasional performance by an artist passing through with a touring company. New Yorkers, for example, were grateful to the Chicago Opera, who, as guests of the Metropolitan Opera House in 1912, presented Mary Garden in the role. The diva had never sung the Gypsy in New York nor ever appeared in any capacity with the Metropolitan Opera proper, but Carmen was part of her repertoire at the Chicago Opera, which was now her home base. And had it not been for visits from Fortune Gallo's San Carlo Opera Company New Yorkers might also have missed Ester Ferrabini, who the critic Frederick Dean considered one of the best Carmens ever to visit the city.[3] The Venetian-born soprano's impersonation "savored of the vampire, rather than the coquette," *Musical America* said, agreeing that it was "one of the most impressive Carmens anywhere"; good enough even "to make you oblivious to her purely vocal limitations."[4]

High on Dean's list as well and seen courtesy of a variety of touring companies, including the San Carlo, was Alice Gentle, a "powerful mezzo-soprano with a brilliant top."[5] Though the pretty native of Peoria, Illinois, created both Preziozilla in *Forza del Destino* and La Frugola in *Tabarro* for the Met in 1918 and appeared as Federico in *Mignon* with Milan's La Scala, she never became a regular with any major company, claiming to prefer life on the road, which gave her a wider repertoire and a better chance for singing leading roles. Carmen was her calling card. Of her performances in Cuba, one critic wrote: "She had moments when we did not know which to admire more: the great singer of splendid schooling, or the great actress who gave to the role the true characteristics of Carmen ... a creature in whose veins flowed the red blood of life."[6] And from San Francisco: "Her reading of the part was "a compromise between the insouciant vulgarity of Maria Gay and the pantherine cruelty of Tarquinia Tarquini. Her protean revelations of the Carmen psychosis were admirably worked out."[7]

The Italian Tarquini, it should be noted, was known for her verismo renderings, notably that of Salome, but apparently not much else, as we gather from the critic who wrote of her appearance at Covent Garden that the soprano was "fully competent to do everything on her own particular lines with the part of Carmen, except sing it."[8]

In any case, Gentele was a trouper in every sense of the word, and would earn still more points a few years later when in Boston with the San Carlo she insisted the show go on even after the bridge on which she had made her entrance broke sending her crashing to the floor and severely bruising her hip. She appeared in three motion pictures, including as an unbilled singer in *Flying Down to Rio*. A 1930 color Vitaphone short, "Alice Gentle in Carmen" reportedly exists.[9]

* * *

But Gotham missed having a celebrity Carmen to call its own, and in 1914 news of the Gypsy's return to the Metropolitan Opera in the person of arguably its most adored diva, Geraldine Farrar, was greeted with enthusiasm. For the comely soprano, now 32, it meant the fulfillment of a long held dream. As a child growing up in Massachusetts, Farrar had seen Calvé in the role and, as she wrote, "completely lost my head over this remarkable performance," resolving then and there that "come what may, I too must someday sing 'Carmen' with the most wonderful cast of grand opera singers in the world, at the Metropolitan in New York."[10] So now it was all coming true; and, buoyed by reviews, which called her recent portrayal of a Parisian prostitute (really a composite of characters) in Charpentier's *Julien*, "superb in her wild recklessness" and "hideously realistic,"[11] and urged on by both Giulio Gatti-Casazza and Arturo Toscanini, she began intense preparation.

Farrar's debut in the coveted part took place on November 19, 1914. The production was brand new; and with Enrico Caruso, Frances Alda, and Pasquale Amato in principal roles and Toscanini conducting, it was star-studded—as in her childhood dream. Reviews, however, were mixed. The *New York Herald* thought it her "happiest" role yet, writing that "her impersonation was free from exaggerations, devoid of all freakishness. She did not slam furniture about the stage, did not drop combs, did not posture before the mirror—in short, she threw to the wind all the conventional stocks in the trade of the usual every day, rubber stamp Carmen."[12] But Richard Aldrich of the *New York Times* thought it not quite there yet. He liked much about her impersonation and felt sure it would "gain in some of the essential attributes that belong to the character," but regretted "a certain lack of rude elemental force in this sophisticated maiden, sometimes too prettily coquettish, too little of the soil."[13] But, as it turned out, a reworking of her portrayal did soon follow—if for the most unexpected of reasons.

For soon after the premiere, Farrar, with a propensity to sing too much, proceeded to sing 11 Carmens, a handful each of Tosca and Madama Butterfly, and her first Madame Sans-Gêne, in addition to recording and concertizing, with the result that in only a matter of months she was beset with vocal problems. It had happened before, and because the best cure is usually to stop singing for a while, an offer to star in three full-length *silent* films to be made that summer in Hollywood—*Carmen* among them—was serendipity.

Geraldine Farrar, the beloved American opera star in the stage version.

As it was, the film industry was still in its infancy and even legitimate actors were staying away, wary of what such an uncertain artificial medium might do to their reputations. Opera singers were big celebrities, who guarded their reputations—Farrar as big as (if not bigger than) any in the eyes of her American public. But if Jesse Lasky, the producer, expected to be refused, he didn't know Geraldine Farrar. For the opera star had always been exceptionally canny when it came to her career. She loved to act as much as to sing, and, beyond getting a chance to rest her weary voice, she sensed the value in being seen by so many more people than could ever see her in the opera house. And so it was that, having assured herself that all her demands would be met, the opera star headed west on a private railroad car with a contract for $20,000 in hand and the assurance that she would be billed as "Miss Geraldine Farrar"—a small distinction to have the additional "Miss" perhaps, but one only accorded stars of the stage, not those of the lowlier film industry. Waiting her arrival: a red carpet, a chauffeur and limousine, a fully-staffed house, living expenses for herself and her entourage, a grand piano, and an orchestra prepared to furnish mood music on the set.[14] She would only work six hours a day, but her young director Cecil B. DeMille did not flinch and finished in just three months.

Geraldine Farrar, the opera star in the silent film *Carmen* (from the photograph edition with its caption "You are the Devil," José said. "Yes," she answered.).

Carmen, the movie, opened on October 2, 1915, in Boston's Symphony Hall with the "Pride of Massachusetts," who had insisted on the venue, in attendance. The critics loved it: "She IS Carmen. She lives the part. Every gesture is one of Carmen's own; every play of the feature is, you feel, as Carmen would have looked;

every action, every decision is made in the exact mood you are sure governed this woman who would walk through fire and not be harmed, who loved love, but not her lovers, whose one ambition was absolute power over men, not for their sake, but for its own."[15]

* * *

Happily, the film is available for viewing today, but because Bizet's score was still under copyright at the time and it is based on the Mérimée novella, there is not a single moment one can believe this Carmen actually loved or even thought she loved Don José. Unfortunately, the beautiful soprano looks disconcertingly matronly. But we can almost forget this as she throws herself into the role with the abandon and energy of one much younger, imbuing it with a physicality not possible on an operatic stage: kicking, scratching, jumping, running, scampering, leaping over rocks and, all the while, keeping her face equally busy with raised eyebrows, frowns, beguiling smiles, and mimed laughter as she smartly makes the most of every close-up. "We acted our parts as if we were engaged in a theatre performance," Farrar later explained, "and I believe, for this reason, we had real expression and feeling, which I find so often lacking in the beautiful but monotonous faces of so many of the screen stars today."[16]

* * *

In any event, Farrar, her celebrity now through the ceiling, had given both the film industry and the opera house an indisputable boost.[17] Film versions of the Carmen story can be traced back to the beginning of the century and approximately 70, in various treatments from burlesque to ballet (but not including the DVDs we see today of live performances of the opera) would appear by the year 2000, several involving opera singers. Farrar's, however, was the first full-length feature film and her personal success in it helped make the new genre respectable for others to explore. Stars of both the legitimate theater and opera—Enrico Caruso and Mary Garden among them—no longer spurned Hollywood on the grounds that the movie industry was beneath them.

In fact, only a year after Farrar's Carmen, the Belgian mezzo-soprano Marguerite Sylva, a veteran of several hundred performances of the Bizet and described as "born to the role,"[18] also portrayed the Gypsy in an eponymous Spanish film—again silently.[19] The first in which we actually hear a Carmen sing was a 1931 British film called *Gypsy Blood* which used synchronized sound and starred Marguerite Namara. Filmed in Spain, the music was recorded in London with the London Symphony under Sir

7. Farrar, Film and Psychology

Malcom Sargent. *Gypsy Blood* appears to be lost, but judging from a 1945 recording of Namara singing the *Seguidilla* to her own piano accompaniment, one can understand why the soprano from Ohio was for at least one listener "the Carmen of Carmens.... Satan re-incarnated: a twisting, snarling, tempestuous Carmen which makes Don Jose's ensnarement easy to see."[20]

* * *

Meanwhile, back in the opera house, critics noticed Farrar's Gypsy indulging in considerably more than the usual hijinks. Was her Hollywood experience to blame—she would ultimately appear in some 15 films—or had her art actually "profited from this work in silent pantomime,"[21] as she believed? Some of her business, such as the slap she landed on her José—Caruso, who would have none of it—and her whistling of the *Seguidilla* in the second act were soon abandoned. But not the realism of her fight with another *cigarière*, which had astonished movie-goers and now made its way into her performances in the opera house. "As in the movies," the unruly one recalled proudly, "in the opera version I fell upon a chorus girl in the provocative first act, seized and kicked her, and bowled her over in an exciting tussle that entertained even her blasé colleagues, looking on."[22]

* * *

In December 1915, after the premiere of the film and before her return to the Met, Farrar gave a long interview that was recorded by the Boston critic Frederic Dean and published in the journal *Bookman* under the title "The Psychology of Carmen." Having by then spent a great deal of time with the original novella, she presents some interesting ideas about the role, based on what she must have learned about the ideas that Mérimée in turn probably got from George Borrows, an English travel writer who had written extensively about Gypsies. Among them, "that gypsies of today are none other than the descendants of these high priestesses of the temple of Thoth and that their books of divination ... have degenerated into the 'Devil's Picture Cards,' ... the ordinary playing-cards with which the present day gypsy tells the fortune." As Farrar read it, Mérimée linked "old Egypt to the modern gypsy," which is "the key to the story and to the psychology of *Carmen*."

She explains:

> The Carmen of his story ... was a high priestess of Fate and a descendant of those other high priestesses who—thousands of years before—had learned the meaning of

the Pictures of Life from the walls of Thoth's temple—the reproductions of which were Carmen's cards of fate.

With perfect faith in the future as it shall be told her among the shuffled spades and hearts, she deals her cards anxiously and with many forebodings—and once realizing the message moves on to her destiny as one who knows and delights in the knowing.

Bizet caught the real meaning of Mérimée's heroine and pictured her as a heroine of Fate. Fate trembles in the violin strings in the orchestral introduction; it is at your elbow, oftentimes but faintly heard, whenever Carmen appears; it proclaims itself even more insistently in the card scene and sweeps everything before it in those leaping crescendos in the final scene of the tragedy.

Her cards never lied to her. And so resignedly, willingly, joyously, she went forth to her fate, for in it was bound a greater love ... a union with a man more worthy of her.... I call Carmen a "high priestess," and she was.... This is the key to the psychology of her character.[23]

Though one has to wonder how much of all this made it into her impersonation, the excellent critic and author H. T. Parker seems to have seen something of it the following spring in Boston:

It was not this Carmen's way to let men go unmastered. Yet, in the interchanges with Jose [Act 2] an implication seemed to steal out of the impersonation that is rather of Mérimée than of Bizet, so far, in his opera. For a moment Carmen was the dour Carmen that sees Fate somehow creeping upon her out of what otherwise is but an ordinary amour....

As Mme. Farrar seems to conceive of the character—and with warrant from text and music, novel and opera that call it into histrionic being—this glimpse of fate fills Carmen with an acrid wantonness and pride of will.... Both pride and wantonness swell out of her coming with the bullfighter to the acclaiming crowd. With a perverse patience or an acrid flash of scorn this Carmen dourly endures Jose's entreaties. Fate hardly flashes upon her eyes or screams in her tones till its knife is in her back.[24]

* * *

And yet, as Mérimée's Don José said, "When that girl laughed, there was no talking sensibly. Everyone laughed with her." And this bright side of the character, as much as the dark, Farrar—herself a woman of great vitality and *joie de vivre*—also played with great effect, as we see in the film and learn from those who saw her in the opera house. Here is as frisky, fun-loving, volatile, alluring scamp as ever there was—"not the wanton that some would have her," as she writes in the *Bookman*, possibly thinking of Gay's rude vulgarity. Rather, Farrar seduced by virtue of her innate charisma and calculated visual effect. "When [Carmen] dashes onto the stage, her appearance alone must be so exciting and magnetic that every man will edge forward on his chair and scheme how to venture past the stage door Minotaur with his orchids," she said. "The seduction of the eye must be instantaneous upon her first appearance."[25]

And in that vein, the dull factory skirt as insisted upon by such standard bearers of naturalism as Calvé and Bressler-Gianoli now gave way to Farrar's preference for "colorful long dresses with 'V' shaped necklines and flounces on the skirts, overlaid with fringed floral shawls. On her bosom she wore a bouquet of roses and for the festive last act outside the bullring added an ornamental comb to her hair."[26]

* * *

Farrar's recordings are a bit of an enigma. "She must have found the recording horn inhibiting, if not intimidating," Robert Baxter has written. "Without sets, costumes and other singers to react against, Farrar could not display the impact she created on stage."[27] Though Baxter was referring to earlier recordings, his comments certainly speak to the extensive selections she made of Carmen, which though sung with clarity, taste, some nice detailing, and lovely tone, offer—in contrast to her charismatic stage personality—little to arrest the listener beyond a delightfully naughty *Habanera* and a nice peal of laughter in an insouciant *Seguidilla*.

A soprano, like most of the era's Carmens, it was Farrar's contention that the role was best sung by the higher voice because mezzos "generally carried too much girth and heaviness of foot to be entirely convincing for the wild cat portrayal of this restless feline."[28] Moreover, her fruity middle register was so ideally suited, one has to wonder why she decided to rewrite certain passages and bother at all with the high options.

What one has to keep in mind, however, is that all these excerpts were recorded shortly after her first season of Carmens. What she would have done with them after her film experience when, to all intents and purposes, she raised the intensity level of her performances up many notches we will never know. But Farrar was arguably the last of the great Carmens still linked to—and committed to—the vocal precepts of the old school, and, as she made no more recordings of the role, it is unlikely Hollywood would have affected her vocal presentation as much as it did the histrionic. Either way,

> by the time of her triumphant debut as Carmen ... Farrar represented an interesting blend of old-style vocal refinement ... and highly fashionable verismo theatricality. Unlike the former generation's sopranos ... Farrar and her successors were to be distinguished by the novelty of what they were to provide on stage. Emotions had at last been emancipated from the repression of nineteenth century morality.... Sopranos who embodied this fresh liberality ... were thoroughly modern stars, and an element of risqué flamboyance or, at least, capricious panache, was expected.[29]

* * *

If not the greatest, Farrar was certainly the most famous Carmen since Calvé—at least in America. For, despite her intense training and early career in Europe, she was an American soprano with an essentially American career. At the Met she enjoyed favored status, and as such virtually owned the Gypsy, performing her some 65 times before retiring from the company in 1922 at the unusually early age of 40. But she continued to concertize and also toured the country with her own traveling production of an abridged *Carmen* with orchestra, scenery, and costumes, herself in the lead, but with no chorus. The idea, she said, was to bring opera to the people and make it more palatable for them. At one point, she claimed, her company mounted "123 consecutive performances in 125 days."[30] What this truncated production did for the country's impression of the Bizet can only be imagined.

In any case, having successfully reconciled old-school vocal training with the new veristic theatricality,[31] Geraldine Farrar marks the end of the transition from old-time singer to modern singer-actress. "That she never overstepped the mark of acceptability and so retained a following in the nation's more sober, cautious, and innocent circle"[32] gave her a power and influence in the United States of a kind Maria Gay and Mary Garden, or—waiting in the wings—Maria Jeritza could never have obtained.

CHAPTER 8

In the Time of Dictators

> "Then I did a Carmen—and although there was nothing courageous in that, we felt a quiver when Carmen sang her hymn to 'la liberté.' That, too, was in 1938."[1]—Goffreso Petrassi (conductor)

Farrar's early retirement left the Metropolitan Opera once again wanting for an outstanding Carmen. In the seven years since her first performances of the role the beloved soprano had been spelled only occasionally: twice by the formidable Romanian Margarete Matzenauer, and—primarily when the company toured—by Florence Easton and Ina Bourskaya. But if Gatti could count on the much-admired Easton to fill any need with her intelligent, well-sung performances, the rather plain-looking English soprano lacked the requisite temperament for the charismatic seductress; and while the Russian mezzo-soprano Bourskaya filled the temperament requirement with a "wild, untamed ... sometimes overact[ed]"[2] incarnation, her performances were uneven and the enthusiasm that had greeted her arrival soon faded. After almost a decade alternating between these unsatisfactory options, therefore, in 1928 Gatti-Casazza set his sights on a Gypsy who, given not only her looks, voice, acting, and temperament but also her star power, had it all; and who, as luck would have it, was already on his roster: Maria Jeritza. No doubt about it. The beauteous blonde had burst onto the New York scene in 1921 with all the glamour and panache of a movie star, leaving some to speculate that perhaps it was no accident that Farrar had chosen to leave at the end of that particular season.

Moravian-born, Jeritza had been the idol of the Viennese since 1912 when, at Richard Strauss's request, she created the eponymous role of Ariadne auf Naxos at the Court Opera. Gatti had sought her services in 1914, but the outbreak of World War I had kept her in Europe until its end, at which time its artists were only too glad to escape the spiraling inflation and political turmoil in their defeated homelands for a share of the boom across the ocean.

Triumphant in her debut as Marietta in the Metropolitan Opera premiere of Korngold's *Die Tote Stadt,* Jeritza continued to win accolades with the company as Sieglinde, Octavian, and other of the German roles for which she was best known. But it was in the veristic roles of Santuzza in *Cavalleria Rusticana* and Tosca that the "Viennese Thunderbolt," as the press dubbed her, electrified New Yorkers. Her startling tumble down the church steps as Santuzza thrilled, as did her *Vissi d'arte* as Tosca, which she sang prone on the floor, "in a pose of unashamed abandon," according to Farrar, who watched from a box.[3]

And therein lay a growing conundrum: for whereas *Tosca* and, especially, *Cavalleria*, were two of the greatest "slice of life" operas to emanate from verismo's birthplace, and required the ultimate in realistic acting, *Carmen*, composed some 15 years before the Mascagni, had nonetheless come to be seen as such. Even the Opéra-Comique was having a hard time maintaining the stylistic refinements of its original presentation. True, critics had once described Galli-Marié and then Calvé as "unbridled" in their portrayals, but those were different times when it took far less to shock an audience. Now, finally free of the corsets, chaperones, and bourgeois prudery that had so long shackled them, women, especially in postwar America, were determined to redefine their place in society, to flaunt their individuality, and, quite simply, to do as they pleased. They smoked, drank, took jobs outside the home, and gave themselves permission to be promiscuous and enjoy sex, just like men—in fact, just like the Gypsy herself. At the opera house, W. H. Henderson had seen it all: "People who were shocked by [Calvé's dance] were living in the age of innocence. The gay '90s were conspicuously naïve. They are now derisively called Victorian.... But in these degenerate days ... we have what the Victorians could not have conceived, the rule of the racket, the high speed mania and the cocktail hour. Calvé's dance would not strike us as wicked. We would say it was an awkward evasion of the candor which we worship."[4]

And so Gatti looked to Jeritza to continue her eye-catching ways and restore *Carmen* to big box-office status, and Jeritza was only too happy to further indulge her veristic side. As expected, the public loved her antics; the critics did not. Said Henderson: "Mme Jeritza was very busy. She made a vigorous attempt at a Spanish dance; she sprawled on tables and chairs, put her feet in men's laps, jumped on tables and off again and smoked cigarettes even while singing.... But with all her energy she did not seem to get far beneath the surface of the role."[5]

8. In the Time of Dictators

And Olin Downes: "It is surprising that a singer of her experience, intelligence and observance of tradition in other roles should have been willing so recklessly, ineptly, crudely, to violate every principle of technic [sic], style, or even effective stage presence as she did on this occasion. Carmen stands many different treatments and many different conceptions of the principal part, but there is a line to be drawn between that which is individual and artistically daring and that which cannot be justified by any sound principles of taste or logic."[6]

Of her performances for Gatti the following season, however, Henderson noted that "she had lightened the color of her hair and darkened that of her voice ... for the better," and that her performance "was evidence of an earnest desire for improvement, and ... a more artistic characterization."[7]

Unfortunately, Jeritza's recordings of the *Habanera* and the *Chanson Bohèmienne*, which she made only days after the performance, are all we have of her bad girl and give no hint of what she must have brought to the stage. For, though she sings prettily enough on these recordings, one doesn't hear a clear characterization. It seems that, not unlike Farrar and Garden, Jeritza needed to be *seen*, not just heard, to truly understand what all the shouting was about.

* * *

While the Weimar Republic struggled to find footing for the homeland after its defeat in World War I, German artists, intellectuals, and musicians flourished in a veritable golden age of expression and experimentation in the brief period before the rise of Adolf Hitler. In Berlin, the center of Weimar culture, one could hear the newest works of such ground-breaking, even radical, composers as Kurt Weill, Paul Hindemith, Anton Webern, and Arnold Schoenberg (some intoned by Mahler discovery Gutheil-Schoder) or attend any number of fresh, robust, imaginative productions mounted at one or another of the capital's many opera houses. For example, the Staatsoper,[8] which in 1925 hosted the world premiere of Alban Berg's *Wozzeck* or the Kroll Opera House, which for a decade challenged enthusiastic audiences with its daring modern productions until 1931, when, accused of left wing propaganda, it was forced to close.

Indeed, not only an encroaching great depression but the rise to power of the ferociously anti–Semitic, anti-modernist dictator Adolf Hitler would bring these and all freedoms to a screeching halt in the early 1930s. A handful of Jews the Nazis considered indispensable if they were to keep enjoying music in the Reich were issued special permits to continue performing in Germany, but most either fled, were incarcerated, or sent to the gas chambers.

How is it that *Carmen* survived such a place in such a time? For given Hitler's campaign to cleanse the Reich of every non–Aryan—Gypsy or Jew—it was odd that an opera about a Gypsy with a libretto by Jews and music by a composer some thought might have Jewish blood was permitted to play at all. Did the new Führer, who was known to occasionally overlook an offending factor in the name of art, simply allow it to slip under the radar? In his brilliant book *Hitler and the Power of Aesthetics*, Frederic Spotts emphasizes that Hitler's love of music, of which we hear so much, was mainly confined to opera: Wagner, above all, and then some Puccini and Verdi. "Otherwise there were few if any non–German composers whose works he could abide."[9] But if those were Hitler's personal choices, Spotts adds that in the Führer's almost fanatical concern for Germany's culture he made every effort to make "acceptable" music—*Carmen*?—available to the people, insisting that opera houses and other cultural institutions be kept open well into the war. And yet another way of looking at it comes from Susan McClary, who writes that "productions of *Carmen* in Nazi Germany—which also exploited the opera for the sake of the political tensions of the moment—functioned to reinscribe (rather than to criticize) racial hatred and the necessity of contaminating Others."[10]

Either way of looking at it, for as long as opera houses stayed open, *Carmen* remained a viable repertory piece and was even performed at Theresienstadt, the "model" concentration camp Hitler allowed foreign visitors to see. And in 1938 someone in the Third Reich, possibly Goebbels, even commissioned the Spanish director Florien Rey to make a movie based on the Mérimée story called *Carmen, la de Triana*—Triana being a Seville neighborhood known for its rich Gypsy life. The popular Spanish film star Imperio Argentina, Rey's wife, starred and also learned German for another version, *Andalusische Nachte* (Andalusian Nights), which was directed by a German and filmed in Germany.[11]

And so, Bizet's masterpiece not only escaped the chopping block but continued to be performed enough for many a Germany-based singer to wisely retain the title role in her repertoire. Lotte Lehmann, in fact, declared Carmen "among the most coveted roles in the Vienna Opera," though the celebrated soprano—a Micaëla in her early career—protested that she herself had no interest in the part and had never seen an entirely satisfactory interpretation. In a bit of a slur on Spanish women, she called the Gypsy "a rather vulgar woman, Spanish to the last drop of her savage blood."[12]

8. In the Time of Dictators

Still, in part owing to the national character, in part to the consonant-laden language with which they had to express themselves, many of the Teutonic and Eastern European Carmens brought a harshness and aggressiveness to the role rarely encountered elsewhere. In Thomas Mann's *Magic Mountain* Hans Castorp describes seeing Carmen portrayed as a "savage creature."[13] Well, maybe not the "savage" of Mann or the "vulgar" of Lehmann, but in the famous Emmy Destinn recording you certainly have one of the scrappiest, fiercest, most uncompromising, and intense of all German language Gypsies. "Famous" because, recorded in 1908, it is billed as the first complete *Carmen* on disc.[14] But more "famous" still because, even today—70 or more commercially recorded portrayals later—the Czech soprano's rendering remains on many lists as one of the most electrifying ever.

Without these discs, the "Divine Emmy," who was only 30 years old when she made them, would almost certainly be remembered more for other roles in her large and diverse repertoire—notably Verdi, Puccini, Wagner—than for her Carmen, which she sang only early in her career and primarily in Germany. Sidney Homer, the husband of the contralto Louise Homer and himself a composer, pronounced Destinn's ravishingly beautiful instrument to be "unique"; her middle voice "like some new wood-wind instrument, the high notes pure, yet charged with emotion ... [her]legato like a river of sound, or a Scotch bagpipe"[15]—all ideal for Carmen. But while these qualities are not readily apparent in the recording, from her straight-out *Habanera* and feather-light *Seguidilla* to her

Emmy Destinn, whose electrifying Carmen can be heard on the first complete recording (1908) (photograph by Verl. Herm. Leiser [Berlin]).

steely defiance in the face of her fate, the role seems tailor-made. Destinn not only possessed the same "fatalistic temperament"[16] but was as tempestuous and disdainful of convention as the wanton one herself.

The number of times Destinn takes the soprano options, adds her own high notes, plays with rhythms, and rewrites whole measures to better suit her spinto soprano may seem excessive even for the period, but this is a Carmen of the moment. And it is as well a Carmen not for the faint of heart. Indeed, in addressing the acoustic, Destinn makes one sit bolt upright in one's chair, arrested not so much by the beauty of her vocalism and wide-ranging palette—stunning as are both—but by the urgency and burning intensity of her delivery.

And it was apparently much the same when she took the stage; even to the point that when in 1897 she sang two Carmen arias for the Prague National Opera in her first audition anywhere, the director told her to go home and pour cold water over her head.[17] (Shades of what a certain critic suggested for Galli-Marié as Carmen.) But Destinn, undaunted, seems to have stayed with her characterization and, after more rejections, ultimately so "surprised" the public in Berlin with the "unusually true character" of her Gypsy that all performances were sold out in advance.[18] On the other hand, though London greatly admired Destinn, it took only two performances of her irreverent hellion for management to replace her with a safer option: the stolid, venerable English contralto, Louise Kirby Lunn.

In any event, the combination of Central European temperament and language tended to result in a rougher, tougher, more aggressive Gypsy than we usually get from artists of other nationalities. One sees it in the photographs and hears it in the recordings, like that of mezzo-soprano Margarethe Klose, a famous Wagnerian, and the volcanic Carmen of the next complete German-language recording, first issued in the 1930s. "Like Brünnhilde at the inn of Lilas Pastia," it was said of Klose.[19] And, indeed, if vocally the role was a walk in the park for most of these singers, stylistically and dramatically it had to have been a challenge.

* * *

In 1924 several European and American capitals had the unexpected pleasure of a visit from the Moscow Art Theater, which included among its unusual presentations a music drama called *Carmencita and the Soldier*. The West was fascinated. "Shorn of all operatic conventions … staged with surpassing originality, employing a single set, only a Greek-style chorus stationed in balconies above, and no Micaëla," it was, said Olin Downes, "an audacious work of genius." Most of Bizet's score was retained, but the libretto had been entirely rewritten to better correspond with the Mérimée novel.[20] "The old conception of realism has been abandoned," its producer Vladimir Nemirovich-Danchenko told a reporter when it played in Berlin, "and everything now is concentrated to bring out the realism of the soul."[21]

Acting, therefore, was of paramount importance, and "the swarthy, sumptuous, fate-ridden beauty" of Olga Baclanova's Carmencita captivated Downes. "Not so accomplished a singer," Baclanova was, regardless, "the embodiment of the mysterious unseen force of the drama," Downes wrote, "an unforgettable figure, one that would have been irresistible in any place or time."[22] So great was her success that, in fact, she decided to stay on in the West—to defect, as it were—where she became a major film actress.

How it was that the Soviet Commissar of Culture gave permission for the company to tour abroad is not told. There had been a time when Russian and Western artists freely mingled in each other's countries, but after the Russian Revolution the great exchange slowed, then came to an abrupt end. Unlike Hitler, who allowed his artists to travel in the belief they were good advertisement for the Reich, Stalin kept the artists of the new Soviet Union sequestered behind the Iron Curtain. If one was ever to be heard in the West, he or she had to have emigrated before the curtain came all the way down, but since emigrating meant leaving one's homeland perhaps forever, most either chose to stay or made the choice too late.

There was opportunity at home, however, even if it meant first meeting with party approval and then following the rules. With four opera houses in Moscow, two in Leningrad, and many smaller cities with companies of their own, most with seasons running through much of the year, there was, as a *New York Times* correspondent reported in 1936, plenty of operatic activity on Soviet stages. Naturally, repertoires favored the Russian historical operas, but Italian, German, and French works were also performed, and *Carmen* was "particularly popular."[23] Happily, of the many Gypsies meeting the demand, two of the most celebrated, Nadezhda Obukhova and Maria Maksakova, both on the Bolshoi roster, left memoirs with entire chapters devoted to their portrayals, though, judging from their writings and recordings, the two could hardly have been more different.

In fact, playing a seductress could not have been easy for Obukhova, who was already 44 years old in 1930 when she first sang the role, and 51 when she recorded excerpts. In her book she recalls the strong impressions and striking differences of other Carmens she had seen: namely, Cecile

Ketten, the Galli-Marié protégé, who was so "spirited, flexible, lively and graceful" in her performance in Nice, and Maria Gay who she found "sometimes short-tempered and rough." Obukhova herself thought of Carmen as "proud, majestic ... cheerful, passionate ... full of life," implacable in her love of freedom, and "not afraid to die." But she makes no mention of the Gypsy's sexual prowess, and goes on to confess that she never imagined herself in the role because of the acting and dancing required. Moreover, her mellifluous, intimate mezzo—though gorgeous to hear in her light-as-a-feather recording of the *Habanera*—sounds a bit mannered for a champion of liberated sex. And so she was probably right in declaring her younger colleague, Maria Maksakova, best in the role.[24]

Maria Maksakova, one of the best Russian Carmens of the Stalin years, 1945.

To be sure, Maksakova, also a mezzo, had come to the role early and over a 30-year period would sing Carmen some 300 times on Soviet stages—always adding to and changing her portrayal, she would write, to keep it fresh and in line with her own aging. Like Obukhova, she viewed the story as primarily about freedom, which is why, she said, her Carmen died with a smile on her face. But there was an edge in both her look and interpretation that seems to have been beyond her gentle older colleague. "A physically attractive singer, her acting was characterized by sparkling temperament, dramatic verve and emotional directness."[25] In her accounting of her Carmen studies, however, she describes the struggle she had reconciling Bizet's colorful, sunny music with Mérimée's dark, primitive story, to which she as a Russian could easily relate.[26]

* * *

Although it is often insinuated that all Stalin really liked about opera was its female singers, Italy's Duce, like Germany's Führer, loved the genre for itself. What Italian didn't? Every Italian town had its own opera house, and every opera house its own opera season. But for all the love for and history behind Italian opera, what was once the national pastime was in trouble. With government increasingly imposing itself on the companies, and cinema, the latest in entertainment, drawing audiences away, many of Italy's greatest singers were being lured away by foreign companies, which paid far higher fees than any their economically stressed homeland could afford. Though Mussolini had expressed an interest in modern works, just to keep their doors open, companies depended on standard repertoire, which, to all intents and purposes, favored the verismo composers—and *Carmen*.

After Galli-Marié introduced the Gypsy to Italy in 1879, native singers were quick to adopt the role for themselves, the younger among them infusing her with the fire in the belly that was verismo's calling card. It is, in fact, in Italy that we encounter most clearly the beginning of a stylistic showdown such as one hears in the recordings of the superlative Claudia Muzio and Fernando De Lucia, artists "who united the searing intensity called for by *verismo* parts with deeply schooled control," as opposed to those for whom "*verismo* licensed shrieking, staggering and playing to the gallery."[27] To be sure, singers' repertoires were changing dramatically, and with them vocal methods and styles. Virtually forgotten were Bellini, Rossini, and Donizetti; in their place Meyerbeer, Gounod, Massenet, Verdi, Wagner and, most recently, Richard Strauss and the Italian veristic composers. The pure instrumental sound of bel canto had given way to an active vibrato; and singers, having once moved freely between roles, undeterred by ranges or other vocal demands, were becoming specialists.

What kind of voice Bizet wanted for Carmen, of course, had never been very clear, but nor had it been a concern. Bizet's troublemaker had, after all, come into the world as really no voice in particular, something mid-range—a Dugazon or Galli-Marié voice, as history books call it—and thus available to any but the lightest voices, so long as they were up to the dramatic challenges. It is not so surprising, therefore, that in her first decades, soprano Carmens outnumbered mezzos by approximately two to one. But now in Italy a major shift to the lower voice was in the works and with it something of a new sound for the popular *gitana*.

The history of singing often sees a time (often a place as well) when a certain type of voice enters a kind of Golden Age. Since the days of Maria Malibran and Marietta Alboni, Italy had rarely wanted for lower female voices—in large part thanks to the important roles Rossini and Verdi created for just their kind. But never had the country produced such a plethora as in the years between the world wars. "Those were the times when contraltos reigned," Lina Pagliughi recalled.[28] As we know, it had initially been sopranos—notably Bellincioni and Germanno-Ferni, the Gypsy's creator at La Scala in 1885—who predominated as Carmen in Italy. But once the country's sumptuous lower voices began intoning her tunes they effectively made the role their own—not only in Italy but everywhere, and, some would argue, for all time. Furthermore, with the sonic change came a corresponding visual one. For while most of these lower-voiced Mediterranean impersonators could produce as passionate a Gypsy as any of their soprano peers, the sheer ripe sensuality of their sound signaled a lustier, more voluptuous physiognomy.

Noted as much for her vivid acting as for her powerful mezzo, handsome Giuseppina Zinetti was so successful in her first assayal of Carmen in Bari in 1918 that she was soon performing throughout Europe, even Australia, and, in the early 1920s, at la Scala. Some anointed her the best Gypsy of the day; recorded excerpts certainly show her to have been a dynamic one.

Another, the exotic, erotic Gabriella Besanzoni,

Gabriella Besanzoni, the colorful Italian mezzo, shown here with an excellent example of the spit curl, around 1929 (photograph by Ernst Schneider).

who was also kept busy in the role, has left us a complete recording (1931) in which she paints her Gypsy in the broad, extravagant strokes of a blustery wench, who laughs heartily and often. But, unhappily, as her rich, rock-solid contralto powers its way through every scene we get few glimpses below the surface and come away with little idea of what she was like on stage. Arthur Rubinstein, who claims to have had an affair with her, wrote that with "something of a wild sensuous animal in her ... though not exactly beautiful, she was the perfect incarnation of Mérimée's gypsy."[29] Vincent Sheean, on the other hand, remembered that given "a voice like very rich black brass" it was all about the singing; that, in fact, she "was content to wear the costumes, to move very little, to act with her face occasionally, and to present the essence of the drama with the voice."[30] Nonetheless, Besanzoni's Carmen traveled far and wide, only missing out at the Metropolitan in New York when Besanzoni appeared there in 1919, because the Gypsy was still the exclusive property of Farrar. A Roman by birth, having made her operatic farewell in the Eternal City as the *diavolessa* in 1939, Besanzoni was buried there in her fourth act costume.[31]

A fine-grained mezzo, almost a lyric, Gianna Pederzini's was the lightest in weight of this heyday of low-voiced Italian women. But having been schooled by the incomparable Fernando de Lucia, she was similarly comfortable in a great range of repertoire from Rossini and Mozart to Richard Strauss, Massenet, and even Verdi's Azucena. But according to the soprano Gina Cigna, the key to her success was that "With a thread of a voice she held the audience spellbound."[32] A beautiful woman—renowned for her legs, according to Franco Corelli—Pederzini sang well into the 1950s, even creating the role of the dying Prioress in Poulenc's *Dialogues of the Carmelites* for La Scala in 1957. But her prime years spanned the interwar period, and during that terrible time she became embroiled in a scandalous affair with one of Mussolini's henchmen, causing much resentment, especially from her mezzo peers who felt sure that her connections impeded their own advancement. Nonetheless, the Gypsy was Pederzini's calling-card, and as she told Lanfranco Rasponi:

> When my Carmen was introduced at La Scala, it exploded like fireworks. After the divine Besanzoni ... the great Giuseppina Zinetti, and Cristoforeanu,[33] it was quite a card I dared play at the gaming table. I was totally different from all the others. I interpreted it as a work of true verismo, which it is. I read a great deal about Galli-Marié ... and the way Bizet really wanted it.... It was never meant to become the huge spectacle that it has turned into today. I followed this original conception: sexy, intimate, snakelike. I never sang to the public, only to the characters on stage. Not only did I win a smashing victory, but it became my warhorse.... I could have eliminated all the other operas and sung only Carmen.[34]

Gianna Pederzini, who "with a thread of a voice ... held the audience spellbound" (photograph by M. Gamuzzi, 1930s).

And then there was Ebe Stignani—though the very idea of this formidable singer in the Bizet surprises. Possessed of a colossal, wide-ranging dramatic mezzo, her renown was as a Verdian. Short and overweight, her looks could hardly have suggested the scandalous enchantress; and though a great actress with her voice, her acting on the stage itself was minimal.

8. In the Time of Dictators

And yet, for a while at midcentury she was famous for the role, and thanks to her 1949 complete *Carmen* recording—actually a soundtrack for a movie that was never made —we know why. Granted, the recorded sound is inferior, but both she and Beniamino Gigli, her José, are on fire. And if one could argue that their effusions are excessive, their words (in Italian) are so fully realized and cleanly delivered, one cannot help but be drawn in.

Other popular Carmens in Italy at this time are the Spaniard Aurora Buades and the Mexican Fanny Anitua, both of whom also left complete recordings of their portrayals. Anitua is interesting in that her vocal approach moves back and forth between soprano and mezzo, which adds to the mercurial aspect of the Gypsy. She's also effective when she declaims passages that were notated to be sung, providing a compelling example of what could be done before conductors brought an end to singers taking such freedoms with the score.

Buades takes her own share of liberties but does not execute them nearly as tastefully. The singing is solid, but rhythms are sometimes distorted and any opportunity to milk a note is taken to the extreme. Hers is an aggressive, mannish Carmen, certainly commanding, but not particularly seductive, nor especially representative of her Iberian origins.

* * *

Both, however, were a far cry from the impeccably sung, stylistically elegant, proud Carmens of Victoria de los Angeles and Teresa Berganza, Spaniards we meet later. But in the same interwar years a lyric mezzo-soprano with a voice and style unlike any other and a "true daughter of Spain,"[35] as she pleased to call herself, mesmerized audiences with a Carmen unlike any other. She was the one and only Conchita Supervia and her career extended from just before World War I to just before World War II, encompassing not only the rise of Mussolini, Hitler, Stalin, and in her country, Francisco Franco, but also the decade of the glamorous Roaring Twenties of which she herself was the spirited personification. And so, though something of an anomaly in any chronicle of important Carmens, the mezzo-soprano from Barcelona crowns this chapter.

To be sure, Supervia enchanted in everything she sang from Spanish songs to operas that ranged from Mozart to Richard Strauss,[36] and included Rossini, who was something of a rarity at the time. Her singular vocalism characterized—especially, it seems, on recordings—by its fast vibrato was not—and remains not—to everyone's taste. But her sound was luminous, her diverse tonal palette endlessly engaging, and her polished

Conchita Supervia, in one of her Lanvin Carmen costumes, which she told an interviewer were "tres chic and also true to Iberian custom."

musicality spot-on. Add to that her infectious personality, tantalizing pulchritude, and magnetic stage presence, Supervia consistently stole hearts and lit up stages across the Western Hemisphere until 1936, when, at the height of her career, her life was tragically cut short in childbirth. That her age at the time was given as only 41 has been questioned; for if she was born in 1895—as the numbers suggests, and the year most research points to—she would have been just 16 years old when in 1911 she created Octavian *(Rosenkavalier)* for Rome and sang her first Carmen in Lecce, Italy. And yet, as described by the noted Chicago critic Edward Moore, she made "a nice, girlish, little Carmen"[37] when she visited his city in 1916, while in a photo from that same visit she even looks a bit like a turn-of-the-century Lolita. This in contrast to a photo from the 1930s, which shows her the epitome of sophistication—and charm, for she could hardly be otherwise—in a dress with a long, sculptural train, coyly holding a huge fan against her chin.

In any event, when in 1930 Supervia first sang the role at the Opéra-Comique, Paris fell in love. Seductive and ironic, she was the "Carmen of Mérimée's imagination," as her "every word conveyed Carmen's intention and her every phrase was colored in response to the music." With a voice that was simultaneously soprano and mezzo, Supervia was, the critic said, a Carmen that "could not be imitated ... and stayed in the memory."[38]

And yet Londoners, though enthralled by her Rossini and Spanish numbers, were not so sure about her Gypsy, which she almost cancelled for vocal reasons when Covent Garden tried to schedule her Carmen before her Cenerentola. The diva won the argument, of course. But, whether it was the Lanvin-designed costumes, modern production involving a revolving stage, dialogue à la Opéra-Comique—insisted on by Supervia against conductor Thomas Beecham's wishes—or the opera house itself, possibly too large for her voice and highly nuanced delivery, her performance "sharply divided critics and public who [two decades later] still cannot make up their minds whether or not she was a great Carmen."[39]

Thank goodness, then, for Supervia's multiple recordings of the role, one in Italian, most in French. Though none are complete, the selections are extensive and her renditions fascinating. What is more, with a voice that is Spanish and a "manner" that is French, we hear the naturalness with which she marries the Spanish protagonist to her French creation, thereby bringing her incarnation "nearest to that 'infinite variety' that marks a true Carmen."[40]

CHAPTER 9

American Idyll

> "A young woman, slender and supple, possessor of the gypsy lure, which is an inevitable attribute of the ideal Carmen, and whose voice fills the requirement of the role, is being sought by the New Opera Company for its projected English version for the Bizet opera."—*Musical Courier*[1]

As part of his customary rant against the United States, Adolf Hitler liked disparaging the young country's lack of culture, including its mere handful of opera houses as compared with the 270 his Reich boasted. The claim was perfectly legitimate, and one that Mussolini could also have made regarding Italy's 300 or more.[2] For while only the American cities of New York, San Francisco, Chicago, Philadelphia, and Boston had houses that offered seasons of any length, in the countries of the Axis, virtually every town and city had an opera house, many of which performed several nights a week in seasons that were sometimes as long as ten months a year. All the same, even as Hitler spoke, opera companies in smaller American cities were quietly beginning to sprout—"like mushrooms," said *Musical Courier*.[3] So much so, in fact, that in 1945, *Opera News* counted some 113 in the United States.

Granted, the new regional companies, as they were called, were hardly comparable in number or in length of season to Germany's and Italy's plenitude. But for America, with no opera tradition of its own, such phenomenal growth was a big step forward, and for American singers a godsend. Finally—just like singers in countries abroad—they could make a living from their art at home. And if *Carmen* was on their résumés, so much the better. It was one of the most popular operas in America, and for mezzos like Coe Glade and Winifred Heidt, its titular heroine virtually constituted their livelihoods. "I sang Carmen about 2,500 times," a long retired Glade told a reporter, happily adding, "It's a role you never get tired of."[4]

* * *

9. American Idyll

So what was it about their portrayals that so appealed to mid-century America? Of Glade we hear, primarily, of her charisma; of Heidt, the earthy wholesomeness. Both were American born, bred, and trained; both from the Midwest; both mezzo-sopranos. Otherwise, they could hardly have been more different.

With "her large, haunting eyes and slight figure, made slighter still by the mass of long, sable-colored tresses it bore, [Glade] was every American's idea of how a Gypsy should look," said Dorothy Kirsten, who made her debut in Chicago as Micaëla opposite Glade, and remembered being "mesmerized by her long, bejeweled eyelashes" and "incredible flamboyance ... a trait which the public absolutely adored."[5] Dissatisfied with the recent portrayals of Mary Garden and the German Maria Olszewska in Chicago, the eminent critic Edward Moore crowed: "At last there is a Carmen.... Glade is the kind of Carmen that makes the lights seem to be turned up a bit when she comes on the stage and the music to sound a little more golden. Not to put too fine a point upon the matter, she has it."[6]

A regular on the rosters of Chicago and the San Carlo Opera—the latter whose savvy manager Fortune Gallo had discovered her in 1926—for two decades Glade took her Gypsy coast to coast, from the Hollywood Bowl, where one critic anointed her "the Calvé of this generation" to Radio City, where she helped open the new theater in scenes with Titta Ruffo as Escamillo and at one time played the role there some four times a day. In Cincinnati, where she was a favorite, they declared the names Carmen and Coe Glade "synonymous."[7] Indeed, probably no other American Carmen of the era stole more hearts.

Except, perhaps, her

Coe Glade, charismatic with "her large, haunting eyes and slight figure" (photograph by Maurice Seymour).

Winifred Heidt, whose earthy, wholesome portrayal stole hearts (photograph by Bruno).

younger colleague, Winifred Heidt. For who could resist the unadulterated gusto the Detroit-born mezzo brought to the role—a Carmen who seduced by virtue of her infectious personality, fresh-faced good looks, and total lack of affectation and female wiles; rather, a free spirit, who lived life to its fullest and took it as it came. And then, the voice; for, to quote Irving

Kolodin, "it would be difficult to imagine a purer, lovelier vocal sound. Rolling tones pealed from her throat and the air tingled with vibrant sound."[8] But Heidt did not make any commercial recordings of opera, and we must content ourselves with just one live performance: her 100th Carmen, broadcast from the Hollywood Bowl in 1946. Somewhat abridged, and in English with spoken dialogue, it nevertheless gives some idea of her glorious vocalism, superb musicality and diction, and vivid impersonation, all of which supports Harold Rosenthal's contention, in writing of her performances in London in 1949, that she was "one of the best postwar interpreters of the role."[9]

As for the Metropolitan, where she briefly sang small roles, her voice alone certainly warranted a chance at leading roles. But even if management had kept her on the roster[10] she might well have been passed over as Carmen, for by then the company's stock of Gypsies had grown considerably.

* * *

Though Gatti-Casazza had taken *Carmen* out of the Met's repertoire in 1932 when Jeritza's waning career left the title role without a star, in 1935, his successor, Edward Johnson, needing good box office for his inaugural season in the midst of a depression, was sure he had exactly that. For since her 1918 opera debut as Leonora in *Forza del Destino* when she was just 18, Rosa Ponselle had been a crowning jewel in the company's already star-studded roster, and now the celebrated Italian-American soprano was going to assume her first Carmen. "And if that's not news I'll bite the dog!" the new manager had crowed in making the announcement.[11]

There were, however, risks: among them, as her own coach cautioned, that he "could only see her as a dramatic heroine in roughly the same tradition as [Claudia] Muzio—a woman of dignity whose constant striving for romantic love was matched by an immense capacity for suffering."[12] Could the public possibly accept Rosa Ponselle as a femme fatale or bad girl, he worried? Still, there was every reason to believe she could make a success of it. "[Carmen's] music fit my voice like a glove," she told a biographer. "[It] was the only role that never made me lose a wink of sleep—no worries at all—as easy as pie."[13] What's more, her large brown eyes, full lips, black hair, feline body—which she would slim down further for the role—and inborn Latin temperament, all pointed to a dramatic fit. And, finally, as important a reason as any: like Hauk, Farrar, and so many others, she loved the character and had the resolve. Given, then, all these positives, having read the Mérimée more than once, Ponselle headed to France to study flamenco with the renowned dancer La Argentina and coach with no less an authority than the Opéra-Comique's Albert Carré.

Tickets for Ponselle's Carmen debut sold quickly; according to the *New York Mirror*, "Nearly a thousand persons were turned away."[14] But while sales were exciting and continued to be regardless of what was written, critics pounced. "We have never seen Miss Ponselle sing so badly, and we have seldom seen the part enacted in such an artificial and unconvincing manner,"[15] Olin Downes began his review, so scathing that audience members wrote letters of protest to the *New York Times*. But Downes was not alone, and because Ponselle was such a star, every piece of printed matter in the city had to have its say. "She sang the Habanera belligerently as if defying the world," *Time* magazine blasted. "She turned on bewildered Don José like a tigress, sidled up to the captain of the guards like an old-time cinema vamp. The stage scarcely seemed to hold her ... [and] she was too busy ranting to do justice by Bizet's music."[16]

In two live broadcasts of Ponselle's Carmen (from Boston and Cleveland), available on CD, the soprano unquestionably makes many poor musical choices and plays fast and loose with the score, leaving conductors and colleagues scrambling to stay with her. There are, in fact, moments that—shades of Jeritza—she sounds altogether like a loose cannon as she exploits the verismo and takes spontaneity to an extreme. And yet, one has to allow that for the most part the performances are exciting and the voice gorgeous throughout.

Ponselle did modify her portrayal somewhat, while the critics modified their response to it. With time, she might have become a great Carmen, as Farrar, Garden, and other colleagues who had leapt to her defense, believed was possible. But it was not to be. Though for two seasons Ponselle played every one of her 15 Carmens to sold-out houses and enthusiastic ovations, hurt by the critics hostility, worn out from the stress of singing in the spotlight for two decades, unable to convince Johnson to mount *Adriana Lecouvreur* for her, and newly married, the soprano, though only 38 years old, abruptly ended her operatic career while on tour with the Met in Cleveland, as chance would have it—or maybe on purpose—as Carmen.

* * *

During Edward Johnson's tenure as manager of the Metropolitan Opera (1935–1950), the company saw some six more Gypsy impersonations. The striking Swedish mezzo Gertrud Wettergren had made her Met debut as Amneris, but, with some 150 performances of the Gypsy abroad already under her belt, replaced an indisposed Ponselle in the role the following month. Despite singing in Swedish while everyone else sang in French due to the short notice, comparisons were inevitable. As though to pour salt into the American's wounds, Downes wrote: "[Wettergren] sang like a true musician, and she conveyed what the composer and librettist intended by means of finesse rather than the exaggerations which have been practiced by nearly all prima donnas who have taken this role of late years."[17] Nevertheless, the company was invested in Ponselle's stardom to shore up box-office—and though Wettergren later sang Carmens in Chicago, she sang only three more—in French—for Johnson.

Then, when Ponselle retired, Johnson turned to Bruna Castagna. The Italian mezzo was experienced, having performed throughout Europe, Australia, and South America; and La Scala had even revived Rossini's *L'Italiana in Algeri* just for her. She had sung her first Carmen in Barcelona, but, anxious to see New York, she had accepted an invitation to sing for Alfredo Salmaggi, and after relearning Carmen in French, opened the impresario's 1934 Hippodrome Opera season in the part. The Met usually scoffed at anyone who sank so low as to sing in the Hippodrome's "poorman's" productions; but after seeing Castagna at Lewisohn Stadium, in 1936 Johnson reversed himself, inviting the mezzo to inaugurate the company's first Spring Season[18] as Carmen, and leaving it to her older soprano sister Maru to fill her Gypsy shoes for Salmaggi.

Taking yet another shot at Ponselle, the critics praised the Italian's "sumptuous voice and excellent musicianship" as well as the "absence from her acting of anything meritorious or cheap,"[19] and their kudos continued the following fall when she joined the regular company. "Castagna is already a better Carmen than Miss Ponselle," Lawrence Gilman declared, though adding, "and if she takes herself in hand and passes the pastry shops with stonily averted face, she may even become irresistible."[20] True, the schoolmaster's daughter was a bit "roly-poly,"[21] as *Time* described her. But she was arguably the most satisfactory Carmen the Met had offered New York since Farrar, and, "beyond question one of the best" Phillip Miller, that brilliant discerner of singing, "ever heard."[22]

Castagna centered the remainder of her career in the United States, a frequent performer not only in New York, performing with the Met until 1945, but also in San Francisco, where she was called "the most voluptuous, rowdy, and altogether exciting Carmen seen here in years."[23] Chicago and Cincinnati also entertained her portrayal, as did Philadelphia, where, as Carmen, she ended her operatic career in 1949.

* * *

Also taking up the slack left by Ponselle's departure was a five-foot-one-inch Russian-born mezzo by the name of Jennie Tourel. With Castagna promoted to the regular season, Tourel had replaced the Italian in the 1937 Spring Season. But when nothing came of her performances of either Mignon or Carmen she had returned to the Opéra-Comique, where, ever since her debut in the Bizet in 1933, she was a star. In 1938, Herbert Peyser, seemingly unaware of her appearances in New York, sounded positively awestruck by Tourel in Paris, writing in the *New York Times*:

> A voice of satin velvet.... I cannot recall a Carmen of such vocal excellence since long before the war.... The most conspicuous feature of the Tourel Carmen is its simplicity. Watching it develop step by step with an inexorable logic of composition, you ask yourself in wonder why it is that the majority of Carmens feel driven to turn themselves inside out in order to get at what they conceive to be the heart of this role, why they need to bring into play all the extravagances and caprices ... to create an impression designed to smash you like a blow between the eye.
>
> Whether this rare characterization would register as perfectly in a larger frame than the ideal one of the Opéra-Comique ... or as part of one of those over-dimensioned and inflated "Carmens" given in opera houses outside of France ... would be quite so memorable and rewarding is something I am not unreservedly prepared to say. In the Salle Favart, at any rate, it is a thing to treasure.[24]

Escaping through Lisbon only a week before the Germans entered Paris, Tourel returned to the United States, however, and rejoined the Met in the mid 1940s. Perhaps, as suggested, the size of the house explains why her Gypsy was never the success there that it was elsewhere in America. But Peyser himself would later vouch that her impersonation was consistent with what he had seen in Paris.

When in 1944 Laszlo Halasz engaged Tourel for the inaugural season of the New York City Opera, her Carmen was transmitted live on radio, and a good portion of Act 2 (from the quintet through *La bas, la bas*) with the mezzo in seamless voice was issued later on a CD. Also included is a 1969 interview in which she talks about the influence the great Supervia, her predecessor in the role at the Opéra-Comique, had on her own portrayal.

* * *

Lily Djanel arrived earlier than expected, but it was also thanks to Hitler that the Metropolitan acquired the Carmen of the Belgian soprano. Having narrowly missed the bombardment of Brussels, the pretty blonde had been singing the Gypsy at the Opéra-Comique only days before the Nazis marched into Paris; like Tourel, she had made her way to Lisbon

Lily Djanel, a vivacious and popular Carmen at the Met in the 1940s.

and, from there, embarked for America. Whereas Olin Downes thought "the part too low for [Djanel]"[25] most reviews and a recording of a live Met performance suggest that the first important French-speaking Carmen to visit America since Calvé and a veteran of some 80 performances of the part on the continent, brought style, admirable diction, a tall, slim figure, and an infectious vivacity to the role. If little else appears to have separated her impersonation from the routine, she would nonetheless remain Johnson's go-to Carmen—including four broadcasts, one of which was issued on CD—through the war years.

In any event, none of the various portrayals by Wettergren, Tourel, Castagna and Djanel, generated the kind of box office of a Ponselle. Star power was needed for that, and in a beauteous mezzo from Deepwater, Missouri, Johnson might have found it.

Though Gladys Swarthout had been on the Metropolitan roster since 1929, at the same time she had also developed a flourishing career as a radio personality and motion picture star, both of which had repaid her with big money, celebrity, and fans that included people who had never even attended an opera but now became interested. In short, the time was ripe for Swarthout to try her wings with Carmen, a role she had long dreamed of playing. Just as Calvé had once inspired Farrar, so too, it seems, had a performance by Farrar herself first inspired the young mezzo. And then—as she often told the story—one night after a performance in which she was singing Mercedes to the Carmen of the great Mary Garden, the diva had suddenly torn her Gypsy shawl in half. She would keep one half for herself, she said, but the other she must give to her Mercedes—the next great Carmen.

But while Swarthout had some success in 1939 with her first Carmens in Cincinnati and Chicago with critics mostly noting the beauty of her voice, figure, and costumes, she did not fare so well at the Met in 1940 where they were merciless, their grim reviews declaring her far too lady-like for the outrageous Gypsy. Now there are Carmens with the inner impulse and Carmens without, and Swarthout, no matter how hard she studied, was a Carmen without. What is more, her portrayal was not only all "learned," but learned at the same time that Hollywood stardom was encasing her in a plastic of her own making. She herself later admitted that because she "found success so fast and so young" she "lost sight of my true artistic goals for a time."[26] The celebrity that came from her long radio career and the five films she made in the late 1930s were both a priority and a distraction.[27] No one faulted her singing, nor certainly her looks. But, "her Carmen could be an adornment to any fashionable cocktail lounge."[28] Indeed, "better suited to the Country Club," wrote the estimable composer and critic Virgil Thomson, who, nevertheless, also allowed that, "in contrast to the fidgety frigidity of her person, the voice is all liquid fire and velvet."[29] She might, in fact, have been ideal in the role had she only had "that combination of flame and profundity that makes for genius."[30]

In any event, in the early 1940s, steely in her determination, Swarthout—"star of opera, screen and radio," as her advertisements proclaimed—took her Gypsy across America to the exclusion of virtually every other of her roles, while "the royalties on her Victor recordings of Carmen arias alone were enough to take care of her for life," she once told a critic.[31] And in her 1943 autobiographical novel *Come Soon Tomorrow*, though Swarthout herself began her career in small roles, it is as Carmen that her protagonist, Emmy, makes her debut at the Met.

* * *

By the end of the 1930s some 45 films had been made on the Carmen theme. And while the enigmatic seductress was, on the one hand, enticing movie studios and beguiling movie goers, back in the opera house her myriad manifestations on screen were inevitably influencing impersonators. Critics had commented that Ponselle's Carmen was more "cinematic" than "operatic,"[32] and when MGM asked her for screen tests in the role, the diva had not hesitated to oblige them. Probably because she set her fee too high—or so rumor had it—nothing came of it. But tests of her singing the *Habanera* and *Chanson Bohémienne* have survived, and it is fascinating to see her attempts at playing to the camera—as opposed to the thousands in the opera house—dressed in the costumes the famous Valentina had designed for her at the Met.

Whereas singers in the first decades of Carmen's life as operatic heroine had worn the kinds of period pieces the genteel 19th-century audiences might have imagined for their prima donnas donned as a Spanish Gypsy—boleros, satins, mantillas—over the decades, modifications, usually in the name of authenticity, were constantly being made. The spit (kiss) curl on the forehead, for instance—in French, called an *accroche-coeur*, fittingly, a "hooked-heart," which suggests a flirt or heartbreaker—was a popular feature that began to catch on in the 1920s, as was the addition of more and more jewelry, which was believed to be the Gypsy custom. And the paintings of the Gypsies that Lucienne Bréval commissioned for her Carmen at the Opéra-Comique, provided just the fodder Marie Muelle, a popular turn-of the century costumer of the stars, needed to dress the diva in "flounced skirts made of the garish handkerchiefs sold to the peasants of Spain ... and prosaic black calico, with large green polka dots on it [in the smuggler scene]." (In the name of realism, Muelle permitted glamour only in the last act.)[33] Could this have been the beginning of polka dots, one wonders—a fabric pattern adopted by Carmens of all nationalities right through the 1960s? Perhaps polka dots seemed trendier, making Carmen more like the girl next door and, consequently, not so threatening.

Then, everywhere, there was the Spanish shawl, which Calvé purported to have introduced.[34] To be sure, elaborately embroidered, usually

Rosa Ponselle, in the controversial Toreador costume Valentina designed for her final act (photograph by the New York Times Studio).

with roses, these fringed shawls—like the one Mary Garden shared with the young Swarthout—were for a time considered *de rigeur* for any self-respecting Carmen. And, in time, shawls of every kind, worn in every way imaginable from simply tied around the waist to engulfing the entire body, found their way into virtually every one of her scenes.

But as the century progressed the shawl would have its day as well, as audiences, attracted by the chic and allure of film and fashion, expected more. Supervia had wowed London in her startling Lanvin creations, and now not only Ponselle but also Swarthout looked to Valentina, the equally renowned designer of celebrity couture.

Gladys Swarthout, who had everything but the temperament.

"I do not believe that the requirements of historical authenticity need limit the fancy," the Russian-born Valentina would say, after putting the slimmed down Ponselle in a highly controversial costume designed to mirror her toreador: a bolero, tight skirt—originally pants, but Johnson had said that went too far—and in place of the traditional mantilla an exaggeratedly wide brimmed version of a matador's hat.

As for her other famous client: Valentina knew her diva well. She had been designing both Swarthout's costumes and street clothes for years, even landing her a spot on America's annual "Ten Best Dressed Women" list more than once. "The personality of Gladys Swarthout in the same part of Carmen ... called for a different interpretation," she said. "Instead of fiery ardor, Miss Swarthout gave an image of tender and lovely femininity which led me to follow her type and personality."[35]

* * *

But as chic and fashionable went out of date, they were replaced by titillating and sexy; and, in 1952, while some found the latest cover of

Newsweek "beautiful," and today no one would give it a second glance, others were so shocked by the photograph showing opera singer Risë Stevens dressed as Carmen with her bosom teetering on the brink of full exposure they just had to protest. Wrote one woman to the editor: "Just when I decided Newsweek was tops, you come out with this. I don't like naked dames. There are things in life besides dames and bosoms." Wrote another: "Frankly, the cover of the Feb. 11 issue came as a distinct shock. Is this sort of flaunting photography necessary?"[36]

For the purposes of our story, though, the question was whether titillation by way of half-exposed bosoms the best a Carmen could muster to "shock" anymore? Was "shock" even necessary? Of course, peasant blouses, with or without a drawstring neckline, had been a mainstay of Carmen's first act costume since her earliest interpreters, and low necklines were certainly not uncommon in the daily life of Spain. Still, Stevens's alluring pose combined with the décolletage created by her off-the-shoulder blouse seems to have been about as provocative as 1950s America could handle.

* * *

Risë Stevens had first played the Gypsy in 1938 at the Neues Deutsches Theater in Prague, where she had made an auspicious debut as Mignon. The company had money only for the most pedestrian costumes, but the mezzo from the Bronx hadn't needed help, and when news of her success reached New York, Johnson had crossed the ocean to judge for himself and follow up with a contract. Returning to America shortly after Hitler invaded Czechoslovakia, Stevens performed a variety of roles, including Octavian, Mignon, and Cherubino, at the Metropolitan. Then in 1941, egged on by her Hungarian husband, an actor who was dissatisfied by the pace of her career in opera, she had gone to Hollywood to replace Jeanette MacDonald as Nelson Eddy's costar. *The Chocolate Soldier* did not impress the Met; but in 1944 Stevens did get its attention playing an opera star gustily singing Carmen's *Habanera* in the classic film, *Going My Way*, which she followed with "an intensive promotional campaign that included everything from advertising Chesterfield cigarettes in her Carmen costume—flower clenched in teeth—to making her first recording of the role."[37]

Taking Johnson's advice, Stevens practiced her Gypsy outside of New York before deftly sliding into the role at the Met, drawing off performances that otherwise would have gone to Djanel, Tourel, and the pretty Russian mezzo Irra Petina. But if her Hollywood exposure helped box-office, critics were not impressed. Of her role debut in the Met's tired old production in 1945, Jerome Bohm described a "stoop-shouldered, sullen figure in the second act ... and in the final scene a melodramatic figure whose scream of fear ... was in the best blood-curdling traditions of the New Star Theater back in 1910."[38] And a year later, Arthur Berger described her portrayal as growing "less and less satisfying.... If she takes more pains than others do to portray the low character of the heroine, she does so with exaggerations and stagy postures."[39] But just as concerning—and Stevens herself recognized it—serious flaws had cropped up in her vocal production to rob it of its former sensuousness and beauty of line. Given all the criticisms and problems, for Stevens's Carmen to have survived the 1940s to become one of the most famous and long-running impersonations in Met history, therefore, is nothing less than remarkable. But that, as next we learn, is exactly what happened.

Chapter 10

Sea Change

"In some day not too remote, potential ticket-buyers may ask who is staging a performance as well as who is conducting or who is singing in it."—*Musical America*, November 1, 1951

Risë Stevens was a good actress. But unable to cast off the Hollywood effect, and rudderless in the Metropolitan's tired-old, cliché-ridden production, her Carmen, as we left it in the last chapter, was foundering badly. Curing what ailed her singing with a new teacher and investing in new costumes as she did in 1949 had not solved much. Nor did it help that, like the new Levittown, a sameness was settling over the country's culture, taking with it opera production. To be sure, no matter in what city Stevens performed her stagey, stereotypical impersonation, it was always the same, and probably would have continued so, had not Edward Johnson retired in 1950 and turned the leadership of the Metropolitan over to a dynamic new manager from abroad. For, having worked with some of Europe's most progressive directors in opera, Rudolf Bing brought with him a vision of opera Americans had rarely experienced. The Metropolitan Opera was rightly lauded for its history of great singing and music making, the Vienna native acknowledged, but now, he declared, it was his mission to provide it with "staging of the first order."[1]

Not only as composer and librettist but as well as stage director for his own music-dramas, Richard Wagner, whose novel idea that singers were not supposed to "be singing an opera" but rather "performing a drama,"[2] had begun the process toward opera as theater in Bayreuth. Verdi had prepared his singers dramatically as well as musically, as had Mahler who, as part of his reforms, also took scenic and lighting design to new heights. And in Russia, as we have seen, innovation with an eye to opera as theater flourished. With so much more still to come, operatic stage direction was becoming an art in itself, and the names of those who practiced

10. Sea Change

it almost as familiar as those of the singers and conductors. At best, opera was total theater, achieved by a collaboration of artists in every department whose first priority was to give the score in hand the fullest and most insightful realization possible.

Such purpose was not totally new in America; movies and the recent arrival of television were making Americans almost as interested in what they were seeing as in what they were hearing. And with refugees from the Nazis and war in Europe taking positions in academic institutions, workshops, and small companies throughout the country, American singers were learning more about the dramatic aspect of their art. To this end, the Russian tenor Vladimir Rosing had formed his own American Opera Company, while the Austrian Herbert Graf, who wrote three books on the subject, not only worked with young singers but also directed opera throughout the country, including at the Metropolitan. And during the war Hans Busch of the recently founded Glyndebourne Festival arrived to help give dramatic plausibility to the relatively innovative productions of the New Opera Company in New York. The upbeat company only lasted three seasons and never did perform a *Carmen*, though it apparently wanted to, as we know from a notice in *Musical Courier* that began: "Ideal Carmen Sought by New Opera Forces."[3] But in the grand scheme of things these were little more than well-meaning gestures; it would take the big house in New York to make more than just a dent in the consciousness.

* * *

Accordingly, his public now apprised of his intentions, Bing opened his first season with Verdi's *Don Carlo*, an opera not heard at the Met since 1922, having engaged as its stage director Margaret Webster—the company's first female in that position—known for her productions of Shakespeare but with no experience in opera. Counting her work a success, thereafter Bing would regularly look to the legitimate theater for directors for all his new productions. As a result, it was not so much Fritz Reiner's *Carmen* or Risë Stevens's Carmen—or even Bizet's *Carmen*—but rather Tyrone Guthrie's *Carmen* that was all the talk when introduced in 1952.

Though best known as the director of England's Old Vic, a company renowned for its productions of Shakespeare, Guthrie, unlike most of Bing's new directors, did have some opera experience, including a 1949 production of the Bizet he had directed for Sadler's Wells in London which Bing just happened to have seen and admired. In it, the British director had dismissed the picturesque to emphasize the downside of life in Seville and, in Anna Pollak, found a singer, who, as he wrote in his memoirs "was not afraid to make Carmen the vulgar, violent slut the story demands."[4] Though this was all a notable departure for the British, they had nevertheless received it well. So now Guthrie brought essentially the same ideas to New York, where he found in Risë Stevens, the Met's presiding Carmen, a singer-actress who welcomed the chance to rethink the role and try new things.

In his biography of Stevens, John Pennino has written in some detail about the mezzo's experience in Guthrie's eye-opening production, which included relocating the final scene from its traditional place outside the bullring to inside Escamillo's dressing room so that Carmen was more convincingly trapped. But, as one critic wrote, it was "impossible to guess how much of [Stevens's] acting represents her own present convictions and how much derives from Mr. Guthrie's instructions."[5] Guthrie was known not to push anything on his actors that bothered them and Stevens reportedly played down his input. He had let her follow her instincts, trusting, one supposes, that whatever interpretation she arrived at by osmosis during rehearsal, could not possibly bear any similarity to her former incarnation. And that, apparently, is what happened. "Alley Cat Carmen," *Time* declared: "Risë Stevens has been singing the role of the wanton gypsy for seven years, but never in such abandoned and sultry fashion…. Heretofore, [her] acting in the role of Carmen has always had a trace of well-bread sorority girl. This time her Carmen was just short of plain alley cat."[6]

Risë Stevens, whose portrayal in the Met's 1952 production *Time* magazine compared to an alley cat.

* * *

10. Sea Change

In his book *Misdirection: Opera Production in the Twentieth Century* (1981) A.M. Nagler identifies two kinds of *Carmen* production: "a 'soft' *Carmen* (lower and upper middle-class, romantic) and a 'hard' *Carmen* (realistic, derived from Mérimée)." Not surprisingly, *Carmen* as "scenic" melodrama was still the preference in most houses, including the Opéra-Comique, which viewed it as "Spain through French eyes" with the Gypsy as a kind of "demimondaine in a pseudo-Spanish milieu" and thereby "soft." But, Nagler wrote, when in 1906 Hans Gregor, the director of the Komische Oper in Berlin, mounted a production that put the emphasis on "character portrayal," by bringing all the realism and fatalism of the Mérimée to the fore, he started a "war against all traditions of the 'soft' version." All the same, Gregor's "hard" approach was as nothing compared to some of the experimental versions to come, notably from Moscow, including Nemirovich-Danchenko's aforementioned *Carmencita and the Soldier* in 1924 and a 1935 Stanislavski presentation that "thoroughly did away with all the bourgeois operatic tinsel," and made of the Gypsy herself "an enchanting vice."[7]

But it wasn't until after the Second World War that the concept of a 'hard,' character-driven *Carmen* really got traction. For, as Europe emerged from its appalling suffering, "the collective unconscious was ... more than receptive to the stark realism of the new productions and to the probing, psychological approach of the new producers."[8] Many point to Walter Felsenstein, who restarted the Komische Opera in East Berlin after the war—the old company having ended soon after Gregor's departure—as leading the movement. The director Lotfi Mansouri, who worked under him for a while, has, in fact, called Felsenstein "the founding father of opera as total theater, a master of externalizing the inner core of the musical drama and renowned for working through a production down to the minutest detail."[9]

But, as everything he did was in the name of dramatic verisimilitude, the German director's lofty aims were often not only extreme but impractical as well. To appear in one of his productions, some of which are available on DVD, was certainly not easy for the singer who was expected to attend as many as 100 rehearsals—thereby keeping international stars away and lowering vocal standards—and at all times put character over singing. "Singing which is not justified emotionally has no business on the stage," Felsenstein insisted. "The audience must never recognize singing as the practice of a professional skill."[10] Hence, "these things in the Habanera must be *said*, not sung," he told one singer. "You are still singing too much from the vocal cords, and not enough from the enjoyment deep inside that you have succeeded with your mesmerism."[11]

Felsenstein mounted his scrupulously realistic and "hard" *Carmen* on at least three different occasions: in 1949 at the Komische, at which time he reinstated the original dialogue and replaced the inferior German translation with one of his own; in 1969 when he took the company to the Stanislavski and Nemirovich-Danchenko Theater in Moscow and performed it in Russian; and in 1972 when he revived the same Moscow production for the Komische, performing it in German but keeping the Russian Emma Sarkissyan, who had previously worked her Gypsy with both Stanislavski and Nemirovich-Danchenko. Of that "deromanticized" production, which had Felsentein's "imprint on every moment of the staging," John Higgins of the *London Times* found Sarkissyan (resembling Yvonne De Carlo) altogether "remarkable" in the role, as she conveyed "the compulsiveness, the erotic flash, the animal reactions for the part, but most of all the directness."[12]

* * *

Lest, however, one has the impression a dark, diabolical *Carmen* was taking over world stages, in actuality, colorful, wholesome productions, befitting an audience raised on the new cinemascope, predominated. The Carmens who performed in them might have imagined themselves the dangerous femmes fatales of the post-war film noir, but more often than not, in keeping with mid-century mores, they tended to be better-groomed and better-behaved than ever—lusty and bosomy, yes; maybe even sexy; but hardly erotic nor even vulgar (an incarnation that seems to have peeked with Jeritza), and certainly not the malevolent temptresses of the new films.

Cecil Smith summed up the disconcerting trend when in 1954 Nell Rankin, a glamorous young mezzo from Alabama, who had been singing at the Met since 1951, was chosen to head an impressive new production, staged by film director Anthony Asquith, at Covent Garden. Disgusted that Rankin's "sole virtues are good looks, good grooming, and a placidly even scale"[13] the venerable critic lamented the "absence of a single singer able to do justice to the part." Perhaps management listened; for the following season Smith rejoiced in Rankin's replacement, writing that Marianne Radev, a mezzo from Yugoslavia, "realized that the way Carmen feels and makes men feel is more significant than the way she looks. I do not mean to imply that Miss Radev looked ugly or plain," he clarified, "but merely that she did not look glamorous. And if there is one quality Carmen should not have, it is 1955 glamour.... Because so many Carmens assume that the role can be treated in terms of decorative appearance and

Nell Rankin, the American mezzo, in a costume designed by the famous Russian George Wakenvitch, presumably around 1953 (photograph by Bruno).

synthetic Hollywood sex, the impact of a singing-actress who gets beneath these tiresome externals is tremendous."[14]

But was it fair to blame it only on the singer? For what, then, was poor Grace Bumbry to do when saddled with a production, such as the one by Jean-Louis Barrault that Bing foisted on New Yorkers in 1967 that seemed only about externals? "Overproduced, overstaged and as artificial as a celluloid Spanish doll with big eyelashes.... No character can be believable under the circumstances," Harold Schonberg had lamented under the headline "Carmen for the Tired Business Man."[15]

* * *

Then again, there was the way Italians liked their Gypsy: "the big, brash Carmen"[16] which flourished up and down the Boot. Properly attended to she might have been reined in, but La Scala and other important Italian houses were busy exhuming the old and premiering the new, leaving the standard repertoire and its singers to fend for themselves. Moreover, though film-making was fast becoming a serious art form in the country as practiced by such pioneering new directors as Fellini, Antonioni, Pasolini, Rossellini, all fearless in revealing the underbelly of their wounded and weary country, their ground-breaking ways had not yet extended to the opera house. But in 1954, inspired after seeing her as Bellini's Norma, Luchino Visconti, famous for his work in film and theater, had asked to direct the rapidly rising soprano, Maria Callas, in a new production of Spontini's *La Vestale* at La Scala. It would be the first in a series of important collaborations and an eye-opener for mainstream audiences to see what an opera—even when practiced within a traditional framework—could look like when drama and music were as one.

Unfortunately, the two never applied themselves to *Carmen,* and Callas never, in fact, performed the role on any stage. But if for that reason the recording she made much later under Georges Prêtre can only be regarded as an aside in this chronicle,[17] it nevertheless provides a glimpse into what this electrifying singing-actress might have done with one of the most discussed roles in the canon, and the excitement that attended its release was palpable. The expectation was that the temperamental diva would unleash a tigress. But while every phrase is fraught with a dark sexuality and sense of danger, Callas's Carmen is even more fascinating for its calculated cool, which gives us only glimpses of the fire smoldering underneath until the tigress is finally released full out at the end.

After Callas's death it was the conceit of Franco Zeffirelli, Visconti's former apprentice, who himself had directed Callas often and staged many a *Carmen* extravaganza, to tantalize Callas's admirers with a film he called *Callas Forever*. In it a producer (Jeremy Irons) convinces Callas, as played by Fanny Arden, to come out of retirement to make a film of the opera. The idea was that because the voice was in ruins, the Callas character would only act the Gypsy but lip-synch her music to her own recording—

that, of course, by the real Callas. The few opera scenes that this film-within-a-film includes are naturally all hypothetical. But Zeffirelli knew the artist and her *Carmen* recording well, and in the final confrontation we see a Carmen not only determined to be free but positively indignant at being stalked. Like any true feminist of the 1980s, this Carmen—or at least Arden playing Callas playing Carmen as imagined by Zeffirelli—is so furious at José for coming after her she goes bodily after him and, so, into his knife.

* * *

In any case, Italian singers, more often than not with no one like a Visconti or even Zeffirelli to work with, continued to exude the Gypsy's exuberant ways with all the verismo abandon of their Italian predecessors and barely a nod to the role's dark side experienced north of the Alps. The country was still producing stunning dramatic mezzo-sopranos who excelled in Verdi and sang Carmen as a lark—as it were. And at midcentury three in particular—Giulietta Simionato, Fedora Barbieri, and Fiorenza Cossotto—upheld the glorious tradition, which would so sadly and inexplicably end in the 1970s. For until very recently, after Cossotto, the line of Italian Carmens ended abruptly.

Though Simionato, born in 1910, was the oldest, she did not come to prominence until well after her rival Barbieri, who was a full decade younger. In fact, when during the war Barbieri burst on the scene at the age of 20 as Azucena, replacing an indisposed Pederzini, Simionato was still singing Mercedes to Pederzini's highly acclaimed Carmen and would not move up to leading roles till that singer's career declined after the war. What's more Pederzini's charismatic incarnation was a hard act for anyone to follow, and

Giulietta Simionato, the Italian mezzo who could perform Carmen in any style (photograph by Semo Mexico, D.F.).

certainly Carmen's hellion ways and seething sexuality did not come naturally to the dignified Simionato. All the same, her velvet mezzo, peerless legato, incisive musicality, and beguiling persona proved enough. For, though once again arriving on Barbieri's heels, she was La Scala's choice for the Gypsy from 1954 to 1963 and for many years was a favorite in the role around the world.

Simionato's Carmen can be seen in only three scenes filmed when on tour in Japan. But it can be heard on any number of pirated recordings as well as a superb studio recording. Singing opposite Nicolai Gedda, the highly disciplined Swedish tenor, and under the Austrian martinet Herbert von Karajan, who had directed and conducted her first Scala Carmens, Simionato delivers a stylish performance in French—measured, nuanced, elegant. This in contrast to some of the pirated performances available in Italian, including one from Palermo in which, even at the age of 50, she so successfully holds her own opposite a passionate young Franco Corelli that the critic Carlo Marinelli was obliged to write: "Von Karajan would surely not have permitted Giulietta to create such a woman of the people, for that matter someone even a little vulgar and impudent, seething with desire and expectation."[18] It would seem then that Simionato could do whatever the language or locale called for.

Simionato sang Carmen in Chicago but never in New York, where she did not appear at all until late in her career. Her nemesis Feodora Barbieri did, however, as a rare replacement for Stevens in the new Guthrie production and, happily, one of her four performances was broadcast. And a fine one it is; for if, as José, her Italian colleague Mario del Monaco made no adjustments for the unaccustomed style and language, Barbieri embraced them. "To anyone who has sung *Carmen* well over a hundred times in Italian, the French language comes as a surprise," she told Mary Jane Matz of *Opera News*, adding, "but a pleasant one.... I much prefer *Carmen* in French to *Carmen* in Italian. The whole color of the opera changes with a change of language, of course, and the principal differences between French and Italian Carmens are differences in color." The usual production is "set in vivid, hot colors ... emphasizing the hot climate of Spain, the bloody quality of the drama," she continued, but the Metropolitan's is "black and white with red accents, returning to the Spanish tradition of the original story."[19] And to prove the point, unlike the beating it takes in a pirated recording from Naples, here Barbieri's beautiful voice all but gleams in its new polished and nuanced rendering.

Indeed, Naples appears to have been a city with a particular penchant for the "big, brassy Carmen" of the kind we see from a stentorian Fiorenza

Cossotto in a 1967 video. Sporting a beehive hairdo and stiletto heels, Cossotto's man-eater seems to prefer marshaling the troops to seducing them, singing more at them than for them. It's as if the further south a singer went the more she felt it necessary to deport herself as the "muscular gypsy ... [who] uses every opportunity to bombard her delighted Italian audience with her granite chest register."[20] To be sure, like Simionato and Barbieri, deftly accommodating her style to suit her audience, the Cossotto who plays Carmen in Naples seems hardly the same as heard on a 1974 live recording from La Scala under George Prêtre in which she scrupulously observes markings while rendering a characterization both nuanced and sensuous. What's more, in a rehearsal segment from that same performance as seen on YouTube, she sings the perilous *Chanson Bohemiènne* with precision and dances with considerable allure with the famed Flamenco dancer Antonio Gades.

Fiorenza Cossotto, the last of the great twentieth century Italian Carmens.

* * *

With the end of war and the arrival of the jet plane, traffic across the proverbial pond picked up and with it the internationalization of operatic performance. While European stars, lured by better fees and conditions, were once again filling choice roles in important American houses, eager young Americans in turn, not having endured anything like the hardship of their European counterparts but rather healthy and prepared, hastened abroad hoping to get experience by filling positions on rosters left in tatters by the fighting.

In 1959, substituting on short notice for an indisposed Simionato,

Gloria Lane of Trenton, New Jersey, became the first American to sing Carmen at La Scala. And when her steamy portrayal earned her a contract for more performances in her own right, even *Time* magazine took note, describing how "dressed in black stockings and a startlingly low-cut shirt ('I never wear a brassiere') she stopped every eye in the house," and how, with a voice that was "opulent and brilliant, rich as plied velvet," she brought it down.[21]

Lane came experienced; in addition to having had leading roles in two Gian Carlo Menotti operas on Broadway, she had sung opera, including multiple performances of the Gypsy, across Europe and America. One, in 1953 in Chicago with the New York City Opera, had made national news when an exasperated David Poleri, her José, suddenly stomped off the stage in the last scene shouting at the conductor Joseph Rosenstock to finish the opera himself and leaving someone else to sing his final lines from the wings and Lane to somehow die without him. Tearful apologies followed but did not save the tenor's job.

* * *

Meanwhile, having enjoyed a long history of superb Carmens from Pauline Lucca to Marie Gutheil-Schoder, in 1955 Vienna acquired "a new darling"[22] in the sultry seductress of Jean Madeira of Cleveland, Ohio, whose first performance all but rocked the Austrian capital, where the young contralto had gone in hopes of furthering her career. At the Met, Madeira had understudied Stevens in the Guthrie production but only managed one student performance. Now, in Vienna, her impersonation earned her "45 curtain calls."[23]

With her tawny complexion, intense green eyes, and lithe figure, Madeira certainly made a most credible-looking Gypsy, a look she sometimes enhanced by pulling her jet black hair back into a sleek knot, nicely complementing the "anthracite sheen"[24] of her rich voice. To be sure, Christa Ludwig, who found herself in the uncomfortable position of having to follow Madeira in the same production, recalled just how "fantastic ... the American with the 'splendid, dark contralto voice' looked, and 'most amazing of all, [how] she could lift her skirt with her teeth.'"[25]

But if Ludwig believed that she herself was temperamentally the "exact opposite of Carmen," as she wrote in her autobiography, she was also determined to succeed in the role and, in a later Vienna production, finally got the help she needed to "create the kind of Carmen that would work for me," from its director Otto Schenk. "I played Carmen as a young woman of the people, a poor factory worker, who lives thoughtlessly and only follows her appetites. I made her shameless, fearless, amoral, and lusty ... and bitterly cold when her passion for Don José dies in the last act."[26] Admittedly, she had trouble carrying this interpretation into other productions. Directors, in fact, with their own ideas as to how to interpret a work were becoming a problem for singers, who, just when they thought they had found an impersonation they could believe in were asked to forgo it for someone else's.

Yet another American to bring her Carmen to Vienna was Bronx-born Regina Resnik. In the 1940s, while building a solid career as a young soprano at the Met, Resnik had sung both Frasquita and Micaëla at the New York City Opera and the Gypsy herself with the traveling Columbia Opera. But when in the mid 1950s Bing disputed her change from soprano to mezzo, she had left for Europe, where her exceptional intelligence, musicality, acting ability, and "warming deep blue"[27] voice brought her accolades in a large and varied repertoire.

Regina Resnik, the American who began her long career as Carmen touring with the Columbia Opera Company in 1945.

Carmen, however, was her calling card—her debut role in Vienna, Stuttgart, London, Buenos Aires and, in 1964, Paris, where *"Le Triomphe de Regina Reznick [sic], Une Carmen extraordinairement envoutante, captivante, troublant"* was but one of the countless glowing headlines that greeted her first appearance.[28] But no wonder the Parisians embraced her, for how often anymore did they get to hear a singer convey the Gypsy's bravado without sacrificing one jot of the music's Gallic grace. Anyone who can filter out Del Monaco's bellowing and barking will hear this rare combination, which she achieves under the baton of Thomas Schippers in her one commercial recording of the role.

Resnik often remarked on the lesson of quietude in acting that she learned from Wieland Wagner with whom she often worked at Bayreuth, and of its importance to her portrayal. Just how Carmen makes her entrance, for example, can be key to establishing her character. Usually we find her bursting on stage, the last of the cigarette girls to leave the factory, and swarmed by the men. But then sometimes she fools us, as did Zélie de Lussan in this unusual bit of staging as far back in 1915: "As the Carmen theme was declaimed ... and the choristers gathered at the back of the stage, dividing on either wing of a side entrance, a strong light was then thrown on the scenery, opposite, which the singer enters sideways from the wings. As she approached, as yet unseen, the light showed up the silhouette of her figure on the scenery gradually coming nearer and nearer till at length she appeared."[29]

Could this extraordinarily original idea have been De Lussan's? Or were these early stage directors more inventive and involved than we thought? Either way it was an impressive accomplishment, given the primitive state of stage lighting at the time, and certainly made a powerful effect, graven as it was in the viewer's memory. In any case, if by no means as stunning, opera lover and author Ida Cook was similarly struck by Resnik's slow, casual descent down the inevitable steps from which one could only infer "she had been up to no good—back there in the factory."[30] Indeed, the lesson of 'less is more' was also important to Shirley Verrett, whose own entrance when she first sang the role at Gian Carlo Menotti's Spoleto Festival in 1962, was directed by Menotti, who "wanted Carmen to be mysterious." And so "instead of Carmen being showcased by entering the stage alone, as the score indicates, he had me enter with some friends ... barely noticed and smoking a cigarette. When the music began, announcing Carmen's entrance, I was already on stage. As I stretched my arms and began rolling my shoulders with suggestive upper body movements, as if emerging from a cocoon, other activity on the stage was minimized.... I dropped my cigarette on the ground, put it out with my shoe, and began my line, 'Quand je vous aimerai.'"[31]

* * *

Verrett belonged to the first wave of African American singers to sing characters assumed to be white-skinned in major opera houses. Indeed, once relegated to performing only with small companies and only in roles that required no make-up—like *Aida*—in recent years these black singers were beginning to perform what were once "whites only" roles with major companies, notably in the United States where the stakes were especially high. Todd Duncan as Tonio in *Pagliacci* in 1945 and Camilla Williams as Madama Butterfly in 1948 at the New York City Opera in 1948; Mattiwilda Dobbs as Gilda in *Rigoletto* and Robert McFerrin as Rigoletto and Valentin in *Faust* at the Metropolitan Opera in 1956 were all big news.

Though it is likely an African American occasionally performed Carmen with a small all-black company, Muriel Smith, it seems, was the first to perform it with a major company, having come to the role by way of *Carmen Jones*, a Broadway musical with lyrics by Oscar Hammerstein and "songs" based on the Bizet score. Transported to a parachute factory in the American South, updated to the present (the Second World War), and cast entirely with African Americans, this quasi-operatic American musical would prove a stepping-stone for several careers, Smith's among them. As Carmen Jones, the New York native had been described as "torridly realistic ... sensuously beautiful, swivel-hipped and salacious ... an unequivocally dangerous woman."[32] And though her career thereafter was comprised primarily of concerts and musicals, in 1957 she would couple those attributes with her throbbing mezzo to render the role in the opera proper for London's Royal Opera.

One might have thought black singers naturals to impersonate the Gypsy: the dusky velvet in so many of their voices, their dark hair and complexions, their supple bodies, their visceral passion, and, above all, their inherent dignity and pride stemming from their ethnic otherness. And yet, there have been surprisingly few in Carmen's chronicle even to the present. Though in the 1960s and 70s, Shirley Verrett and Grace Bumbry were counted among the most celebrated Carmens of their time, neither particularly liked the role in large part because of the cliché association with their skin color. "Carmen is the same sickness for black mezzos as Aida is for black sopranos, Bumbry complained."[33] All the same, for both of them the part was a ticket to recognition in their early careers.

From Spoleto, Verrett had taken her Gypsy to the Bolshoi (1963), and from there to companies around the world, among them La Scala, the Metropolitan, Covent Garden. Her preference remained, however, for smaller stages and more intimate productions, like Menotti's in Spoleto, and Franco Enriquez's in Florence, where she found, she said, her "definitive Carmen."

> I captured Carmen's mystery by not flaunting her. In most productions everyone onstage circles around Carmen. She is the center of attention. In this production, I positioned myself off in a corner. I spoke with a veiled quality to my voice—a quality achieved by lowering my voice, dropping my shoulders and body, or lowering my

head. I turned my body away from the audience. Carmen was calmer, more human and down to earth, more attainable. The audience could relate to her.

I loved this version of Carmen, because it was not a giant production, but more *musica da camera* (chamber music).[34]

Though a few years younger than Verrett, Bumbry reached international renown faster partly owing to a sensational debut in Bayreuth—the first black singer to perform in the prestigious festival—as Venus in Wagner's *Tannhäuser* in 1961, which followed her first Carmen in Basel, Switzerland, where she had a contract. In her mind the Gypsy was "just not a positive character." But she knew the part fit her "like a glove," and a 1967 film of the opera, conducted and staged by Herbert Von Karajan—based on his Salzburg production—brought her portrayal worldwide acclaim. Prerecorded, the lip-synching and Hollywood style studio sets take some getting use to. But the camera work, especially the close-ups, adds a new dimension, which Bumbry, not just dark-skinned but dark-minded and altogether spellbinding even in her absurdly glamorous costumes and hairdos makes the most of.

Indeed, like recording at the turn of the century, now, as *Carmen* approached its 100th birthday, film—be it a commercial venture or a video of a live performance—was beginning to play a critical part in making opera more accessible to a larger audience and thereby impacting how singers performed. For better or for worse, nothing escaped the zoom lens; singers knew the very veracity of their portrayals were at stake, and most seized on the lessons of this new technology and incorporated them into their work.

* * *

Meanwhile, scholars were resurrecting other aspects of *Carmen* performance. A slew of new editions of the Bizet score, most particularly one by the German Fritz Oeser, which opened up old cuts and restored the dialogue, presented other challenges. Felsenstein, who provided the German translation for Oeser's critical edition, was just one who welcomed the return to the original dialogue in the belief that the sung recitatives caused an "unwarranted lyricism—a bourgeois romanticizing—which Bizet ... could not have intended."[35] But not everyone agreed; for example, in 1971, at the height of the excitement over the Oeser, Regina Resnik, agreed to direct a new production for Hamburg—in French (with Huguette Tourangeau) and in German (with Tatiana Troyanos)—but insisted on keeping the Guiraud recitatives in the belief it was obvious Bizet would have preferred *Carmen* as grand opera.

10. Sea Change

In any event, it was all very confusing and a bit of a dilemma. For while Oeser's claims and conclusions could not be dismissed out of hand, at the same time other new editions were surfacing. What to cut, what recently uncovered music to restore, and, above all, whether to stay with the Guiraud recitatives or reinstate the original dialogue resulted in any number of approaches, the matter of the spoken dialogue throwing fear into those singers whose inferior French would be exposed. And then, ironically, just as the dialogue option was becoming accepted around the world, Paris reversed itself and prepared to hear Guiraud's recitatives for the first time ever. It was almost 85 years since its birth at the Salle Favart, but now *Carmen* had been ordered to leave its home with the city's subsidized Opéra-Comique[36] and take up residence at the Palais Garnier, the subsidized home of grand opera, where dialogue was prohibited.[37] Its first performance there was to be one of three gala events planned by André Malraux, Charles De Gaulle's Minister of Culture, whose purpose it was to remind the world of the greatness of French culture.

And so it was that on November 10, 1959, Bizet's masterpiece joined the repertoire of Paris's famous Opéra before a veritable who's who of dignitaries, artists, and celebrities.[38] Directed by the actor and film director Raymond Rouleau, the mammoth production boasted 100 musicians in the pit and, on stage, horses, donkeys, supers, and 350 choristers, representing every conceivable Seville type in costumes inspired by Goya. "So realistic is the producer's touch," the correspondent for the *London Times* reported "one might almost say that in Rouleau, Julien [the company's new director] has found his Felsenstein."[39] What's more, to show off at a time many thought the country's singing in decline the cast was—with the exception of the José, Australian Albert Lance—entirely French, even if the Parisian-born Carmen, Jane Rhodes, had the most un–Gallic of names.

Jane Rhodes had made her debut with the Opéra in Berlioz's *La Damnation de Faust* in 1957, having spent several years performing in the French provinces. With a voice of neither distinctive size nor color, she vacillated between the mezzo and soprano repertoires. But she was such a superb actress that she was almost as famous for her Tosca and Salome as for her Carmen, which, while fiery and seductive, she nevertheless rendered with notable restraint, taste, and insight. As one critic extoled: *"Sans aucun doute cette Carmen mérite une place dans l'histoire de l'Opéra aux cotés de Violetta de Claudia Muzio et de la Médée de Maria Callas."*[40] Production and Gypsy were the talk of the city and in 1960 the Metropolitan flew Rhodes over for a single Carmen in Guthrie's production.

With Guthrie long gone and such Carmens as Blanche Thebom, Nell Rankin, Belan Amparan, and Rosalind Elias occasionally replacing Stevens, however, the production had lost its focus. But now "two new Carmens infused fresh blood into the title role, each of them presenting conceptions of the part that were radically different from the kind of Hollywood vamp to which [Met audiences] have become accustomed in recent years." The Swede Kerstin Meyer, the critic described as a "Scandinavian seductress, vibrant and slender, resembling one of the existential heroines of Bergman or Strindberg ... passionate and cruel."[41] The French Jane Rhodes, on the other hand wearing her own costumes and looking like "a grown-up Brigitte Bardot moves about the stage less than any other Carmen in memory, relying upon a flashing pair of eyes to summon men to her bidding."[42] "A rather languorous, aristocratic, even ladylike Carmen," Harold Schonberg thought, but "capable of violent rages and swift changes of temperament ... [and] one of the most brilliant Carmens of recent memory."[43]

Meanwhile, others followed Rhodes in the Opéra's new production, including not only Resnik and the excellent French mezzo Denise Scharley, who sang 62 performances, but also, in the fall of 1960 (while Rhodes was in New York), an American we met earlier, who had made her stage debut as Amneris at the Garnier the previous season. When a photograph appeared in the French papers of two Carmens at Orly airport about to take off with the new production for Japan, one white, the other young Grace Bumbry—"*la Carmen noire,*" as the French had dubbed the mezzo—it seemed *Carmen* was "clearly taking off for new adventures, adventures that seemed poised less to escape than to continue to play out the historically complex set of attitudes toward the exotic other embodied in the various formulations of Carmen, from Mérimée on."[44]

Chapter 11

100 and Counting

> Carmen is the most exciting role in the entire musical literature. And some of the ladies who have played her are the most colorful women in opera. I can't imagine any other heroine being given a birthday party, not even Madama Butterfly.—Joanna Simon[1]

> Today, Carmen would have José committed, or at least enjoined by the courts from molesting her. Her free evenings would be spent in karate classes and at NOW meetings, soaking up the wisdom and tactical knowhow of Steinem, Atkinson, and Jong.—Donal Henahan[2]

One hundred years had passed since the night Bizet's provocative protagonist began her inexorable march to "Seductress of the Century."[3] And in New York City, the magazine *Opera News* and the French Embassy on Fifth Avenue teamed up to celebrate with champagne toasts to the opera and a repast befitting the Gypsy's lesser-known reputation—so engagingly depicted by Mérimée—as gourmand. In addition to a handful of Josés, Micaëlas, and Escamillos, some 11 Carmens, past and present, attended, among them the venerable Régine Crespin, the latest to assay the role at America's world renowned opera house.[4]

Casting the French diva as the archetypal siren had struck many as questionable. Though a welcome rare opportunity to hear a French voice in the role, was it not unsuited to her temperament and vocal strengths, her reputation having been founded on such soprano heroines as Strauss's Marschallin and Wagner's Sieglinde? Moreover, at the age of 48, was she not a little old, especially considering it was her first time?

In fact, Crespin wasn't so sure about the idea herself. But when the conductor Alain Lombard suggested she try her *gitanilla* in a concert version he was planning for Miami, once she had studied the score she found herself as snake-bitten as any of her predecessors. And so it was that with success in Miami under her belt, Régine Crespin put all reservations aside, and, when the Metropolitan called, declared herself ready.

The Met's production was in its fourth season. Though conceived by Gören Gentele, whose idea it had been to personally direct a new *Carmen* to inaugurate his first season as the company's manager, the Swede's death in an automobile crash only weeks before the 1972 opening night had sent the production into a tail-spin and into the hands of his assistant, one Bodo Igez. At the time, Gentele's ideas were known primarily from conversations. But as he had already agreed to Joséf Svoboda's massive, stark, grey and white shapes as sets, it seemed he was poised to present the same kind of dark Bergmanesque production he had directed earlier in Sweden with Kerstin Meyer as Carmen. Also known was his plan to focus more on the role of José—the rationale being that José narrates the story from prison in the Mérimée and Carmen is simply the catalyst for his downfall. Such a directorial approach was not entirely new. Remembering how José was spotlighted even during the card scene, Verrett would later rail: "In those days it seemed that many productions of *Carmen* were trying to rename the opera *Don José*."[5] The concept, however, remains popular with directors to this day.

In his book *Carmen Chronicle,* Harvey E. Phillips has documented many of the problems the production encountered after Gentele died. Among them: the singers' insistence that the prompter's box, which Gentele had wanted removed, be restored, and that the carpet, which Svoboda wanted to cover the entire stage as a uniting factor, but which the singers feared would affect their sound, be removed. (The prompter's box was restored; the carpet remained.) And, disregarding the immense size of the new house and the fact that most of the cast didn't speak French, because Gentele had wanted to use the original spoken dialogue instead of the sung recitative, countless additional hours were given over to preparing the singers to deliver idiomatic French.[6]

While anticipation for the new production with Leonard Bernstein as its conductor was high, it was the casting of Marilyn Horne in the title role that created the most buzz. Gentele had accepted Horne and James McCracken for the leading roles in part because the two stars had already been contracted for the *Tannhäuser* that his predecessor Rudolf Bing had planned to open the season. But whereas McCracken was already a highly regarded José in Europe, Horne's experience as Carmen—beyond that of providing the singing voice for Dorothy Dandridge in the movie *Carmen Jones*—was limited. No one questioned the appropriateness of her sizeable mezzo, but neither the bel canto repertoire on which her career was founded nor her chubby physique and brassy personality pointed to a fit. Nevertheless, just as over the decades singers with even less to recommend them for the role have made a success of it by finding a piece of the Gypsy's infinite variety within their own makeup, so too did Horne, which was something Harold Schonberg captured in his review of opening night, September 19, 1972:

> Marilyn Horne sang the title role and she acted it in a manner unlike any orthodox Carmen of the immediate past. Hers was not a hip-waving, sensual kind of Carmen. She is not built for that, and she wisely refrained from throwing herself around.
> What she brought to the role was an earthy quality, yet with plenty of temperament and even some pointed humor. Rather than giving us idealized sex, or the femme fatale bit, Miss Horne tried to make Carmen a woman—coquettish at times, angry at other times, in love, out of love, eternally fascinating.[7]

That she also sang "magnificently" (Schonberg's word) we know from the recording that followed. Even allowing for the kind of patching that comes with all commercial recording and excepting a few tasteless additions,[8] some of which Bernstein protested but ultimately accepted, Horne's was a carefully considered rendering, delivered cleanly and vividly.

But now, a year later, here was Régine Crespin, a rarity in the role for the Met not only because she was a soprano but also because she was French; audiences were finally to be treated to a portrayal that included all the taste, charm and dramatic expression of a true Mediterranean. Little attention, however, was given Crespin's contention that Carmen was suicidal; the idea seemed incompatible with the heroine's *joie de vivre*. But in an essay Crespin wrote for *L'Avant-Scène*, she explained how something in Carmen's character reminded her of "those comics who hide their sadness, their hopelessness, under the smile of *Paillasse* [Pagliacci]."[9] "[Carmen] is a double-face, a person who laughs all the time," she told an interviewer, "but inside has a suicide wish."[10] Peter Davis understood, and in his review of her performance describes how she implemented this difficult concept.

> For the first act and a half this Carmen is nonchalant, vaguely amused by the influence she exercises over men but detached and blasé. When José throws her to the floor just before singing his Flower Song, the violent gesture seems to crystallize in Carmen the realization that her ultimate freedom lies in death and that José is the means to achieve this goal. From that point until she virtually embraces her lover's knife, Carmen is transformed into a bitter, taunting, self-destructive woman as she goads José to murder—and the instant of death when she reaches out to caress José becomes a moment of almost unbearable pathos. Only the greatest artistry could bring off such an unusual interpretation, and Crespin holds one in thrall every instant she is on stage.[11]

* * *

Régine Crespin, the French soprano in her first Carmen, at the Metropolitan in 1975 (copyright Beth Bergman 1975, NYC).

Rare as it was to find a Frenchwoman playing Carmen, however, just as rare was a Spaniard. There was precedent, of course: Maria Gay, Conchita Supervia, Aurora Buades; but now the enchanting Victoria de los Angeles was tasting the waters. Though considered a lyric soprano and known for her mild manner and genteel bearing—a natural as Micaëla, a role she performed often—she had recorded Bizet's charmer under Sir Thomas Beecham in the late 1950s. The conductor had been skeptical, but the Barcelona native's voice had, in fact, proved to have the metal—copper, bronze—to render the middle and lower passages with beauty and ease. Moreover, alive to every innuendo, color, and turn of phrase, if for some tastes too cultivated, she nevertheless projected charisma at every turn with the result that her performance on record—though arguably more loveable than dangerous—remains one of the most admired. That the lightness and high spirits of her recorded Carmen were lost when she took her portrayal to the stage almost two decades later, however, was probably to be expected—and regretted. For by then—the late 1970s—de los Angeles was well past her prime and had taken on the challenge primarily, she told Donal Henahan in 1977, to redress the wrongs done [Carmen] by current interpreters. "They don't understand Spanish women.... Even the common gypsy women have a pride and reserve. They stay faithful to one man at a time, no matter what. That is my Carmen."[12]

* * *

"Redressing the wrongs" was also on the mind of Teresa Berganza, yet another Barcelona native,[13] who, after much soul-searching, finally agreed to test herself in the role when offered the chance at the Edinburgh Festival in Scotland in 1977. As it had for de los Angeles and Crespin, the offer came late in her career and, given her smallish mezzo and quiet demeanor, she too doubted her suitability. In her personal life she had always been "the submissive wife," she said, far better suited therefore to a role like Charlotte in *Werther*. Moreover, renowned for her Rossini and Mozart, Carmen, in every respect, constituted a total about-face and major risk. And making matters even more stressful, her husband of 20 years, who was also her pianist and mentor—and who, like José, was Basque and possessive—hated the opera, which meant she would have to sing it not only against her better instincts but also against his will. Once met, however, the challenge proved both life and career changing. "Because of Carmen, through her honesty and uncompromising refusal to lie, which became part of me, too, I found the courage to separate from my husband," she later disclosed.[14] "This total freedom of the gypsy is what I associate with Carmen, whom I look upon and love as a friend who liberated me from my yoke and restored my *joie de vivre*."[15]

And so, dropping most of her other roles, Berganza began taking her proud Romany to Hamburg, Paris, London, Zürich, Paris, Seville, Zürich—smaller theaters suiting her best. Directors would have to make adjustments, not only for her seeming inappropriateness but also for her strong beliefs as to how the opera and her part should be presented, beliefs she laid out in a long letter to Peter Diamond, the director of the Edinburgh Festival, which read in part: "The essence of Carmen lies in her total awareness of her role as a woman.... I'm convinced that this is what Mérimée himself conceived; a woman secure in the knowledge and acceptance of her own femininity.... Today one could regard Carmen as an ideal; a fully emancipated female, liberated, and therefore free, independent and wholly responsible for her actions.... This does nothing to detract from Carmen's inherent female characteristics, but serves, on the contrary, to underline them."[16]

In Edinburgh the stage director Piero Faggioni helped her overcome her inhibitions and find the impersonation that worked for her, and we see the result in a video of her 1980 performance at the Opéra-Comique with Faggioni again the director. With a voice the color of amber, pliant and warm, and an artistry alert to every inflection and detail; with her girly mischief-making, constant preening and giggling with friends, light carriage, graceful idiomatic dancing, pretty princess dresses and French twist updo, Berganza, initially, appears to be as fetching and altogether feminine a Gypsy as ever there was. But then, as she had further written Diamond, in reading the cards, "the intensity and depth of character which enable Carmen to accept her own destiny, and even her death, with such dignity and poise, lead us to compare her with some of the heroines of ancient tragedy."[17] And in this way we see this modern woman execute Carmen's tragic transformation with such grave and noble determination that suddenly the French twist seems just right.

Carmens combining the "elegance of French style and pride of Spanish spirit,"[18] as we saw from de los Angeles, Crespin, and Berganza, did not stay long however. With another wave of the women's liberation movement cresting, a portrayal of singular persuasion was filling movie houses around the world, the impact of which would set interpretations on their heads for sometime to come.

* * *

In 1984 reporter Enrique Fernández of the *Village Voice* pondered the reasons for so many new artistic offerings based on the Bizet opera and its famous Gypsy. "Carmenmania is upon us," he wrote, noting a recent dance film by Carlos Saura based on the story with music from the Bizet score; a film (*Prénom Carmen*) directed by Jean-Luc Godard, loosely based on the story but without the music; *La Tragédie de Carmen*, a minimalist adaptation of the Bizet by the director Peter Brook, which explored the profundity and complexity that had been missing from the opera in recent decades; and, making the biggest impression, a film spectacular of the complete opera shot in Spain and directed by Francesco Rosi.

"Obviously," ventured Julia Migenes-Johnson—the star of the Rosi film—responding to Fernández, "it has something to do with women's lib. In our day men can no longer expect women to be a certain way, to have hormones that make you want to clean the house, for example. Carmen stands as a model of female independence and men are fascinated by a woman like Carmen because they realize that's what women are like more and more."[19] Moreover, Fernández reasoned, taking it a step further, with Carmen "somehow keeper of her country's mysteries ... the Carmen boom must be read, then, in the light of Spain's recent entry into full-blown modernity, a modernity that is inexorably shaped by the political emergence of women and its corollary: the politicization of sex."[20]

Whether these views are what audiences actually took away from Rosi's impressive film is hard to know. But, undoubtedly, ever since the death of Franco in 1970, Spanish women were claiming a new place for themselves and might well have cheered the irreverent, in-your-face, guttersnipe that was tiny Migenes-Johnson, a 39-year-old American-born daughter of Puerto-Rican and Greek parents. Noting her "childlike naughtiness ... twitching thighs" and "combative stance" the film critic Pauline Kael declared the soprano "the chief glory of the production."[21] When, indeed, had anyone ever seen a Carmen—frizzy-haired, freckle-faced, makeup-free, armpits- unshaven—spread her legs wide for José (Placido Domingo) "to fuck his eyes out." After all, "Carmen's got balls," the lithe soprano told Mr. Fernández, who aptly titled his piece: "Carmen Cojones."[22]

The impact of this film cannot be overstated. Even today people speak of it as the spark that ignited a passion they didn't realize they had for opera in general and *Carmen* in particular, while many a singer has noted the inspiration of Migenes-Johnson's singular incarnation. "For me, [Migenes-Johnson] is absolutely *the* Carmen," Elina Garanča would say a generation later.[23] And, though she had never performed the role on the stage and came primarily from musical theater and television, in command of a warm and pliant, albeit smallish, soprano, Migenes-Johnson—"The *Yenta*-Puerto Rican Carmen of all Carmens"—so naturally and completely inhabits it that "there has been none quite like her."[24] Nonetheless, while it was one thing to be swept up by the portrayal in the movie house, could it succeed in a conventional opera house, where prettified Carmens with inflated voices, coiffed hair and shiny Gypsy costumes, too plastic to be particularly erotic or dangerous, still prevailed?

* * *

Russian—Soviet—singers had not enjoyed international careers for a long time. But with the death of Stalin in 1953 a thaw in relations with the West had made it possible for two of the best to try their Carmen portrayals outside the Iron Curtain. Irina Arkhipova's chance had come in 1959 when the Bolshoi invited the Italian Mario Del Monaco to sing José with the company as a guest, and, worried that the Soviet's most famous Carmens were all too old, engaged the young unknown to play opposite the exciting tenor. A remarkable video was made of excerpts of their high-powered performance in which the fetching Russian, who sang in her native tongue, showed herself quite capable of keeping up with the feisty Italian, who sang—when not lapsing into French—in his. But, presumably, Arkhipova relearned it in Italian; for the next thing she knew, Del Monaco had invited—and the Soviet government had permitted—her to perform the opera with him in Naples and from there across Europe.

Making an even bigger impact in the West, however, was Elena Obraztsova, Arkhipova's younger colleague, who can be seen leading a new production from Vienna that its director Franco Zeffirelli arranged to be filmed for TV in 1978. By then Obraztsova's glamorous Gypsy was well known in the West. For not only had she performed in the earlier Otto Schenk production in Vienna but she had also made such an impression in New York during a Bolshoi tour that the Met had engaged her for a variety of dramatic roles. Of her portrayal as Carmen there, Joseph Horowitz wrote that he admired her "commanding presence" and "big sultry mezzo," which "enfolds the tessitura with ease" but generally found her interpretation "too one-dimensional ... a happy-go-lucky gypsy."[25] To be sure, the Vienna film corroborates the "happy-go-lucky" Gypsy of the first scenes, but, thereafter, her organ-toned contralto, painfully sad in the *Air des cartes*, becomes a force of nature that under the legendary baton of Carlos Kleiber carries the drama full throttle to the end.

* * *

In the 1980s two startling new portrayals arrived, so fully inhabited and potently rendered that audiences, whether they liked what they were seeing or not, found it difficult to look away. Such was certainly the unglamorous, unsmiling, unsympathetic, uninhibited, hard-voiced Carmen of Agnes Baltsa, whose grim intensity and goat-like physicality might well have stemmed from the remote Greek island of Levkas where she was born and grew up, as was London's experience in 1983 when one critic wrote:

Agnes Baltsa, wild, intense, riveting; shown here at the Metropolitan in 1987 (copyright Beth Bergman 1987, NYC).

> [Baltsa] sang and played the role with total absorption and a wild power.... In every way she did exactly what she wanted, and so riveting was her presence, so uncannily true her vocal projection, that what she wanted came very forcefully across. It might all easily have appeared self-indulgent had it not been done with a total lack of self-regard, for Miss Baltsa seemed, and made Carmen seem, quite unconscious of herself, charging, leaping and staring through the drama like an animal, or like an earth spirit.... The very strength of her interpretation gives her the right to toy with the part, as she toys with those on the stage, and as she toys with the audience.[26]

The mezzo had sung her first Carmen in Houston, Texas, in 1971 when she was only 27, but feeling herself too young for the role and in need of better stage direction, she had waited for Jean-Pierre Ponnelle in Zürich in 1982 to perform it again. Since the revered Swiss director's practice was to stage a production according to his cast, his conception of the protagonist for Baltsa was therefore "tailor made"[27] to her quirky ways. Her Carmen quickly took flight and, especially when partnered with the José of the handsome Spanish tenor, José Carreras, was soon—divisive though it was—one of the most in demand of the decade. Of her first performance at the Met in 1987, Thor Eckert of *The Christian Science Monitor* wrote: "Baltsa is unlike any Carmen you are apt to encounter—a totally rethought concept that stresses an aggressive, feline side to the role.... Baltsa makes an unusually multifaceted Carmen, riveting in the unfolding of both the character and the drama in which the character is placed.... Vocally she is equally compelling. She uses her chest voice—the lower potentially brassy part of the instrument—more than one might think is wise. Yet almost every musical moment is that of a singer secure in what she is trying to achieve with the instrument."[28]

And yet, of the same series of performances, Donal Henahan found her "a determinedly unsympathetic Carmen, a shrill tight-lipped harridan who gave one little reason to care about her."[29] Such were the two sides of looking at it and they would follow her portrayal everywhere.

As for her 1982 recording under Herbert von Karajan, Baltsa herself would say that "while Ponnelle gave me the wildness, the grit in Carmen, Karajan gave me the perfume, the whipped cream, all the delicate filigree work."[30] And, indeed, with no more than a microphone to consider, her singing under the aging Karajan is warmer and more sensuous than that we hear on the telecast of her Met Carmen—a telecast, it should be noted, that she was awarded in place of the equally enthralling—but totally unlike—Gypsy of American mezzo Maria Ewing, who, on being denied the telecast, thereupon dramatically quit the company.

* * *

11. 100 and Counting

Born in Detroit, Michigan, of a Danish mother and a father with Scottish, American Indian, and African American ancestry, small and lithe Maria Ewing with her copper complexion, large, dark lidded eyes, luxurious dark hair, and sensuous protruding lips could have stepped straight out of the Mérimée story. Her silky lyric mezzo (later soprano) had made her an obvious candidate for the comic and trouser roles in which she first excelled, but to Peter Hall, directing her as Dorabella at Glyndebourne, her rightness for Carmen, a role she had studied with Jennie Tourel, was readily apparent. Happily their collaboration (which would result as well in marriage) on the Bizet is available on DVD. It is "a performance of daring variety ... [which] insist[s] on our attention."[31] Right from her entrance, wearing only a drab black dress and apron, cigarette in hand—the color black and cigarettes are constant—we know this Carmen is trouble. And if some men might be put off by her dusky sullenness, she nevertheless draws them in like the proverbial black widow spider—no stock 1950s hussy here.

Much criticism has been leveled on this brooding, seemingly anarchic realization. But while Ewing pushes boundaries, she never oversteps them. And, in her vocalizing of the role she achieves a spontaneity akin to extemporizing, occasionally bordering on spoken song. When she and the production moved to the Met the following year, her portrayal was as controversial as Baltsa's. Compare, for example, Donal Henahan in the *New York Times*: "The doom-haunted gypsy, in the person of Maria Ewing, slouches in from the wings and stands for a long while with her back to the audience. We guess at once that this is a pouty teenager determined not to ingratiate herself with us in any way, and, as it turns out, we guess right. Miss Ewing pursues this eccentric concept to the end, which might be more plausible if her light mezzo were a true Carmen voice. It is not.... Miss Ewing's Carmen, no doubt molded by a firm directorial hand, fell only a little short of complete travesty"[32] with Andrew Porter in the *New Yorker*: "As Carmen, Maria Ewing gave an electric performance. She employed an uncommonly large range of vocal devices, from richly throbbing vibrato to bleached, desolate tone, from faint (but always audible) murmuring to full-throated cries. She phrased with the verbal incisiveness and subtlety of a cabaret singer.... Miss Ewing's kaleidoscopic approach to the role displeased some people, but I thought I had never heard Bizet's music brought to life with so much variety, intensity, and detail."[33]

Three commercial DVDs of three separate productions of Ewing's Carmen provide a chance to consider how much is the result of the direction and how much comes innately from the artist. The earliest, the

Maria Ewing, brooding, enigmatic, mysterious, shown here at the Metropolitan in 1986 (copyright 1986 Beth Bergman, NYC).

previously noted Glyndebourne production (1985), is followed by a 1989 production performed in the round in the gigantic arena known as Earl's Court in London. Given the difficult venue, it is effectively staged—with extra music, a great deal of dancing, and performers counting in the hundreds—by Gavin Taylor, whose conception of Carmen as exotic "other" follows naturally on the somber one Ewing had built under Hall's aegis, including the costumes. But even in a more conventional performance, like that staged by the Spaniard Nuria Espert in 1991 for the Royal Opera, her red skirt and girlish smiles and flirtations are barely a cover for her "otherness." Ultimately, Ewing presents as an artist who never abandons her personal truth for the sake of the production, merely adjusts to its trappings.

* * *

In the mid–1990s the Met decided to reverse course again. New York audiences had seen enough of sullen Gypsies and dingy Sevilles, they reasoned. They would bring back the sun and some color; Carmen herself would follow suit, and the opera would thereby regain its popularity at the box office. And so, once again, management turned to the famous Italian director Franco Zeffirelli, master of the lavish and picturesque, who, as Met manager Joseph Volpe tells it, just happened to be able to offer the company the production he was doing in Verona at the moment, which was similar to the one that had been so popular in Vienna (and still plays there at this writing.) But there was a sticking point: Zeffirelli wanted the African American Denyce Graves as his Gypsy, while music director James Levine wanted the German Waltraud Meier. "Meier, one of the world's most formidable Wagnerians, had never sung *Carmen*," Volpe writes. "But she was a redhead with a blazing stage presence, and if she could pull it off, the Met would make international opera news."[34] Actually, Teutonic Carmens were not so plentiful as they had once been. Brigitte Fassbaender, a highly regarded mezzo from Munich, was a rarity in the role, who, according to Arthur Bloomfeld, writing of her 1970 performance in San Francisco, played it "almost [like] the girl next door, only one who has gone a little wrong."[35] In any case, Meier was engaged, and, to read Mathew Gurewitsch in *Opera News*, the Met and Levine got—if not quite the girl next door—just the sunny, colorful Carmen they wanted: "Waltraud Meier's Gypsy arrives as a breath of fresh air.... She flies on like a girl let out of school, radiant in the sunshine, itching to play. Her mind is quick, her spirits high. She has no dark side. This Carmen is no tragedy queen. Too self-centered and vivacious to be possessive, she follows her whims,

Denyce Graves, the African American mezzo who played Carmen her way, shown here at the Metropolitan Opera in 2002 (copyright Beth Bergman 2002, NYC).

bearing no grudges.... Above all, Meier's Carmen reflects the clear, bright Mediterranean sparkle of the Bizet score"[36] though on the other hand, *New York Times* said: "Waltraud Meier has approached the role by taking it apart. Every phrase, every vocal gesture and every theatrical move has been painstakingly considered, making Carmen more a collection of calculated details than an entity in itself. If it is the most thorough enactment I can remember, it is also the blandest."[37]

Readers can decide for themselves by checking out the video of her March 25, 1997, performance on Met Opera on Demand. Regardless, Meier herself wasn't happy with the production and Zeffirelli got his girl.

* * *

Neither a commercial DVD nor a recording of a complete *Carmen* with Denyce Graves exists, which is curious in that throughout much of the 1980s, '90s and well into the 2000s, the mezzo was one of the busiest of all practicing Gypsies. In fact, by the time of her 1985 Met debut in the Hall production, her impersonation had already been acclaimed in capitols from San Francisco to Berlin, Paris, and London. Since Verrett's and Bumbry's impersonations two decades prior, there had been no important African American in the role. But to the pantherine grace, inherent eroticism, and smoky, burnished mezzo of these same singers, the free-spirited Graves now added an empowerment befitting her designation of "a Carmen for the post-feminist era."[38]

There was nothing especially controversial about the Graves portrayal. She fit the image perfectly and sang it easily. What's more, wrote Anne Midgette, "she has worked her interpretation into a polished whole that seems impregnable."[39] So secure was she as to her portrayal, in fact, that when in 1986 she finally did appear in Zeffirelli's overstuffed picture postcard of a production, the headline "Mezzo Does Battle with Zeffirelli's 'Carmen,' and Wins" was right to the point. "It was as if she was saying," the critic Anthony Tommasini wrote, "'I don't care what kind of clunky production is going on around me, the people came to see a Carmen, and they're going to get one.'"[40]

Indeed, to judge from pirate videos and multiple reviews, Graves played her Carmen her way no matter who was in the director's chair. She would be one of the last. For empowered as women were beginning to feel, thereby fulfilling the legacy of the rebel siren herself, those who impersonated her were increasingly finding their personal interpretations subject to someone else's dictates.

Chapter 12

Game Change

> Carmen should be directed in a modern way, and by that I mean as a modern woman, not just a weird production.—Vesselina Kasarova[1]

> By the Way, the Singers Were Good, Too—Donal Henahan[2]

Elina Garanča undoubtedly had her own ideas and in another time would have answered easily. But if the question posed at intermission as to her interpretation of the Gypsy left the beauteous mezzo from Latvia a little tongue-tied before the millions watching the Met's HD performance of *Carmen*, there was good reason. Her halting response that "from production to production it changes, one looks for more sex, one for more freedom—or something" was the new order of things. Directors, now at the top of opera's pecking order, dictated interpretation, and singers were expected to comply, even if Carmen, as the mezzo added, "changes all the time" anyway.[3]

Garanča, after all, would know. She may initially have prepared the role as she imagined the composer wanted. But, as directed by one Andrejs Zagars, clips on YouTube of her first assayal at the Latvian National Opera in 2007 show her not as a sexy Gypsy in romantic Spain but rather as a street-smart chick in Castro's 1950s revolutionary Cuba. "Very modern, very vivid, and very much about freedom," which, "at that time," she would recall, "fit me like a glove."[4] Though certainly colorful, not always pretty: as when José impulsively grabs a bottle from a vendor's cart, breaks it and swings the broken glass at her throat, spewing blood all over her stilettos, gold belt, sleek white top and pedal pushers. No mantillas here.

Plenty, however, for the picture postcard Gypsy she next portrayed in Rome's Caracalla Baths and then again in a production—extravagant and busy enough to rival even Franco Zeffirelli's—by the American director Francesca Zambello at London's Royal Opera, where, compared to the heat previously generated by the exciting Italian, Anna Caterina Antonacci, for whom the production was made—a visceral Carmen, replete with heaving, sweaty bosom, skirts pulled up to her hips, and legs spread wide—the Latvian's cool manner, not withstanding the beauty of her lush, limpid vocalism, some critics found wanting. Now, Garanča can lift her skirts with the best of them and did as directed; but "business" that might come naturally to one singer does not necessarily work for another, a problem that often happens when a singer is engaged for a production built around another temperament.

Less a problem, however, for orthodox productions or for those lacking a strong point of view, such as the Met's 2009 production as directed by Richard Eyre, which gave the world Garanča's first and best Gypsy on DVD by way of the aforementioned HD from the Met. For with no concrete directorial agenda, we see the mezzo free to deliver a Carmen she can believe in—one that categorically proves that cool can in fact smolder. Remote, elusive, indifferent even, and yet as dangerous, sensuous, and desirable as any in the Met's long procession of seductresses, Garanča's Carmen under Eyre laughs not for joy but clinically, wickedly even, all the while oozing a sexuality bordering on frightening—a *femme fatale* for the 21st century. In any case, the Met now had a production modern enough to appease its critics, yet vague enough in concept to allow for any number of other temptresses from the languorous Russian Olga Borodina to the animated American Kate Aldrich. Garanča herself would reprise the Eyre production in 2015, but in the interim take her Carmen, sometimes as a blonde (her natural color) around Europe, including to Milan, where, also in 2015, she made her La Scala debut in a production already notorious for the vulgar conceits of one Emma Dante.

* * *

Roundly booed when it opened the season in 2009, Dante, best known as an experimental theater director, may have thought that loading the Bizet with confusing religious symbols, writhing whores, and unrelenting misogynistic violence, including José's attempted final rape of Carmen—to keep himself from killing her, perhaps?—was taking the opera into the new century. But in the opening performance, streamed live, it appeared more a convoluted parody of the feminist lore of a bygone time. That Anita Rachvelishvili, a native of Tbilisi, Georgia, who was making her professional opera debut at the age of 25 in the title role, still came out on top is a wonder. But, possessed of a voluptuous mezzo that was widely acknowledged as promising, if her attempts to be sexy were awkward, repetitive, and a bit stale, Rachvelishvili fascinated the audience as, by turns gamin and demon, she conjured up Mérimée's unholy sprite. Consequently her *diavolessa* was soon in demand around the world, and by the time of her own Met HD in 2014, she had, as she told an interviewer, "probably done fifty different stagings of *Carmen* in fifty different styles, in different periods and with different types of costumes."[5] Her plump figure, rich mane of dark, curly locks, smoky doe eyes, and light copper skin tone had not changed, but her large mezzo had by then developed an alluring fruitiness, and the musical and verbal detail to which she had clearly given much thought gave new dimension to her increasingly insightful characterization. Moreover, since Eyre happened to be in the house directing another opera at the time, he had been able to work one on one with her and, as a result, add some of the violence and physicality that had suited her so well in her portrayal under Dante.

* * *

Had he lived to see the Dante himself, we can be sure the estimable critic Henry Pleasants would not have been pleased with it. In his 1989 book *Opera in Crisis* he had devoted a scorching chapter, titled "The Plague: Produceritis," to the ills directors, like her, were inflicting on opera, and, among many examples, included a *Carmen* the British director David Pountney had "set in a automobile graveyard somewhere in Latin America." But an even greater abomination would most certainly have been the *Carmen* of the avant-gardist director, Romanian Lucian Pintilie, a kind of improvised fantastical play within a play performed in a "nightmarish" circus arena peopled with midgets, clowns, and "screaming children."[6] Though originally mounted by the Welsh National Opera, when reprised for the Expo 86 World Festival in Vancouver, a performance was broadcast from which a video was made. In it the Carmen, Jean Stilwell, a fine Canadian mezzo, "caricatures her own considerable sensuality, strikes phony-alluring poses, rubs her body everywhere during the Habanera (and I do mean everywhere), [and] taunts José mercilessly."[7] Though arguably surpassing any irreverent directorial imagining for *Carmen* before or since, the production that initially seemed scandalous proved a kind of success. A "riotous avant-garde" romp," the critic Martin Bernheimer wrote, that "in its own madly iconoclastic way ... was wonderful ... a brilliant, daring, illuminating reexamination of a masterpiece."[8] Presumably, Pleasants, from the old school, never saw it.

Though "Producerits" has prompted endless discussion, the history of the operatic stage director's rise from a position of virtual non-existence to one of total preeminence in the operatic hierarchy does not belong in these chapters, fascinating as it is. But agreement has been growing that a director is a bad thing only when he allows his ego to take precedent over the composer's score and intent in such a gratuitous and groundless way as to turn everything on its head and make the work at hand unrecognizable. When, on the other hand, the score and intent are respected, a director's reimagining can challenge audience's expectations and thereby widen their horizons, move them to greater understanding, and altogether transform what might have become a tired old work for them—even a masterpiece like *Carmen*—into living theater.

From the singer's viewpoint, working with a director in an enlightened production towards a greater understanding of the character, is wonderful. What is not wonderful is being made to feel like a "prop" in some crazy staging that makes no sense and disrespects the composer. What's more, as the trend has grown, in good productions and bad, these same singers notice, and mind, that with the exception of a few superstars, their names—singers' names having once blazoned across billboards—are now relegated to fine print, while their performances—an individual singer's performances having once filled inches of copy in the press—receive a few lines at best. So that, when Donal Henahan titled an article "The Singers Were Good, Too," they knew exactly of what he spoke, but knew as well that to be difficult about this new state of affairs could put a career in jeopardy.

Regardless, the confluence of "Directoritis" (Henahan's word for it) with videos of live performances and subtitles enabling audiences to know exactly what was going on at all times, worked in everybody's favor. For, as a singer's every word was considered and every move and look enlarged and scrutinized, so too was born "a whole race of physically attractive young singers ... to meet the demands of the ascendant producers."[9] Acting reached new heights, and incumbent as it was on singers to present themselves as the "whole package," directors were better able than ever to invest their productions—be they conventional or high concept—with new and illuminating insights.

* * *

Though many still believed a successful *Carmen* required a picturesque, romantic treatment, new thinking about it all was clearly in order; and with the turn of the millennium at hand in 1999 the Catalan director Calixto set out to expose *Carmen*'s "innards" in a way no one ever had. It doesn't happen often that a *regie* staging of the Bizet or in fact of any opera survives more than a season or two or, for that matter, is mounted other than by the company for which it was created. But ever since its premiere in Spain's Festival Castell de Perelada with Annie Vavrille as Carmen and Roberto Alagna in his role debut as José, the demand around the world to see the Bieito *Carmen*, as it is known (usurping even the composer's name in billboards and references) has not let up, and a DVD of a live performance at Barcelona's Liceu in 2009 has cemented it for posterity. Stripped of all nonessentials from parading picadors to superfluous dialogue, and closer to the ambience of the Mérimée than we usually see, Bieito's perspective of *Carmen* "as a contemporary and relevant tale of domestic violence, clash of cultures and the impossibility of freedom"[10] might well be what Bizet would have wanted had his hands not been tied by the times in which he lived and the circumstances of the premiere. In any case, the Catalan's creation stands on its own—imaginable even on Broadway.

In all these years the Bieito *Carmen* has seen both many stagings and casts.[11] But the one commercial DVD of the production stars Béatrice Uria-Monzon and, unless another is made, much of the its success consequently stands on her shoulders, even if, unquestionably, she is a little past her prime both visually and vocally. Though her long and distinguished career in a wide repertoire includes non-commercial recordings and videos of her Gypsy in a variety of productions, her portrayal here, moreover, will almost certainly be the one for which she is best remembered,[12] and in our long chronicle of Carmens it presents a modern incarnation as credible and sustainable as any today.

Ever since her first in Paris in 1993 Carmen had been something of a calling card for Uria-Monzon, the French-born daughter of the Spanish painter of that name. Her classically beautiful figure and face, idiomatic French, Mediterranean sensibility and gleaming mezzo with soprano reach explain much of her appeal in the role, though some have found her demeanor too proper. She has, in fact, admitted that initially she felt no connection to the Gypsy, nor even wanted to portray her; and yet, unlike most, she comes across as both relevant and sympathetic, even in traditional productions. And nowhere are those distinctions more in evidence than in the Bieito where we first see her—her work smock opened to reveal a black slip—arguing with someone in a telephone booth as the men outside plead for her love. Pausing just long enough to angrily tell them she doesn't know when—if ever—she'll love them, she returns to tell the "someone" on the phone (presumably a lover) that it certainly won't be today and slams the phone down (on the chord) before gathering herself for what begins as a contemplative Habanera. And so it is that we learn right from the beginning that this Carmen is not only a real woman but also a modern woman with real and modern problems.

To be sure, life is lived on the edge in this sad evocation of late Francoist Spain, where Carmen's prized freedom seems so unattainable. We see her affection for and loyalty to the pimps, junkies, and low-lifes of all kinds who traffic in old Mercedes Benzes and the latest electronics—like Gypsies, they too must live by their wits— and who make up her world. But we also see that she is better; that she doesn't belong—that, in truth, she is "other" even among her own people. And the strength and independence Uria-Monzon's

Uria-Monzon, the French mezzo, who, under Calixto Bieito's direction, gave us a modern interpretation that works, shown here at the Metropolitan Opera in 1998 (copyright Beth Bergman 1998, NYC).

"other" exhibits in the first acts only make that much more heartbreaking the vulnerability and honesty she exhibits in confronting the situation in which she finds herself as their consequence. Several who have played Carmen believe she truly loves José. We know Uria-Monzon to be one. And in the Bieito rendering it is clear as, almost tearfully, the knife already at her throat, she gently presses the ring into José's hand instead of throwing it defiantly away.

* * *

Updating *Carmen* to the Spanish Civil War and Franco's Spain was not new with the Bieito production however. In 1984, for example, the director Frank Corsaro upset many —very likely Mr. Pleasants—by turning the smugglers into gunrunners for the Loyalists, whose political activities were a continuous distraction. Several singers took on the title role in this troublesome but interesting production at the New York City Opera, but it was Victoria Vergara's performance that the television series "Live from Lincoln Center" broadcast, and though the beautiful Chilean mezzo certainly had all the necessary attributes for the role, with so much of the focus on Carmen as Freedom Fighter, she had little opportunity to show what she might really do.[13]

Then, again, directors have also built productions around the hard life of poverty and the marginalization that accompanies it: as when another American director David Kramer transferred the Bizet to a 1970s trailer park in Seville, Ohio, a hick town where boredom prevails and Carmen is "not just a sexy tart but a broken woman who knows only violence and abuse."[14] Premiered by Opera North in Leeds in 2011 with a hot Heather Shipp in the title role, while some critics praised Kramer's concept for its relevancy, others made so much of the flagrant sex and violence that the company felt obligated to refuse admittance to children under 12. Viktoria Vizin, who has globetrotted Carmen from Beijing to the Met and was engaged for the Kramer production when it was reprised at the Vlaamse Opera in Antwerp the following year, had her doubts but soon changed her mind, telling an interviewer that the production was, in fact, the "closest, deepest" telling of the story she had ever done.[15]

Unquestionably, moving the story to places and times of not only revolution and war—the preferred setting being Franco's Spain—but also of oppression and corruption, has opened up a whole new way of looking at Carmen and how she is portrayed. Whereas traditional productions tend to make little of the difficult circumstances of her existence, by delving deeper and exposing the downtrodden and desperate society into which she was born and out of which she can only dream of escaping, she becomes a far more sincere and tragic figure than we realized.

* * *

Early in the new millennium's first decade a young Russian beauty, Marina Domashenko, arrived to hold the Carmen spotlight for several years, and in this time gave us a rare opportunity to compare her in two opposing extremes of production—the orthodox and the avant-garde—on video. On a commercial DVD of a live performance in Verona's huge arena in 2003, her melting vocalism and fine-tuned musicality, which can also be heard on a complete recording, and her vivid impersonation of the quintessential bad girl are as good as it gets for a traditional approach. What's more, this native of frigid Siberia can be as hot as any Latin, which only makes her transformation a year later to icy mystery goddess or dominatrix in skintight black leather—one can imagine her with a whip—that much more astonishing. Directed by Martin Kusej for Berlin, the production was filmed with Domaschenko in the title role in 2006. Set on a slanted concrete block that revolves to suggest the various locales, the opera opens and closes with José being executed by firing squad. But there are still more gratuitous brutal death scenes as when José stabs Zuniga to death; José mistakenly shoots and kills Micaela; Escamillo is gored to death (off stage) and ceremoniously carried on stage by people in white face. In other words, everyone dies. But if such changes to the plot seem an unacceptable violation of the original, the fatal attraction, so consummately played out by Domashenko and Rolando Villazón, between whom a symbolic red scarf continually passes, is riveting.[16]

In 2008 the venturesome Zürich Opera mounted a similarly heretical—but totally opposite in conception—creation with the Bulgarian mezzo Vesselina Kasarova making her role debut as perhaps the oddest, most off-putting and perplexing Carmen on commercial DVD. Directed by Matthias Hartmann we are once again presented with a minimalist set; in this case just a raked disc with a few suggestive props that change: a beach umbrella and up front a stuffed dog that can even wag its tail in keeping with the early levity of Act One; a single tree and the carcass of a bull's head (replacing the happy dog) for the tragic conclusion.

No question that it's all rather odd. But Kasarova herself is an unusual artist, and the production works well with her idiosyncratic vocal delivery and unsentimental, cerebral, physically awkward, but altogether mesmerizing characterization. Wearing the same simple dress and apron throughout—removing the apron as the only gesture of celebration for her bullfighter in the last act—she thoroughly confuses and overwhelms her guileless José, brilliantly played by Jonas Kaufmann, while at the same time both her sensitive response to the Flower Aria and frantic efforts to keep from being killed remind us that this seeming psychopath has real feelings, not too unlike our own. Such a conflicted interpretation, however, appears to have come naturally to Kasarova; for, even in Vienna the critic, while lauding her for lifting Zeffirelli's antiquated staging out of the doldrums, caught the quirky play between "unorthodox" and "human."[17]

But if Kasarova has not given Carmen a place of importance in her repertoire, the role has been a calling card for her compatriot, the mezzo Nadia Krasteva, and with good reason. A video of Krasteva in the same Zeffirelli in Vienna, where she was a regular, does not do her justice. But others give a good gauge of her many attributes, including the earliest, her 2005 appearance at the beautiful St. Margarthen Summer Festival in Austria, said to be the largest outdoor natural setting in Europe. Miked for a space that can accommodate 150,000 and handicapped by the stage's vast reaches, Krasteva's voice nevertheless maintains its plush, plummy resonance while her portrayal builds from funny and feisty to one of unmitigated ferocity in her defiance of the man she no longer loves.

But two other unusual arena settings, also on video, provide backdrops for Krasteva in provocative updatings: a modern staging in 2009 by the Canadian Robert Carsen in Amsterdam, in which both audience and chorus effectively surround the action in an indoor arena; and another in the far larger outdoor space of the Gold Line Arena in Hamburg, memorable both for the beauty of the setting and visual effects, as well as for the original staging. Krasteva with her long, straight, dark tresses, big eyes, and sleek physique, delivers powerful fatalistic incarnations in both of these intelligent, inspired productions. One has to wonder, though, how the mezzo ever came to terms with the much-maligned 2008 creation for the Bolshoi—the first in 25 years at that theater—by David Pountney; the very one who, as we know, staged an earlier production in an "automobile graveyard." For this time Pountney has the entire opera play out inside the cigarette factory with only a few select props to indicate changes of location. "An oppressively sealed off space from which there

Vesselina Kasarova, the Bulgarian mezzo in a minimalist production by Matthias Hartmann at the Zürich Opera in 2008 (photograph by Suzanne Schwiertz. © Suzanne Schwiertz).

is no way to escape," said a press release from the company, adding, "It is the illusion which rules the day here ... the illusion of freedom, the illusion of love, which in point of fact deteriorates into violence and cruelty."[18]

* * *

The reader cannot have failed to notice how many of these Carmens come from the former Soviet Union. In fact, in large part thanks to Glasnost and Gorbachev, Western opera companies have been flooded with any number of outstanding new Slavic voices in recent years. And, isolated as they have been from outside influences for such a long time, these voices still retain much of their original distinctive timbre, above all, the plaintive colorings that work so well for our ill-fated adventuress come down from the mountains to work her exotic allure in the Mediterranean sun. It is as though the artists of this melancholy and repressive land were predisposed to the Gypsy's same *duende* and hunger for "*la liberté*."

Regretfully, Olga Borodina, one of the first of this impressive parade, has left us neither a commercial recording (not even an aria) nor a video of any kind of her celebrated Carmen. "In her initial attempt anywhere at the role" in San Francisco in 1996, a year after her debut there as Rossini's Cenerentola, one critic wrote "she is merely the company's finest in almost two decades— a smoldering, intense, potent protagonist who evades routine every bar of the way." The "teasing, lightly ironic approach was the key,"[19] and we hear it for ourselves on the only decent recordings—pirates both—we have: one from 1997 (with no less

Olga Borodina, the Russian mezzo, languid but smoldering as Carmen, shown here at the Metropolitan Opera in 2008 (copyright Beth Bergman 2016, NYC).

than Valery Gergiev conducting and Anna Netrebko as Micaëla); another under Neeve Järvi from the Opéra Bastille in 2000. At the outset, in place of the big plush voices some mezzos employ—and Borodina herself possessed—often making them sound older, she lightens and brightens hers to give us a Carmen who is youthful and fun-loving, unmindful of the portentous events ahead. It is only as the story darkens and intensifies that she imparts the same by way of her extraordinary instrument, always mindful, however, of the Gypsy's volatility which she establishes with a dizzying array of vocal colorings and carefully considered musical and textual details.

That said, however, one aspect of Borodina's Carmen to regularly receive criticism was its seeming listlessness, something she herself has said came so naturally to her that it was one reason she initially avoided the role. "I am rather phlegmatic by nature, so I couldn't identify with or find the energy for a scenically 'busy' Carmen."[20] And, to be sure, the somewhat busy Eyre production at the Met did not sit as well with her leisurely incarnation as had the earlier sprawling Zeffirelli. But no matter the production, Borodina's "extraordinary sangfroid brought its own meaning to this famously protean role. She was a force too monumentally assured to let any man overcome her."[21]

* * *

If, however, pride of place in the new century arguably goes to the Slavic and Eastern European Carmens, there have been any number of representatives from other geographical regions who have revealed interesting aspects of the protagonist. For globalization has yet to entirely erase all the special properties that comprise national differences. Countering the dreamy Borodina or cool of some Slavic singers might be, for instance, the easy exuberance for which Americans are famous, with no better example than the pulchritudinous Kate Aldrich, possessor of a dark, lustrous mezzo, whose own appearance in the Eyre, was startling in its contrast with that of Garanča, her sultry predecessor in the same production. Was she out of sync with what Eyre wanted or was his concept just so unspecific that the American's *joie de vivre* (not only cartwheels in Act 2, but has any Carmen looked more pleased with herself as this movie star beauty as she entered on the arm of Escamillo in the last act?) simply proves that, when not pressed in one direction or another, a singer's individual interpretation can still take wing, even if, as we can see on pirate videos of other productions—one set in a red light district for Oliver Py in Lyons; another in a house of cards for Louis Désiré in Orange—no matter what concept is handed her, Aldrich embraces it without equivocation.

* * *

A famous singer playing against type always raises eyebrows. So in 2002 when it was announced that Anne Sofie von Otter—a tall, blue-eyed, blond Swede, whose cultivated persona and pure, silvery mezzo rendered her ideal for early and Baroque music—was, at age 46, going to perform her first Carmen, many eyebrows went up. But, as it turned out, von Otter surprised even the most serious of skeptics. "Ice Princess Sizzles as Carmen" was typical of the many reviews that greeted her first staged performance and virtually all suggested it wasn't such a crazy idea after all. And when, on the video, we first see her running down the steps, plunging her head into the fountain to cool off, launching into the Habanera with a cigar clenched in her teeth in David McVicar's new production for Glyndebourne, it is clear that she and the director were going to do everything possible to crack the preconceptions. Indeed, even within the bounds of the relatively traditional setting—albeit as grungy as a Dickens novel and updated only as far as the period of the opera's composition (she will die in a Victorian bustle)—no piece of business is too much for this ballbuster of a Carmen in her red wig, who, throwing caution to the wind, delivers perhaps the most visceral hellcat on film.

Anne Sofie von Otter, the Swedish mezzo in a production set in Franco's Spain (photograph by Ken Howard © Ken Howard, 2006).

Who then could have imagined the about-face she would make four years later at the Santa Fe Opera Festival in New Mexico where, as directed by her compatriot Lars Rudolfsson in a production set in a bleak port city in Fascist Spain, she metamorphosed from brazen hussy into "desperate young woman, drained of belief, who found nothing to nourish her in the ambient bleakness."[22] With no video of the performance I might not have believed the reviews had I not seen it with my own eyes. But if only for the feeling of the utter hopelessness she conveyed, this Carmen by von Otter—probably her last—stays in the mind. And as to whether her particular lyric mezzo was wrong for the role, she herself would answer: "I like to think I can get my way around that problem by really using the words and acting with the voice."[23] And that is exactly what she did as she imbued the familiar lines with such nuance and clarity and with such fresh insight that one listens as though hearing them for the first time.

* * *

Carmen was not mounted in Santa Fe again until 2014 when the British director Stephen Lawless set the Bizet on Mexico's border with the United States, and the Puerto Rican soprano Ana Maria Martinez excelled as "not only a political firebrand but a boiling vat of sexuality."[24] But back in Glyndebourne the McVicar was reprised often over the years with multiple promising young singers taking over for von Otter. Rinat Shaham, who had sung Carmen as early as 2001, headed the McVicar cast in 2004 and thereafter sang it around the world non-stop. As seen primarily in conventional stagings, the role seems a perfect fit for the beautiful Israeli—vocally, visually, temperamentally. Eyes flashing, long black curls flying, nimble and lithe, svelte, sexy, intense, fierce, witty, and quick, her Gypsy stays two steps ahead of everyone else and in charge at every turn. Commanding too is her dusky wide-ranging mezzo and—belying her petite frame—powerful deep chest tones. Unfortunately, however, thus far Shaham's only complete Carmen available on a commercial DVD comes from Sydney Harbor, Australia, where an ill-considered, albeit fairly orthodox, production and the demands of negotiating the huge outdoor stage while unattractively miked seriously diminish her considerable effectiveness.

The most recent McVicar Gypsy is Stéphanie D'Oustrac, a French mezzo who, best known for her work in the Baroque repertoire, sang her first Carmen in Lille in 2010 in a highly intelligent, semi-stylized modern production by Jean-François Sivadier. Possessed of a glassy lyric, D'Oustrac delivers the score with gratifying Gallic clarity and nuance, and on the video her quixotic, unnerving smile, and eyes like a cat looking to pounce, remind us that indeed Carmen was, as José knew, the devil incarnate,

12. Game Change   161

or, at the very least, a "sorceress." Though her success in Lille was newsworthy, she did not return to the role until 2015, when Glyndebourne nabbed her for its third and arguably best revival of the McVicar thanks in large part to D'Oustrac, who, it was said, ignited the stage as though born to the part.

* * *

In addition to D'Oustrac and Uria-Monzon, there are more French Carmens now than there have been for decades: Nora Gubisch, Clémentine Margaine, and Sylvie Brunet to name but a few. And there are a number of Hispanics, notably Nancy Fabiola Herrera, Ana Maria Martinez, and Alicia Nafe. Teutonic Carmens, once so abundant, however, are far fewer these days, which is surprising considering the many important German directors interested in taking risks with the Bizet, as we saw with Martin Kusej's iconoclastic production in Berlin, and Matthias Hartmann's surreal perspective in Zürich. But most curious is that since Fiorenza Cossotto, only Anna Caterina Antonacci has proved to be an important representative of the Italians. In two productions available on commercial DVD, her glowing dark beauty and robust physicality fairly mesmerize. Even in pirated clips of a panned production at the Bastille, set during Spain's late 1970s and early 1980s counter-culture movement known as the Movida, in which she appears in a blonde Marilyn Monroe wig, surrounded by drugs, debauchery, and drag queens, there is not a moment that she is not arresting. And in the previously mentioned Zambello production at the Royal Opera, starring opposite Jonas Kaufmann, we see her give a virtual clinic in verismo acting which two years later, she wisely scales down for the much smaller, newly restored Opéra-Comique, without losing any of its impact.

Antonacci's hybrid voice—she has called herself both soprano and mezzo-soprano—is warm, clear, well-forward, and resonant and, despite the present generation's preference for sumptuous mezzo voices in the role, is a good example of why the argument for soprano voices will not likely ever go away. Viewing Carmen as "almost an evanescent creature," she has said. "I have always felt that the music needed a lighter, brighter sound."[25] (To be sure: think Calvé, Supervia, de los Angeles, Galli-Marié, Farrar.) Moreover, her delivery of the French, for which she clearly has an affinity, remains elegant and supple, as she takes care to infuse every syllable, every word with purpose. How Bizet would have loved to hear the words of his Habanera, which he personally struggled so long over, enunciated with such eloquence and implication. Happily, Antonacci has given the role a certain pride of place in her extensive repertoire.

* * *

Be the production conventional or high concept, directors have in recent years introduced all sorts of well-considered new stage business, which has at times given significant new dimension to the character. For example, some have shown Carmen as having a particular affection for children, which adds to her humanness, and more importantly, to her place in the Gypsy (or "other") community; while washing herself when she first appears in Act 1—popular with many directors these days—is not only colorful and sexy but helps establish the conditions in which she works. And some directors have recognized the importance of finding a moment in which to show José giving Carmen a ring, giving weight to their relationship and greater meaning to her final defiant gesture of liberation when—in any number of ways depending on how the moment is interpreted—she returns it to him. Which brings us to the bigger matter of how she dies. Yes, the score tells us José stops her from entering the stadium by stabbing (or striking) her, and directors (and even singers) have found any number of ways to achieve this end. But might, as we remember Régine Crespin believed, Carmen be suicidal? "It is as if she were flirting with fate and asking for the last card, the card of death," the singer explained. "She laughs and jokes, shows off on the surface, fights a great deal. In fact, though, she pushes José to kill her."[26] Or might the murder even be almost accidental? After all, we know José did not go to the stadium planning to kill her. In Nuria Espert's production for the Royal Opera, when Carmen (Maria Ewing) throws his ring away, she just happens to throw it in the direction of the arena and as he goes to retrieve it José (Luis Lima) finds himself face to face with a cattle hook which just happens to be hanging outside. There is an excruciating flash of recognition: he is desperate; it is a weapon; he grabs it, and he kills her with it. There is no knife; he never came with one. To be sure, when the goal, first and foremost, is to create a coherent theatrical experience, all sort of possibilities as to staging open up; sometimes telling us something new, sometimes simply explaining or enlightening the old story.

But what dilemmas directors confront when trying to create a *Carmen* that both resonates with modern audiences and at the same time maintains the integrity of the original composition. If he (or she) takes the story out of 19th-century Spain, will it not conflict with the strongly romantic and Iberian character of Bizet's music? If he sets it in a place where there is no cigarette factory, can Carmen and her coworkers remain as cigarette girls; should he—may he—change the words or just ignore them? If he surrounds Carmen with beautiful writhing bodies and gratuitous sex, does he diminish her as an object of unattainable sexual desire? If he makes José the central character, does he forfeit the energy that is Carmen herself? If he substitutes drug dealers, prostitutes, and degenerates for the Gypsies and the Gypsy culture of the Mérimée and Bizet, does Carmen lose not only her gravity and *duende* but as well her identification with the supernatural, with the Devil, with Fate? And, just as important, what happens to her "otherness"—the "otherness" that allows her to function outside the social norms and that fascinates us so? And if he presents her as some kind of alien dark lady, psychopath, or even superwoman, what happens to that which we love most about her: the free spirit, charm, love of life of this troublesome bad girl who works, lives, and lusts just like us—only so much more so.

Directors keep trying to recapture some of the original shock. But having Carmen raise her skirt to her crotch, spread her legs wide, and simulate sex whenever possible, as we see so often nowadays, can't possibly have the kind of shock effect on jaded modern audiences that Galli-Marié's "foul-mouthed, brazen ... small-time gutter prostitute"[27] had on the 19th-century bourgeoisie. It's the spectator who has changed. No longer the scandalous, treacherous anti-heroine she was in 1875, Carmen is for today's audience a heroine: courageous and principled—flawed, unquestionably—but a heroine nonetheless.

For that matter, today's audiences don't particularly see her as a *femme fatale* either—the deadly treacherous woman out to seduce a man in order to destroy him as in the film noir of the 1940s, or even the watered-down version of the '50s. Nor do they particularly want to see her confined to the time warp of woman's liberation, equal rights, and the sexual revolution. "The contemporary Carmen, measured against traditional moral standards, is in truth an 'impossible' being."[28] Indeed, one can place her virtually anywhere in time, and directors will continue to dream up new concepts to suit the period's social and cultural history, but the fact remains that "one interpretation can emphasize only some of her many aspects.... She is simply about too much."[29] And no one understood this better than Bizet and Mérimée themselves, who, in creating their heroine of a thousand faces knew to "mix light and dark in such a way that a variegated and ambivalent *chiaroscuro* results."[30]

* * *

The changes in the way opera is produced today have certainly sent the singer scrambling to meet the challenges and understand her new place. But, whatever the concept, it will always be subject to the givens of a singer's voice, talent, looks, temperament, personality, ethnicity, and thinking. True, the days of the individual portrayal as chronicled throughout this book are to all intents and purposes over; the staging, the costume, the interpretation are probably someone else's. But if the audience wonders just whose Carmen they are seeing, ultimately the role belongs to the singer before their eyes, as it always has. And because, as we remember Geraldine Farrar pointing out over a century ago, "each one of us probably sees something that the others have not seen—or thinks she does,"[31] the procession of Carmens, some not yet imagined in even the most visionary of minds, will continue. To be sure, having thus far given us Galli-Marié's demon, Hauk's charmer, Calvé's rapscallion, Stevens's alley cat, Baltsa's wildcat; Migenes-Johnson's guttersnipe, Ewing's sphinx, how could it be otherwise?

Appendix A.
Alphabetical Listing of Singers Mentioned in the Text

Aldrich, Kate
American mezzo-soprano; b. Damariscotta, ME, 1973.

Amparán, Belén
Mexican-American mezzo-soprano; b. El Paso, TX, 1927; d. Mexico, 2002.

Anitúa, Fanny
Mexican contralto; b. Mexico, 1887(8); d. Mexico City, 1968(9).

Antonacci, Anna Caterina
Italian mezzo-soprano; b. Bologna, Italy, 1961.

Arkhipova, Irina
Russian mezzo-soprano; b. Moscow, Russia, 1925; d. Moscow, 2010.

Arnoldson, Sigrid
Swedish soprano; b. Stockholm, Sweden, 1861; d. Stockholm, 1943.

Arral, Blanche
Belgian soprano; b. Liège, Belgium, 1864; d. New York, 1945.

Baclanova, Olga
Russia mezzo-soprano; b. Russia, 1893; d. Switzerland, 1974.

Baltsa, Agnes
Greek mezzo-soprano; b. Lefkada, Greece, 1944.

Barbieri, Fedora
Italian mezzo-soprano; b. Trieste, Italy, 1920; d. Florence, Italy, 2003.

Bellincioni, Gemma
Italian soprano; b. Monza, Italy, 1864; d. Naples, Italy, 1950.

Berganza, Teresa
Spanish mezzo-soprano; b. Madrid, Spain, 1935.

Besanzoni, Gabriella
Italian mezzo-soprano; b. Rome, Italy, 1888; d. Rome, 1962.

Borisenko, Vera
Russian mezzo-soprano; b. Bolshaya Nemka, 1918.

Borodina, Olga
Russian mezzo-soprano; b. St. Petersburg, Russia, 1963.

Bourskaya, Ina
Russian mezzo-soprano; b. Ukraine, 1888; d. Chicago, 1954.

Branzell, Karin
Swedish contralto; b. Stockholm,

Sweden, 1891; d. Altadena, California, 1974.

Bressler-Gianoli, Clotilde
Swiss soprano; b. 1874, Geneva, Switzerland; d. 1912, Geneva.

Bréval, Lucienne
Swiss dramatic soprano; b. Zürich, Switzerland, 1869; d. Neuilly-sur Seine, France, 1935.

Brohly, Suzanne
French mezzo-soprano; ? 1882; d. ?. 1943.

Buades, Aurora
Spanish contralto; b. Valencia, Spain,1897; d. Florence, Italy, 1965.

Bumbry, Grace
American mezzo-soprano, later soprano; b. St. Louis, Missouri, 1937.

Callas, Maria
American-born soprano of Greek parentage; b. New York City, New York, 1923; d. Paris, France, 1977.

Calvé, Emma
French soprano; b. Decazeville, Aveyron France, 1858; d. Montpellier, France, 1942.

Castagna, Bruna
Italian mezzo-soprano; b. Bari, Italy, 1901; d. Buenos Aires, Argentina, 1982.

Castagné, Marie
French mezzo-soprano; b. Toulouse, France, 1859; d. France, ?

Cavalieri, Lina
Italian soprano; b. Viterbo, Italy, 1874; d. Florence, Italy, 1944.

Cernay, Germaine
French mezzo-soprano; b. Le Havre, France, 1900; d. Paris, 1943.

Chenal, Marthe
French soprano; b. near Paris, 1881; d. Paris, 1947.

Cossotto, Fiorenza
Italian mezzo-soprano; b. Crescentino, Italy, 1935.

Crespin, Régine
French soprano; b. Marseilles, France, 1927; d. Paris, France, 2007.

Cristoforeanu, Florica
Romanian mezzo-soprano; b. Romania, 1887; d. Rio de Janeiro, Brazil, 1960.

Davidova, Maria
Russian mezzo-soprano; b. St. Petersburg, 1889; d. Paris, 1987.

de Belocca, Anna
Russian mezzo-soprano: b. Russia, 1854.

Delna, Marie
French contralto; b. near Paris, France, 1875; d. Paris, 1932.

de los Angeles, Victoria
Spanish soprano; b. Barcelona, Spain, 1923; d. Barcelona, 2005.

de Lussan, Zélie
French mezzo-soprano of American birth; b. Brooklyn, NY, 1861; d. London, England, 1949.

Destinn, Emmy
Czech soprano; b. Prague, Czechoslovakia, 1878; d. Ceské Budejovice, 1930.

Djanel, Lily
Flermish soprano; b. Belgium, 1909; d. ?

Dolaro, Selina
English soprano; b. London, 1849; d. New York, NY, 1889.

Domashenko, Marina
Russian mezzo-soprano; b. Kemerovo, Russia, ?

D'Oustrac, Stéphanie
French mezzo-soprano; b. Rennes, France, 1974.

Easton, Florence
English soprano; b. England, 1882; d. New York City, NY, 1955.

Ehnn, Bertha
Hungarian soprano; b. Budapest, Hungary, 1845; d. Aschberg, Austria, 1932.

Ewing, Maria
American mezzo-soprano; b. Detroit, Michigan, 1950.

Farrar, Geraldine
American soprano; b. Melrose, Massachusetts, 1882; d. Ridgefield, Connecticut, 1967.

Fassbaender, Brigitte
German mezzo-soprano; b. Berlin, Germany, 1939.

Ferni-Germano, Virginia
Italian soprano; b. Turin, Italy, 1849; d. Turin, 1934.

Ferrabini, Ester
Italian soprano; b. Venice, Italy, 1884; d. Italy, 1984.

Fremstad, Olive
Swedish soprano; b. Stockholm, Sweden, 1871; d. New York City, NY, 1951.

Friché, Claire
Belgian soprano; b. Brussels, 1875; d. Chantilly, France, 1966 (68).

Galli-Marié, Célestine (Marie-Célestine-Laurence Galli-Marié)
French mezzo-soprano; b. Paris, France, 1840; d. Vence, France, 1905.

Garanča, Elīna
Latvian mezzo-soprano; b. Riga, Latvia, 1976.

Garden, Mary
American soprano of Scottish birth; b. Aberdeen, Scotland, 1874; d. Scotland, 1967.

Gay, Maria
Spanish mezzo-soprano; b. Barcelona, Spain (?), 1879; d. Barcelona, 1943.

Gentle, Alice
American mezzo-soprano; b. Peoria, Illinois, 1885; d. Los Angeles, California, 1958.

Gerville-Réache, Jeanne
French contralto; b. Orthez, France, 1882; d. New York City, 1915.

Glade, Coe
American mezzo-soprano; b. Chicago, Illinois, 1900; d. New York City, NY, 1985.

Gonzalez, Eulalia
Spanish mezzo-soprano; no further information.

Graves, Denyce
American mezzo-soprano; b. Washington, D.C. 1964.

Gutheil-Schoder, Marie
German soprano; b. Weimar, Germany, 1874; d. Thuringia, Germany, 1935.

Hauk, Minnie
American soprano; b. New York City, NY, 1851; d. Lucerne, Switzerland, 1929.

Heidt, Winifred
American mezzo-soprano; b. Grand Rapids, Michigan, 1906 (?); d. Boynton Beach, Florida, 1986.

Herrera, Nancy Fabiola
Spanish mezzo-soprano; b. Caracas, Venezuela, 1965.

Hersee, Rose
English soprano; b. London, England, 1845; d. London, 1924.

Horne, Marilyn
American mezzo-soprano; b. Bradford, Pennsylvania, 1934.

Hunt-Lieberson, Lorraine
American mezzo-soprano; b. San Francisco, California, 1954; d. Santa Fe, New Mexico, 2006.

Jeritza, Maria
Czech soprano; b. Brno, Czechoslovakia, 1887; d. Orange, New Jersey, 1982.

Juyol, Suzanne
French soprano; b. Paris, 1920; d. Paris, 1994.

Kasarova, Vesselina
Bulgarian mezzo-soprano; b. Stara Zagora, Bulgaria, 1965.

Kellogg, Clara Louise
American soprano; b. Summerville, South Carolina, 1842; d. New Hartford, Connecticut, 1916.

Ketten, Cecile
French soprano; no further information.

Klose, Margarete
German mezzo-soprano; b. Berlin, Germany, 1902; d. Berlin, 1968.

Krasteva, Nadia
Bulgarian mezzo-soprano; b. Sofia, Bulgaria, ?

Labia, Maria
Italian soprano; b. Verona, Italy, 1880; d. Lake Garda, Italy, 1953.

Lane, Gloria
American mezzo-soprano; b. Trenton, New Jersey, 1930.

Leblanc, Georgette
French soprano; b. Rouen, France; 1875; d. Le Cannet, France, 1941.

Lehmann, Lilli
German soprano; b. Würzburg, Germany, 1848; d. Berlin, Germany, 1929.

Lucca, Pauline
Austrian soprano; b. Vienna, Austria, 1841; d. Vienna, 1908.

Ludwig, Christa
German mezzo-soprano; b. Berlin, Germany, 1928.

Lunn, Louise Kirby
English contralto; b. Manchester, 1873; d. London, 1930.

Madeira, Jean
American contralto; b. Centralia, Illinois, 1918; d. Providence, Rhode Island, 1972.

Maksakova, Maria Petrovna
Russian mezzo-soprano; b. Astrakhan, Russia, 1902; d. Moscow, 1974.

Margaine, Clémentine
French mezzo-soprano; b. Narbonne, France, 1984.

Marié de L'Isle, Jeanne
French mezzo-soprano; b. Paris, 1872; d. Paris, 1926.

Martinez, Ana Maria
Puerto Rican soprano; b. San Juan, Puerto Rico, 1971.

Matzenauer, Margaret
Romanian soprano; b. Romania, 1881; d. California, 1963.

Mazarin, Mariette
French soprano; b. Digne, France, 1877; d. 1952.

Meier, Waltraud
German mezzo-soprano/soprano; b. Würtzburg, Germany, 1956.

Mei-Figner, Medea
Italian mezzo-soprano, later soprano; b. Florence, Italy, 1859; d. Paris, France, 1952.

Merentié, Marguerite
French soprano; b. ?, 1880; d. ?

Meyer, Kerstin
Swedish mezzo-soprano; b. 1928, Stockholm, Sweden.

Alphabetical Listing of Singers Mentioned in the Text

Michel, Solange
French mezzo-soprano; b. Paris, France, 1912; d. Bourges, France, 2010.

Migenes-Johnson, Julia
American-born soprano of Greek and Puerto Rican parents; b. NYC, NY, 1945.

Moe, Olfine
Norwegian soprano; b. Bergen, Norway, 1850; d. As, Sweden, 1933.

Nafe, Alicia
Argentine mezzo-soprano; no further information.

Namara, Marguerite
American soprano; b. Cleveland, Ohio, 1888; d. Marbella, Spain, 1974.

Niehoff (also Edling), Dina
Swedish mezzo-soprano, b. 1854; d. 1935.

Obraztsova, Elena
Russian mezzo-soprano; b. St. Petersburg, Russia, 1939; d. Leipzig, Germany, 2015.

Olszewska, Maria
German contralto; b. Ludwigsschwaige, Germany, 1892; d. Klagenfurt, Austria, 1969.

Otero, Caroline
Spanish soprano; b. Barcelona, Spain, 1868; Nice, France, 1965.

Pasqua, Giuseppina
Italian soprano, later mezzo-soprano; b. Perugia, Italy, 1851; d. Bologna, Italy, 1930.

Patti, Adelina
Italian coloratura soprano; b. Spain of Italian parents, 1843; d. Wales, 1919.

Pavlovskaya, Emiliya
Russian soprano; b. St. Petersburg, 1853; d. Moscow, 1935.

Pederzini, Gianna
Italian mezzo-soprano; b. Trento, Italy, 1900; d. Rome, Italy, 1988.

Perelli, Lucy
French mezzo-soprano; b. ?, 1895; ? 1974.

Pollak, Anna
English mezzo-soprano; b. Manchester, England of Austrian and Russian parents, 1912; d. Kent, England, 1996.

Ponselle, Rosa
American soprano of Italian parents; b. Meriden, Connecticut, 1897; d. Baltimore, Maryland, 1981.

Rachvelishvili, Anita
Georgian mezzo-soprano; b. Tbilisi, Georgia, 1984.

Radev, Marianna,
Romanian mezzo-soprano; b. Konstanza, Romania of Croatian parents, 1911; d. Zagreb, Croatia, 1974.

Rankin, Nell
American mezzo-soprano; b. Montgomery, Alabama, 1926; d. New York City, NY, 2005.

Raveau, Alice
French contralto; b. Paris, France (?),1884; d. Paris, 1951.

Renard, Marie
Austrian mezzo-soprano, later soprano; b. Graz, Austria, 1864; d. Graz, 1939.

Resnik, Regina
American soprano, later mezzo-soprano; b. New York City, NY, 1922; died, NYC, 2013.

Rhodes, Jane
French mezzo-soprano; b. Paris, France, 1929; d. Neuilly-sur-Seine, 2011.

Roze, Marie
French soprano; b. Paris, France, 1846; d. Paris, 1926.

Rubio, Consuelo
Spanish mezzo-soprano; b. Madrid, Spain, 1927; d. Madrid, 1981.

Sarkissyan, Emma
Russian mezzo-soprano; b. 1935, Woronesch, Russia.

Shaham, Rinat
Israeli mezzo-soprano; b. Haifa, Israel, 1980.

Shipp, Heather
British mezzo-soprano; no further information.

Simionato, Giulietta
Italian mezzo-soprano; b. 1910, Forli, Italy; d. 2010, Rome, Italy.

Slavina, Maria
Russian mezzo-soprano; b. St. Petersburg, Russia, 1858; d. Paris, France, 1951.

Smith, Muriel
American mezzo-soprano; b. New York City, NY, 1923; d. Richmond, Virginia, 1985.

Stevens, Risë
American mezzo-soprano; b. Bronx, New York, 1913; d. New York City, NY, 2013.

Stignani, Ebe
Italian mezzo-soprano; b. Naples, Italy, 1903; d. Imola, Italy, 1974.

Stilwell, Jean
Canadian mezzo-soprano, b. Toronto, Canada, 1955.

Supervia, Conchita
Spanish mezzo-soprano; b. Barcelona, Spain, 1895; d. London, England, 1936.

Swarthout, Gladys
American mezzo-soprano; b. Deepwater, Missouri, 1900; d. Florence, Italy, 1969.

Sylva, Marguerita
Belgian mezzo-soprano; b. Brussels, Belgium, 1875; d. Glendale, California, 1957.

Tagliana, Emilia
Italian soprano; b. Mailand, Italy 1854; d. 1902.

Tarquini, Tarquinia
Italian soprano; b. Colle di Val d'Elsa, Italy, 1882; d. 1976?

Tarquini D'Or, Mathilde
French soprano; b. 1863; d. 1945.

Thebom, Blanche
American mezzo-soprano; b. Monessen, Pennsylvania, 1915; d. San Francisco, California, 2010.

Tourangeau, Huguette
French-Canadian mezzo-soprano; b. Montreal, Canada, 1938.

Tourel, Jennie
Russian-born American mezzo-soprano; b. Vitebsk, Belarus, 1900; d. New York City, NY, 1973.

Trebelli, Zélia
French-born contralto; b. Paris, France, 1838; d. Étretat, France, 1892.

Troyanos, Tatiana
American mezzo-soprano; b. New York City, NY, 1938; d. New York City, 1993.

Uria-Monzon, Béatrice
French mezzo-soprano; b. Agen, France, 1963.

Vallin, Ninon
French soprano; b. France, 1886; d. Lyon, France, 1961.

Vavrille, Annie
French mezzo-soprano; no further information.

Alphabetical Listing of Singers Mentioned in the Text

Vergara, Victoria
Chilean mezzo-soprano; b. Chile, ?

Verrett, Shirley
American mezzo-soprano; b. New Orleans, Louisiana, 1931; d. Ann Arbor, Michigan, 2010.

Veselovskaya, Maria
Russian soprano; no further information.

Vix, Genevieve
French soprano; b. Le Havre, France, 1879; d. Paris, 1939.

Vizin, Viktoria
Hungarian mezzo-soprano; b. Kecskemet, Hungary, ?

von Otter, Anne Sofie
Swedish mezzo-soprano; b. Stockholm, Sweden, 1955.

Wettergren, Gertrude (also Gertrud Palson-Wettergren)
Swedish mezzo-soprano; b. Sweden, 1897; d. ?, 1991.

Wyns, Charlotte
French mezzo-soprano; b. Paris, France, 1868; d. ?

Zbrueva, Evgenia
Russian mezzo-soprano; b. Moscow, Russia, 1868; d. Moscow, 1936.

Zinetti, Giuseppina
Italian mezzo-soprano; b. Ferrara, Italy, 1889; d. Milan, 1973.

Appendix B. Chronology of Premieres and Significant Performances[1]

(Any performance in a language other than French is noted, when known.)

3/3/1875	World premiere at the Opéra-Comique in Paris with Célestine Galli-Marié; 36 performances in first season.
10/23/1875	Vienna premiere with Bertha Ehnn; in German.
11/15/1875	Second series of 13 performances at Opéra-Comique, with Galli-Marié.
2/3/1876	Brussels premiere with Maria Dérivis.
4/1/1876	Antwerp premiere (with Galli-Marié?).
10/28/1876	Budapest premiere; in Hungarian.
1877	Reprised in Brussels with Galli-Marié.
early 1878	Angers, France, premiere with (Rita?) Lelong.
2/16/1878	St. Petersburg Bolshoi (Stone) Theater premiere with Bertha Ehnn, in Italian.
3/22/1878	Stockholm premiere with Olfine Moe, in Swedish.
6/22/1878	London premiere with Minnie Hauk, in Italian.
9/9/1878	Dublin premiere with Minnie Hauk, in Italian.
10/23/1878	American premiere at the Academy of Music in New York City, with Minnie Hauk, in Italian.
10/25/1878	Philadelphia premiere, with Clara Louise Kellog, in Italian.
1/3/1879	Boston premiere with Hauk.

Chronology of Premieres and Significant Performances 173

2/5/1879	First performance by the Carl Rosa Company with Selina Dolaro, in English.
2/27/1879	First performance by Pauline Lucca in Vienna, presumably in German.
3/5/1879	Canadian premiere in Toronto with Clara Louise Kellogg, in Italian.
summer/1879	Australian premiere in Melbourne with Rose Hersee, in English.
11/15/1879	Italian premiere in Naples, Teatro Bellini, with Galli-Marié, in Italian.
12/18/1879	New Orleans premiere, possibly with Emilie Ambré, in Italian.
1/31/1880	Hamburg premiere, in German.
2/21/1880	New Orleans, St. Charles Theater, in English.
3/12/1880	Berlin premiere with Emilie Tagliana, in German; Lucca took over soon after; by World War I, Berlin had mounted 910 performances of *Carmen*, more than any other opera.
3/29/1880	Prague premiere in German.
12/3/1880	Berlin premiere, in German.
12/16/1880	Milan premiere at Teatro del Verme with Stella Bonheur, in Italian.
12/24/1880	Geneva premiere.
1881	Nietsche sees *Carmen* in Genoa with Galli-Marié.
1881	Malta, in Italian.
1/14/1881	New Orleans first performance in French.
1/19/1881?	Zürich premiere, in German.
2/11/1881	Mexico premiere.
3/2/1881	New York first in English at Haverly's Fifth Ave. Theater.
5/23/1881	Rio de Janeiro premiere.
8/2/1881	Barcelona premiere with Galli-Marié.
8/9/1881	Buenos Aires premiere.
Fall/1881	Dieppe, with Galli-Marié.
Winter/1882	Galli-Marié performs it at Genoa, Lyon, and Liege in Belgium.
2/1882	Cairo premiere, with Finnish mezzo Elisabeth Frandin, probably in Italian.

Appendix B

5/27/1882	First Covent Garden performance with Pauline Lucca.
1883	Santiago, Chile, premiere, in Italian.
4/24/1883	Return to Opéra-Comique with Adèle Isaac who sings it 27 times before turning it back to Galli-Marié.
5/18/1883	Latvia premiere, in German.
6/7/1883	Mexico City, in Spanish.
10/27/1883	Revised new production at Opéra-Comique with Galli-Marié.
12/22/1883	One hundredth performance at the Opéra-Comique with Galli-Marié.
1/5/1884	Metropolitan Opera premiere in Boston with Trebelli, in Italian.
1/9/1884	Metropolitan Opera premiere with Trebelli, in Italian.
12/13/1884	Romania premiere.
1885	Milan at the Dal Verme with Stella Bonheur.
3/12/1885	Estonia premiere.
9/1885	Performance in St. Petersburg at the Mariinsky, Slavina.
11/1885	Lisbon premiere.
11/25/1885	Lilli Lehmann debut at Metropolitan Opera, first in German.
1886	Galli-Marié in London at Her Majesty's Theater.
1/22/1887	Amsterdam premiere, in Dutch.
4/24/1887	Copenhagen premiere, in Danish.
11/2/1887	Madrid premiere, with changes and an adapted libretto, at the Teatro de la Zarzuela with Eulalia Gonzales, in Spanish.
3/1888	Madrid Teatro Real, with Giuseppina Pasqua, in Italian.
2/10/1889	Helsinki premiere (in Russian).
7/28/1890	First Covent Garden performance in French with De Lussan.
12/1890	Gala performance at the Opéra Comique to raise funds for Bizet memorial; with Galli-Marié, Melba, De Reszke and Lasalle.
11/25/1892	Calve sings first Carmen ever, at Opéra-Comique.
12/2/1892	Command performance Queen Victoria at Windsor Castle, with Zélie de Lussan.

Chronology of Premieres and Significant Performances

6/18/1893	Zagreb, Croatia, premiere.
12/20/1893	Emma Calvé's first at Metropolitan Opera is the Met's first in French
1895	Cape Town, South Africa, premiere.
2/23/1896	La Scala premiere with Virginia Ferni, in Italian.
1898	First performance at the Bolshoi.
12/8/1898	Inauguration of new Salle Favart with Georgette Leblanc.
5/7/1900	Oslo, Norway, premiere, in Norwegian.
5/14/1900	Negro troupe, Theodore Drury Opera Co. plays Lexington Opera House in New York.
1900	Vienna under Mahler with Gutheil-Schoder.
1902	Maria Gay sings her first ever Carmen in Brussels.
12/23/1904	Opéra-Comique celebrates the 1,000th performance of *Carmen* with Calvé.
12/21/1907	The first and only performance of *Carmen* at L'Opéra de Paris until it enters the repertoire in 1959, with Marguerite Merentié.
1908	First complete recording of *Carmen*, with Emmy Destinn, in German.
3/9/1912	Sofia, Bulgaria, premiere.
8/1/1914	First performance in the Verona Arena, with Maria Gay.
11/19/14	Farrar sings the first of her 65 performances at Metropolitan Opera.
1915	First performance at Teatro Colon, with Genevieve Vix.
1918	China premiere in Shanghai, in Russian.
1919	Japan premiere in Yokohama.
1922	Yugoslavia (Belgrade) premiere.
4/30/1923	A rare Gala performance at the Opéra-Comique performed with Guiraud's recitatives, with Suzanne Brohly.
1925	San Francisco Opera premiere, with Anima Allegra.
11/10/1925	Tel Aviv, Israel, premiere.
11/1931	Athens, Greece, premiere, in Italian.
2/24/1935	Tokyo premiere, in Japanese.
1947	Carl Rosa in England and the Columbia Touring Opera in U.S. perform Carmen with what may be the first

	performances with spoken dialogue outside of France. In 1953 Covent Garden tries dialogue but abandons it.
5/4/1959	Last performance at Opéra-Comique, with Isabelle Andreani.
11/10/1959	In Paris, *Carmen* is officially transferred from the Opéra-Comique, where it had played 2,899 times to the Opéra at the Palais Garnier with Jane Rhodes; it did not return to the Opéra-Comique until 1980.
3/3/1975	The world celebrates the 100th birthday of *Carmen*.

Appendix C. Discography

Listed in alphabetical order by artist singing Carmen; all recordings, including those of live performances, have at some time been released commercially on CD, though as these sometimes appear on more than one label, I note only the label of the recording in my possession. I do not include those released only on LP. Countless other noncommercial options (some better than others) can also be found on such sites as Premiere Opera and House of Opera. Single aria recordings are included only for singers mentioned in the book who did not made complete recordings. All are in French unless otherwise noted; all use the Guiraud recitatives, those using spoken dialogue are noted.

Alperyn, Graciela
Giorgio Lamberti (José), Alexander Rahbari (conductor)
1991, 1994
Naxos, complete and highlights

Amparán, Belén
Franco Corelli (José), N. Sanzogno (conductor)
In Italian
1956
Myto, complete

Arkhipova, Irina
Mario del Monaco (José); Alexander Melik-Pesheyev (conductor)
In Russian, Italian and French
1959
Myto, complete

Arkhipova, Irina
Vladislav Piavko (José); Yuri Simonov (conductor)
In Russian
Live from the Bolshoi, 1975
Irina Arkhipova Foundation, excerpts

Baltsa, Agnes
José Carreras (José); Herbert von Karajan (conductor)
With spoken dialogue
1982
Deutsche Grammophon, complete

Barbieri, Fedora
Mario del Monaco (José); Fritz Reiner (conductor)
Live from the Met, 1953
Myto, complete

Appendix C

Bardon, Patricia
Julian Gavin (José); David Parry (conductor)
In English, with spoken dialogue
New Urtext edition by Richard Langham Smith
English National Opera, 2003
Chandos, complete

Bellincioni, Gemma
Habanera and Air des cartes, 1905
In Italian
Marston, The Creators of Verismo, Vol. 1

Berganza, Teresa
Placido Domingo (José), Claudio Abbado (conductor)
1978
With spoken dialogue
Deutsche Grammophon, complete and highlights

Besanzoni, Gabriella
Piero Pauli (José), Carlo Sabajno (conductor)
1931
Arkadia, complete
(Besanzoni's brother, Ernesto Besanzoni, sings Escamillo)

Borisenko, Vera
Georgi Nelepp (José); Wassii Nebolsin (conductor)
In Russian
1952
Hamburger Archiv fur Gesangskunst, complete

Bressler-Gianoli, Clotilde
Chanson Bohème and Air des cartes
Harold Wayne, Vol. 30
Symposium

Brohly, Suzanne
Henri Saint-Criege (José); Albert Wolff (conductor)
1930
Polydor, abridged

Buades, Aurora
Aureliano Pertile (José); Lorenzo Molajoli (conductor)
In Italian
1933
Phonograph, complete

Bumbry, Grace
Jon Vickers (José); Rafael Frühbeck de Burgos (conductor)
With spoken dialogue by actors
1970
EMI, complete and highlights

Callas, Maria
Nicolai Gedda (José); Georges Pretre (conductor)
1964
EMI, complete

Calvé, Emma
Many recordings of arias and excerpt, including:
Emma Calvé: The complete 1902 G&T, 1920 Pathé, and "Mapleson Cylinder" recordings on Marston
Emma Calvé: the complete Victor recordings (1907–16) on Romophone

Castagna, Bruna
Air des cartes
1938
Great Operas at the Met: Carmen

Cernay, Germaine
Raymond Berthaud (José); D.H. Inghelbrecht (conductor)
With spoken dialogue
Recorded for radio, 1942
Malibran, almost complete

Červená, Soňa
Rolf Apreck (José) Herbert Kegel (conductor)
In German
1960
Eterna, selections and complete

Cossotto, Fiorenza
Placido Domingo (José); George Prêtre (conductor)
Live from La Scala, 1974
Gala or Opera d'Oro, complete

Discography

Crespin, Régine
Gilbert Py (José); Alain Lombard (conductor)
1971
Ultima, selections

Crespin, Régine
William Lewis (José); Henry Lewis (conductor)
With spoken dialogue
Live broadcast from the Metropolitan Opera House, 1975
Bella Voce, complete

D'Alvarez, Marguerite
Habanera, 1920/22; Séguidille 1929
Club 99

Davydova, Vera
Nikandr Khanev (José); Melik-Pesheyev (conductor)
In Russian
1937
Melodiya, complete

Delna, Marie
Habanera, Séguedille Air de Cartes
1903
Marston, Marie Delna: Published Recordings
Malibran, Marie Delna

de los Angeles, Victoria
Nicolai Gedda (José); Sir Thomas Beecham (conductor)
1958, 1959 (first in stereo)
EMI, complete

de Lussan, Zélie
Habanera
1903
Great Operas at the Met: Carmen

Destinn, Emmy
Karl Jörn (José); Bruno Seidler-Winkler (conductor)
In German
Berlin, 1908
Marston, complete (this was the first complete recording; originally released on 18 double-sided discs, some 12-inch, some 10-inch, each of which was sold individually)

Djanel, Lily
Raoul Jobin (José); Sir Thomas Beecham (conductor)
Live Metropolitan Opera Broadcast, 1943
Walhall, complete

Domashenko, Marina
Andrea Bocelli (José); Myung-Whun Chung (conductor)
With spoken dialogue
2005
Decca, complete

Farrar, Geraldine
Giovanni Martinelli (José)
1914–15
Geraldine Farrar in French Opera
Nimbus, excerpts

Fassbaender, Brigitte
Ludovic Spiess (José); Giuseppe Patané (conductor)
In German
1972
Berlin Classics, highlights only

Fremstad, Olive
Séguedille
1911
Great Operas at the Met
Three American Sopranos, Marston

Garden, Mary
Air des cartes
1929
Mary Garden: Complete Victor Recordings
Romophone

Gay, Maria
Air des Cartes (Great Operas at the Met: Carmen and Covent Garden, Vol. 2)
Habanera (Golden Age of Singing, Vol. 2)
Chanson Bohème (Record Collector, Vol. 2, 1997)

Final duet, in Italian, with her husband Giovanni Zenatello (Giovanni Zenatello, Vol. 1, Lebendige Vergangenheit)

Gerville-Réache, Jeanne
Habanera
Air des Cartes
Opal/Pearl

Gheorghiu, Angela
Roberto Alagna (José), Michel Plasson (conductor)
2003
EMI, complete
(also includes one of the 12 alternative versions Bizet wrote for the *Habanera*, using the same text)

Giannini, Dusolina
Habanera and Air des Cartes
1932
Dusolina Giannini (Lys and Lebendige Vergangenheit)

Heidt, Winifred
Ramon Vinay (José); Leopold Stokowski (conductor)
In English with spoken dialogue
Live from the Hollywood Bowl, 1946
Eklipse, almost complete

Höngen, Elisabeth
Torsten Ralf (José); Karl Böhm (conductor)
In German
1942
Presier, complete

Horne, Marilyn
James McCracken (José); Leonard Bernstein (complete)
With spoken dialogue
1973
Metropolitan Opera Production, complete
Remastered by Pentatone in 2014

Juyol, Suzanne
José Luccioni (José); Jules Gressier (conductor)
1947
Malibran, complete

Juyol, Suzanne
Lebero De Luca (José); Albert Wolff (conductor)
Opéra-Comique, 1951
Paperback Opera, complete

Klose, Margarete
Rudolf Schock (José); Ferenc Friscay (conductor)
In German
1951
Audite, highlights (no Escamillo selections)

Kozena, Magdalena
Jonas Kaufmann (José); Simon Rattle (conductor)
With spoken dialogue
Concert performance, 2012
EMI, complete

Larmore, Jennifer
Thomas Moser (José); Giuseppe Sinopoli (conductor)
With spoken dialogue
1995
Teldec, complete

Ludwig, Christa
Rudolf Schock (José); Horst Stein (conductor)
In German
EMI, complete, 1961

Ludwig, Christa
James King (José); Lorin Maazel (conductor)
Vienna State Opera, live 1966
Orfeo D'Or, complete

Madeira, Jean
Nicolas Filacuridi (José); Pierre Dervaux (conductor)
1957
Paperback Opera, complete

Discography

Maksakova, Maria
Air des Cartes
Maria Maksakova: Lebendige Vergangenheit

Malaniuk, Ira
Hans Hopf (José); André Cluytens (conductor)
In German
1958
Walhall, complete

Marié de l'Isle, Jeanne
Leon Beyle (José), Hector Dufranne (piano)
1904/05
Marston, selections

Mérentié, Marguerite
Agustarello Affré (José); Francois Ruhlmann (conductor)
With spoken dialogue
Opéra-Comique, 1911
Marston, Pathé Opera Series

Meyer, Kerstin
Arne Hendriksen (José); Sixten Ehrling (conductor)
In Swedish with spoken dialogue
Recorded for radio, 1954
Bluebell, complete

Michel, Solange
Raoul Jobin (José); André Cluytens (conductor)
With spoken dialogue
Opéra-Comique, 1950
EMI, complete

Migenes-Johnson, Julia
Placido Domingo (José); Lorin Maazel (conductor)
From the film by Francesco Rosi, Warner classic, release date 2010

Milcheva-Nonova, Alexandrina
Nikola Nikolov (José); Ivan Marinov (conductor)
1985
Capriccio, complete and highlights.

Milinkovic, Georgine von
Rudolf Schock (José); Eugene Jochum (conductor)
In German with spoken dialogue
1954
Walhall, complete

Mödl, Martha
Habanera, Séguedille and Air des Cartes
Presier, Martha Mödl

Moffo, Anna
Franco Corelli (José); Lorin Maazel (conductor)
1979
RCA, complete (made for a proposed movie of Carmen)

Mooney, Janet
Mark Luther (José); Roderick Dunk (conductor)
In English
1995
Traveling Opera Company
IMP Classics, highlights

Norman, Jesseye
Neil Shicoff (José); Seiji Ozawa (conductor)
1988
Philips, complete and highlights

Obraztsova, Eleana
Placido Domingo (José); Carlos Kleiber (conductor)
Vienna State Opera, live 1978
Golden Melodram, complete

Obraztsova, Elena
Vladimir Atlantov (José); Jury Simonov (conductor)
In Russian
Melodiya, complete

Olszewska, Maria
Habanera, Séguedilla, Air des Cartes
1922–1927
Maria Olszewska: Lebendige Verganenheit, in German

Pantos, Pamela
Corneliu Murgu (José), Roberto Paternostro (conductor)
1998
Empire Opera Classics, complete

Pederzini, Gianna
Air des Cartes, 1928;
Habanera and Sèguedilla, 1940
Air des Cartes, 1941
Gianna Pederzini: Lebendige Verganenheit, in Italian

Perelli, Lucy
José de Trévi (José); Piero Coppola (conductor)
1928 (first electrical)
Malibran, complete

Ponselle, Rosa
René Maison (José), Louis Hasselmans (conductor)
Broadcast of the Met on tour in Boston, 1936
Eklipse, complete

Ponselle, Rosa
René Maison (José); Gennaro Papi (conductor)
Broadcast of the Met on tour in Cleveland, 1937
Walhall, complete

Price, Leontyne
Franco Corelli (José); Herbert von Karajan (conductor)
1963
RCA, complete and highlights

Qing, Miao
Li Jin Yuan (José); Jean Périsson
Opéra Central de Pékin; Jan. 1, 1982, live
In Chinese
Rondine, complete

Radev, Mariana
Habanera
The Best of the Opera

Resnik, Regina
Mario del Monaco (José); Thomas Schippers (conductor)
1963
London, complete

Rhodes, Jane
Albert Lance (José); Roberto Benzi (conductor)
l'Opéra de Paris, live 1959
Malibran, complete

Rubio, Consuelo
Leopold Simoneau (José); Pierre-Michel le Conte (conductor)
1959
Urania, complete

Simionato, Giulietta
Franco Corelli (José); Fritz Reiner (conductor)
In Italian
1953
Archipel, complete

Simionato, Giulietta
Nicolai Gedda (José); Herbert von Karajan (conductor)
1954
Gala, complete

Simionato, Giuietta
Franco Corelli (José); Herbert von Karajan (conductor)
1955
Great Opera Performances, complete

Simionato, Giulietta
Franco Corelli (José); Gian Giacomo Guelfi (conductor)
In Italian
1959
Gala, complete

Stevens, Risë
Jan Peerce (José), Fritz Reiner (conductor)
1951
RCA, complete

Stevens, Risë
Richard Tucker (José); Fritz Reiner (conductor)

Discography

Live from the Metropolitan, 1952
Walhall, complete

Stevens, Risë
Richard Tucker (José), Tibor Kozma (conductor)
Live from the Metropolitan, 1954
Immortal Performances, complete
I believe this is the best of the multiple recordings by Stevens

Stevens, Risë
Giuseppe di Stefano (José); Max Rudolf (conductor)
live from the Metropolitan, 1956
Opera Live, complete

Stevens, Risë
Mario del Monaco (José); Dimitri Mitropoulos (conductor)
Live from the Metropolitan, 1957
Nuova Era, complete

Stignani, Ebe
Beniamino Gigli (José); Vincenzo Bellezza (conductor)
In Italian
recorded live for radio, 1949
Allegro, complete

Supervia, Conchita
1927–1928
In Italian
Marston, the Complete Conchita Supervia, Vol. 1, three excerpts

Supervia, Conchita
Gaston Micheletti, tenor, and Gustav Cloëz conductor
1929 and 1931
Marston, The Complete Conchita Supervia, Vol. 3, ten excepts

Supervia, Conchita
Gaston Micheletti, tenor, and Gustav Cloëz
1929–1930
EMI, three excerpts

Swarthout, Gladys
Charles Kullman (José); Wilfrid Pelletier (conductor)

Live from the Metropolitan, 1941
Immortal Performances, complete

Tassinari, Pia
Franco Corelli (José); Arturo Basile (conductor)
1957
In Italian
Cetra, highlights

Tourel, Jennie
Joseph Rogachevsky (José); Lazlo Halasz (conductor); Regina Resnik (Frasquita)
1944
radio broadcast from the New York City Opera
Eklipse, Act 2 excerpts and an interview in which Tourel talks about Carmen and Supervia.

Troyanos, Tatiana
Placido Domingo (José); Sir Georg Solti (conductor)
1975, 1985
London, complete

Uria-Monzon, Beatrice
Christian Papis (José); Alain Lombard (conductor)
1995
With spoken dialogue
MPO, complete and highlights

Vallin, Ninon
1927 and 1928; excerpts, including 2 versions of the Habanera et Séguedille
Marston Pathé Art Label Recordings

Vallin, Ninon
Villabella (José); Ruhlman and Andolfi (conductors)
excerpts, including the final duet; also Vallin singing Micaela's aria and duet, and Manon selections
Malibran, 1929

Verrett, Shirley
Placido Domingo (José); Sir Georg Solti (conductor)

With spoken dialogue, one of the first recordings to use the Oeser edition
Live from Covent Garden, 1973
Grand Tier, complete and highlights

Visconti, Raymonde
Georges Thill (José); Élie Cohen (conductor)
Opéra-Comique, 1928
Historic Sound, complete but without dialogue or recitative; also Malibran

Wyns, Charlotte
(see Bressler-Gianoli)

Appendix D. Videography

Videos are listed alphabetically by the artist in the role of Carmen. All have at one time been released commercially on DVD. (Many non-commercial performances not listed here can be found on such sites as Premiere Opera and House of Opera.) All are in French unless otherwise noted. All are live performances unless otherwise noted. For those wanting to look further into the Carmen legend on film, I strongly recommend *Carmen on Film: A Cultural History* by Phil Powrie, Bruce Babington, Ann Davies, and Chris Perriam. According to these authors only Dracula outnumbers the Gypsy in adaptations.

Amparan, Belan
Franco Corelli (José), Nino Sanzogno (conductor), Franco Enriquez (director)
Filmed at the RAI Studios in Milan (June 13, 1956)
Sung in Italian
Hardy Classic Video

Antonacci, Anna Caterina
Jonas Kaufmann (José), Antonio Pappano (conductor), Francesca Zambello (director)
Royal Opera House, London (2007)
Decca

Antonacci, Anna Caterina
Andrew Richards (José), John Elliot Gardiner (conductor), Adrian Noble (director)
L'Opéra Comique (2009)
FRA Musica/Opéra Comique

Arkhipova, Irina
Mario del Monaco (José); Alexander Melik-Pashayev (conductor)
In Russian, French, and Italian
Live excerpts from the Bolshoi (1959)
VAI

Baltsa, Agnes
José Carreras (José)
James Levine (conductor), production by Peter Hall
Metropolitan Opera (1987)
Deutsche Grammophon

Bonfitto, Angela
Jevgenij Taruntsov (José)
Elisabetta Maschio (conductor), Giovanna Nocetti (director)
Teatro Coccia, Novara (2008)
Kicco Classics

Appendix D

Bumbry, Grace
Jon Vickers (José)
Herbert von Karajan (conductor and director)
A film, made in 1967 in Munich, of the 1966 Salzburg production, with dubbing
Deutsche Gramophone

Domashenko, Marina
Marco Berti (José)
Alain Lombard (conductor), Franco Zeffirelli (director)
Arena di Verona (2003)
TDK

Domashenko, Marina
Rolando Villazon (José)
Daniel Barenboim (conductor), Martin Kusej (director)
Berlin (2006)
This production can now be rented on Amazon Video.

Ewing, Maria
Barry McCauley (José)
Bernard Haitink (conductor), Peter Hall (director)
Glyndebourne, 1985
Kultur

Ewing, Maria
Jacques Trussel (José)
Jacques Delacote (conductor), Steven Pimott (director)
Earl's Court, 1989
Image Entertainment

Ewing, Maria
Luis Lima (José)
Zubin Mehta (conductor), director (Nuria Espert)
Royal Opera, 2001
Image Entertainment

Garanča, Elina
Roberto Alagna (José)
Yannick Nézet-Séguin (conductor), Richard Eyre (director)
Metropolitan Opera, 2010
Deutsche Gramophone

Kasarova, Vesselina
Jonas Kaufmann (José)
Franz Welser-Möst (conductor), Matthias Hartmann (director)
Opernhaus Zurich, 2009
Decca

Krasteva, Nadia
Aleksandrs Antonenko (José)
Ernst Märzendorfer (conductor), Gianfranco de Bosio (director)
St. Margarethen, 2005
Euroarts

Krasteva, Nadia
Bojidar Nikolo (José)
Ralf Weikert (conductor), Bernard Broca / Rian van Holland (directors)
Color Line Arena, Hamburg, 2006
Companions Opera, Amsterdam

Migenes-Johnson, Julia
Placido Domingo (José)
Lorrin Maazel (conductor), Francesco Rossi (director)
Filmed on location, 1984
Olive Films

Obraztsova, Elena
Placido Domingo (José)
Carlos Kleiber (conductor), Franco Zeffirelli (director)
Vienna State Opera, 1978
TDK

Rice, Christine
Bryan Hymel (José)
Constantinos Carydid (conductor), Francesca Zambello (director)
Royal Opera, originally filmed in 3D; 2015
Opus Arte

Semenchuk, Ekaterina
Carlo Ventre (José)
Henrik Nánási (conductor); Franco Zeffirelli (director)

Arena di Verona, 2014
Bel Air

Shaham, Rinat
Dmytro Popov (José)
Brian Castles-Onion (conductor); Gale Edwards (director)
Opera on Sydney Harbour, 2013
Opera Australia

Sofie von Otter, Anne
Marcus Haddock (José)
Philippe Jordan (conductor); David McVicar (director)
Glyndebourne Festival Opera, 2002
Opus Arte

Surguladze, Nino
Phillipe Do (José)
Carlo Montanaro (conductor); Dante Ferretti (director)
Sferisterio Festival, Macerata, 2008
Dynamic

Uria-Monzon, Béatrice
Roberto Alagna (José)
Marc Piollet (conductor); Calixto Bieito (director)
Gran Teatre del Liceu, Barcelona 2011
Unitel Classics

Walewska, Malgorzata
Mario Malagnini (Don José)
Giorgio Croci (conductor); Wolfgang Werner (director)
St. Margarethen, 1998
Classic World

Chapter Notes

Introduction

1. Risë Stevens, quoted in *Opera News*, December 13, 1975.
2. Mérimée, *Carmen*, Oxford University Press, 48.
3. Geraldine Farrar, "The Psychology of Carmen," *The Bookman*, January 1915, 414.
4. Peter Conrad, "Fatal Charms," *Opera News*, March 15, 1986.
5. Farrar, *The Bookman*, 415.
6. *Opera News*, March 14, 1987.
7. D.C. Parker, *Bizet*, 38.
8. Prosper Mérimée, *Carmen and Other Stories*, Oxford University Press, 36.
9. *Ibid.*, 52. *Calli* is another word for Gypsy.
10. *Ibid.*, 15.
11. *Ibid.*, 42.
12. *Ibid.*, 43.
13. *Ibid.*, 40.
14. *Ibid.*, 51.
15. *Ibid.*, 30.
16. *Ibid.*, 16.
17. *Ibid.*, 46.
18. Milton Brener, *Opera Offstage*, Walker and Company, 1996, 132.
19. From the *Mémoires* of Céleste Vénard, quoted by Brener, 130.
20. As the story is similar in every account, this telling of it is a compilation taken from two newspapers: *The Advertiser*, September 30, 1907, and the *Marlborough Express*, January 28, 1908. There was much more discussion about it in the Parisian press, and more recently, Gail Lavielle mentions it in her *Carmen: The Seduction of the Century* as does Robert Potterton in his article "Bizet and his Carmen," *Opera* (July 1975). There is also a major article about it in *The Bookman*, Vol. 32, No. 2, October 1910.
21. Risë Stevens, quoted by Steven Blier in "The Carmen Challenges," *Opera News*, December 1998.
22. Lorraine Hunt-Lieberson, quoted by Steven Blier in "The Carmen Challenges," *Opera News*, December 1998.
23. Prosper Mérimée, *Carmen et Autres Nouvelles*, Editions Rencontre Lausanne, 1967, 305. "On ne s'ennuyait pas auprès de cette fille-là." Translation by the author.

Chapter 1

1. "Je suis, oui, fascinée par Carmen! Quelle richesse expressive, que de possibilities dramatiques: je non dors plus." Letter and translation courtesy of Claude-Pascal Perna.
2. Letter, dated September 1873, cited in P. Berton, *Souvenir de la Vie de Théâtre*, 237, and quoted in Mina Curtiss, *Bizet and His World*, 357.
3. Paul Lhérie created the role of Don José.
4. Curtiss, 357.
5. Even a ballet was created around the character with choreography by a still little known Petipa. *Carmen et son Toréro* was first performed in Madrid in 1845 or 1846. By the end of the century dozens more had followed.
6. All reminiscences by Ludovic Halévy

are from an article he wrote, "La Millième Représentation de Carmen," that was published in *Le Théâtre*, No. 1 (January 1905) and appears, translated, in Michael Rose, *The Birth of an Opera*. Anyone wanting to know details of the harrowing story of the birth of *Carmen* cannot do better than to consult the chapter on *Carmen* in Rose's excellent book.

7. Halévy, quoted in Rose, 217.

8. I have yet to find any source to convince me that Bizet actually said about this aria, "If they want trash, I'll give them trash," as has been widely reported.

9. Mina Curtiss, *Bizet and His World*, 378.

10. Soon after Bizet would hire Vincent D'Indy, then a student at the Conservatory, to play just enough harmonium in the wings to keep him on.

11. Halévy, quoted in Rose, 223.

12. Charles Pigot, *Georges Bizet et Son Oeuvre*, 193. Making matters worse, the sets having been finished only just in time, scene changes were interminably long.

13. Lesley Wright, ed., *Georges Bizet, Carmen, Dossier de Presse Parisienne (1875)*, i.

14. Victorin Joncières, *La Liberté*, March 8, 1875, quoted in the *Dossier*, 41, 42; translated by the author.

15. Winton Dean, *Bizet*, 226.

16. M. de Thémines, *La Patrie*, quoted in the *Dossier*, 55; translated by the author.

17. Oscar Commetant, *Le Siècle*, April 23, 1883; translated in Curtiss, 403, 404.

18. Unnamed critic, quoted in Curtiss, 358.

19. Thomas rewrote parts of it for the soprano Christine Nilsson who was the first to take it to England and subsequently the United States.

20. Unnamed columnist, quoted in Curtiss, 355. Though Malherbe in *Carmen*, 291, says that Galli-Marié knew it had been offered to Bouffar, explaining her early ill humor, the author has found nothing to corroborate this.

21. Roze letter to Bizet, September 7, 1873, quoted in Curtiss, 355.

22. Letter from Galli-Marié to du Locle, December 18, 1873, quoted in Curtiss, 364.

23. *Ibid.*, January 2, 1874, quoted in Curtiss, 368.

24. After Bizet's death Geneviève married the lawyer Emile Straus. Her salons, visited by the intellectuals and artists of the period, were renowned. A friend of Marcel Proust, she is said to have been the model for Oriane, the Duchess of Guermantes in *Remembrance of Things Past*.

25. Curtiss, 406.

26. Unnamed critic, quoted in Curtis, 358.

27. Prosper Mérimée, *Carmen and Other Stories*, Oxford, 28, 44.

28. Henry Malherbe, *Carmen*, 176.

29. Félia Litvinne, *Ma Vie et Mon Art*, 25.

30. Théodore de Banville, *Le National*, March 8, 1875, quoted in Wright, *Dossier de Presse Parisienne*; translated by the author.

31. Modest Tchaikovsky, quoted in David Brown, *Tchaikovsky: The Crisis Years*, 58.

32. Mérimée, *Carmen and Other Stories*, Oxford, 14.

33. Léon Escudier, *L'Art Musicale*, March 11, 1875, quoted in Wright, *Dossier*, 105.

34. Evan Baker, *From the Score to the Stage*, 230.

35. Karen Henson, *Opera Acts*, 84.

36. Merimée, *Carmen*, Oxford, 20, 21.

37. Henri Blaze de Bury, quoted and translated in Henson, 87.

38. Klein, *The Golden Age of Opera*, 128.

39. When Minnie Hauk became a famous Carmen in London in 1878 she told the impresario Strakosch that she regretted she had never met Bizet, only to be told that, in fact, she had. For Bizet had been the young man who accompanied her in some songs she sang at a party given by Théophile Gautier in 1869. More incredibly, Mérimée was at the same party. Hauk, 52.

40. Klein, *Golden Age of Opera*, 129.

41. Blanche Arral, *The Extraordinary Adventures of Blanche Arral*, 73.

42. Though Bizet's friend Ernest Guiraud has written that Carmen's first aria underwent 13 rewritings at the instigation of Galli-Marié, the Bizet scholar Lesley A. Wright questions both the number and Galli-Marié's involvement. In any case, one of the earlier versions, which has been recorded by both Angela Gheorghiu and Elina Garanča, can only be described as a charming but routine showpiece.

43. Henri Blaze de Bury, *Revue des Deux*

Mondes, March 15, 1875; quoted from Wright and translated in Henson, 50.

44. Unnamed critic after her debut in 1862 in Pergolesi's *La Serva Padrona*, quoted in Curtiss, 358.

45. Letter from Hector Berlioz to Pauline Viardot, September 21, 1862, quoted in Rémy Stricker, *Georges Bizet*, 226, and translated by the author.

46. Brown, *Tchaikovsky, The Crisis Years*, 58.

47. Mathilde Marchesi, *Marchesi and Music*, 197.

48. Saint-Saëns, quoted in D. C. Parker, *Carmen*, 38.

49. Arral, 73.

50. Named for the French soprano Louise-Rosalie Dugazon (1755–1821), a *dugazon* voice–sometimes referred to as a Galli-Marié voice–was a light mezzo or dark-hued soubrette soprano.

51. Curtiss, 365

52. D. C. Parker, *Bizet*, 37.

53. Arral, 73.

54. Klein, 129.

55. Quoted in Malherbe, 296, *Entrée de Carmen: Absolument le Costume et l'Entrée Indiquée par Mérimée*. This author, however, has never seen those instructions in a published score.

56. Merimée, *Carmen*, Oxford, 20–21.

57. Winton Dean, *Bizet*, 126.

58. Charles Pigot, quoted by Curtiss, 420.

59. Ernest Reyer, quoted and translated by Curtiss, 421. Reyer's actual words appear on p. 308 in Reyer's *Quarante Ans de Musique* as a footnote provided by Emile Heriot, who also wrote the preface. According to Heriot, Reyer, who was Bizet's friend, wrote the full description of the "anecdote" on a piece of paper, dated 21 November 1875. It reads in full: *"Un soir madame Galli-Marié ressenti une impression inaccoutumée en lisant dans son jeu des presage de mort. Son coeur battait a rompre, et il lui semblait qu'un froid malsain était dans l'air. Rentré dans la coulisse, après des efforts violents pour aller jusqu'a la fin du morceau, elle s'évanouit. Quand elle revint a elle, on essaya de la calmer, de la reassurer, la meme pensée l'obedésait toujours, le meme presentiment la troublait. Mais ce n'était pas pour elle qu'elle avait peur: elle chanta donc, puisqu'ill fallait chanter. Le lendemain, madame Galli-Marié apprenait que, dans la nuit, Bizet était mort! Je sais bien que les esprits forts hausseront les épauls."* Pigot gives a similar account, also as a footnote, in his book *Georges Bizet et Son Oeuvre*, 247. His description, he says, was given him by Bizet's friend Ernest Guiraud, who witnessed it.

60. Quoted in Curtiss, but with no citation.

Chapter 2

1. Minnie Hauk, *Memories of a Singer*, 172.

2. Though, according to Gaudier and Pigot, Bizet signed the contract shortly before he died, he apparently had known about Vienna's interest in it before. In a letter, dated June 7, a friend, Léon Husson, describes seeing Bizet the day before he left for Bougival, where the composer told him, he looked forward to making the changes needed for the opera to be produced in Vienna. This letter is quoted in Hervé Lacombe's *Bizet*, 677.

3. As Guiraud could only partially complete this huge task in time for the premiere, it seems the first Vienna performances were a mix of dialogue and sung recitative.

4. Just one month after creating Carmen for the city, Ehnn would sing Elisabeth in the Vienna premiere of *Tannhäuser* with Wagner conducting.

5. *Neue Freie Presse*, October 26, 1875.

6. Henri-Étienne Dérivis and Prosper Dérivis, respectively.

7. Ludovic Halévy, *L'Art du Théâtre*, January 1905, quoted in Parker, 69.

8. Charles Gaudier, 40. The Brussels premiere was performed without the ballet but with Guiraud's recitatives (now intact).

9. Hauk, 161.

10. *Ibid.*, 144.

11. *Ibid.*, 149.

12. *Ibid.*, 159.

13. *Ibid.*, 163.

14. Klein, *The Golden Age of Opera*, 66–67. Later, Klein would write even more positively in *The Gramophone and the Singer*.

15. Luigi Arditi, *Reminiscences*, 194. Arditi both conducted Hauk in the role and knew her well personally.

16. Hauk, 164.
17. Herman Klein, *The Reign of Patti*, 225–226.
18. "Mme. Patti as Carmen," *New York Times*, April 19, 1887.
19. Klein, *The Reign of Patti*, 227.
20. *New York Times*, January 10, 1884.
21. Klein, *Golden Age of Opera*, 69.
22. G. B. Shaw, *Dramatic Opinions and Essays*, Vol. 2, 12.
23. *Neues Wiener Tagblatt*, February 28, 1879.
24. Marcel Prawy, *The Vienna Opera*, 41.
25. Henry T. Finck, *Success in Music*, 129.
26. Lilli Lehmann, *My Path Through Life*, 80.
27. Finck, 128.
28. Herman Klein, *The Golden Age of Opera*, 90.
29. Joseph Bennett, *Daily Telegraph*, as quoted in Klein, *The Golden Age of Opera*, 90.
30. *Times*, June 29, 1882.
31. Henry Krehbiel, *Review of the New York Musical Season 1886–1887*, 180.

Chapter 3

1. *Sydney Morning Herald*, December 6, 1880.
2. Georges Bizet, letter to Galabert in 1865, quoted in Curtis, 430.
3. All material on the Swedish premiere and Olfine Moe, including the recollections of Fröding, can be found in "Olfine Moe (1850–1933): Sveriges förste Carmen," by Johanna Grut, Moe's great granddaughter. I am indebted to Hans Gränbeck for sending the essay to me and to Winifred Hallwachs for translating the relevant portions of it.
4. Anne Sofie von Otter, *Opera News*, May 1997.
5. Boris Schwarz, *Music and Musical Life in Soviet Russia*, 266.
6. Julie A. Buckler, *The Literary Lorgnette, Attending Opera in Imperial Russia*, 64.
7. Félia Litvinne, *Ma Vie et Mon Art*, 102.
8. Sergei Levik, *The Levik Memoirs: An Opera Singer's Notes*, 198.
9. *The Argus*, Melbourne, May 16, 1879.
10. *The Age*, Melbourne, May 15, 1879.
11. *The Herald*, Melbourne, May 15, 1879.
12. Winton Dean, "*Carmen*'s Place in History," liner notes to Solti recording.
13. *New York Times*, March 28, 1880.
14. *El Correo Catalan*, August 1, 1881, quoted by Elizabeth Kertesz and Michael Christoforidis in "Confronting *Carmen* beyond the Pyrenees: Bizet's opera in Madrid, 1887–1888," 80.
15. In 2014, the Teatro de la Zarzuela, again attempting to make the connection between opera and zarzuela, used much of the same Spanish translation.
16. Kertesz and Christoforidis, "Confronting Carmen," 98–99.
17. Pasqua had begun her career as a soprano, having made her debut as Oscar in *Un Ballo in Maschera* in Perugia in 1868. She changed to mezzo in 1876.
18. *New York Times*, October 24, 1878.
19. *New York Times*, November 2, 1878.
20. Clara Louise Kellogg, *Memoirs of an American Prima Donna*, 290.
21. *Philadelphia Bulletin*, October 26, 1878.
22. *New York Times*, October 16, 1880, and March 20, 1881.
23. Schwerke, "Salute to Minnie Hauk," *Opera News*, March 19, 1945. Schwerke knew Hauk and says that of her many titles she liked it best when they called her "The Inventor of Carmen."
24. Kellogg, 291. "Other times, other manners."
25. In New Orleans the Carmen was probably Emilie Ambré, whose portrait in the role by Eduard Manet now hangs in the Philadelphia Museum of Art.

Chapter 4

1. Leon Kerst, *Le Voltaire*, November 29, 1883. *Enfin! Carmen nous est rendue*.
2. See Appendix B for *Carmen*'s complete progress.
3. Letter form Galli-Marié to Geneviève Bizet, August 1881, quoted in Curtiss, 430. Describing its reception in Barcelona as "a great success," however, contradicts the indifference paid it as noted by Kertesz and Christoforidis and remarked upon in the last chapter.
4. Letter from Galli-Marié to Geneviève Bizet, June 1882, quoted in Curtis, 432.

5. It is possible that Carvalho scheduled the first performance just after the premiere of Delibes's *Lakme* in the hopes it would be overshadowed by the Delibes. Lesley A. Wright describes the whole event in a fascinating article, "Rewriting a Reception: Thoughts on *Carmen* in Paris, 1883," *Journal of Musicological Research*, 28.

6. Pierre Veron, *Le Charivari*, April 24, 1883; translation by author.

7. Arnold Mortier, *Le Figaro*, April 22, 1883, quoted by Lesley A. Wright, "Rewriting a Reception: Thoughts on *Carmen* in Paris, 1883," *Journal of Musicological Research*, 28, 2009, 288.

8. Charles de Sivry, "Reprise de Carmen," *Ville de Paris*, 23 April 1883, 2; quoted in Wright, 288.

9. Halevy quoted in Strickland, 283. From a letter to du Locle dated April 1883.

10. Wright, 293

11. Alphonse Duvernoy, "Musique," *La République Française*, October 31, 1883, as quoted in Wright.

12. This is clear in photographs. Moreover, Malherbe calls her "round."

13. Quoted in Curtiss, 435.

14. *New York Times*, December 14, 1890. Galli-Marié would live out her life with her second husband in Nice, where she taught till her death in 1905.

15. This move is described in a later chapter. But shortly before the Second World War, as government subsidies dried up, it was determined the only way that the Opéra-Comique could survive was to join the larger Opéra de Paris. By then the contracts described at the beginning of this chapter were long gone. The move was successful for a while, but the larger company slowly absorbed the smaller, which closed completely in 1972, not to reopen until 1990 back at the Salle Favart.

16. The company played in other theaters while waiting for the Favart to be rebuilt. This was actually the third Salle Favart as the first had also been destroyed by fire. The theater was declared an historic monument in 1977.

17. Georgette Leblanc, *Souvenirs*, 52.

18. Though Carl Van Vechten supplies this translation in his "Music of Spain," 128, the original article in French by Fierens-Gevaert is found in *Le Guide Musical*, no. 40, June 10, 1895, under the title "Une Chanteuse."

19. Leblanc, *Souvenirs*, 161.

20. Albert Carré, *Souvenirs de Théâtre*, 239; translated by the author.

21. Leblanc, 164.

22. Carré, 240.

23. Fedora Barbieri in "Many Colored Carmen," as quoted by Mary Jane Matz, *Opera News*, January 26, 1953.

24. Byrant Manning, interview with Natalie Dessay, *Time Out Chicago*, Issue 187, September 25–October 1, 2008; Chicago.timeout.com.

25. Charles Gounod, quoted in "Decline and Fall" by Barrymore Lawrence Scherer, *Opera News*, December 6, 1986.

26. Lorraine Hunt-Lieberson, as quoted in "The Carmen Challenge," Steven Blier, *Opera News*, December 1998.

27. This, Arnaud's one and only performance with the company, is actually better remembered as the performance when the bridge in Act One collapsed, sending eight choristers to the ground.

28. Anna Arnaud, "Pleads for a Better Carmen," *Musical America*, January 16, 1909.

29. D.C. Parker, *Bizet*, 39.

30. Jeanne Marié de l'Isle, as quoted in Gabriel Bernard, "Carmen and Carmens," *La Revue Théâtral*, January 1905; translated by Alison Jourdet.

31. Available on the Marston label.

32. Though we don't hear it in these recordings, Parker writes that it was Marié de l'Isle who introduced the *"tambour de basque"* (tambourine) in the *Chanson Bohemiènne*.

33. John Culshaw, *Opera News*, December 13, 1975.

34. *Comment on ne doit pas interpreter Carmen, Faust, et Pelléas*, Heugel, 1923.

35. Vincent Sheean, *First and Last Love*, 73.

36. Alberto Innaurato, "Anatomy of a Seduction," *Opera News*, May 1996.

37. Arthur Bloomfield, *Fifty Years of the San Francisco Opera*, 61.

38. Tarquini D'Or, quoted in Bernard "Carmen and Carmens."

39. Marie Castagné, quoted in "Carmens et Carmen."

40. *New York Times*, December 26, 1909.
41. Breval, Lucienne, "De l'interprétation de Carmen" *Musica-Noël*, No. 87, December 1909.
42. *Gil Blas*, February 25, 1909.

Chapter 5

1. Quoted in Arthur Wisner, *Emma Calvé, Her Artistic Life*; no date given.
2. Carl van Vechten, *Music of Spain*, 125
3. *Sunday Times of London*, December 4, 1892.
4. Marie of Romania, *Story of My Life*, Vol. 1, 234–236.
5. Queen Victoria had studied singing with the famous bass Luigi Lablache.
6. Extracts from the *Queens Journal* were provided to the author by the Sophia Smith Collection, which houses the De Lussan archives.
7. Charles Darcourt, *Le Figaro*, 15 December 1892, as quoted by Van Vechten in *The Music of Spain*, 127.
8. Harry P. Mawson, found in a scrapbook; probably from *Musical America*.
9. Helen Sheehy, *Eleanora Duse*, 32–33.
10. Calvé, *My Life*, 60.
11. Quoted in William Weaver, *Duse*, 216. Duse and Calvé would become friends.
12. Klein, *Golden Age of Opera*, 159.
13. See the chapter Breaking Away.
14. G. B. Shaw, *Dramatic Opinions and Essays*, 14.
15. Henry T. Finck, *Evening Post*, December 21, 1893, as quoted in *Success in Music*, 149.
16. W. H. Henderson, *New York Times*, December 21, 1893. Henderson's name, however, does not appear on the review.
17. Henderson, *New York Times*, December 11, 1896.
18. Emma Calvé, *My Life*, 81.
19. Frederic Dean, *New York Times*, October 31, 1920.
20. Peggy Wood, "I Remember Emma," *Opera News*, February 6, 1971.
21. Shaw, Vol. 3, 226.
22. Susan Rutherford, *The Prima Donna and Opera*, 269.
23. Helen Sheehy, *Eleanora Duse: A Biography*, 5.
24. *Musical America*, interview with Calvé, April 20, 1907.
25. W. H. Henderson, quoted in Rupert Christiansen, *Prima Donna*, 273.
26. Emma Calvé, quoted in Christianson, 273.
27. Arthur Pougin, *Le Ménestrel*, December 18, 1892, as quoted in *Music, Theater and Cultural Transfer*, 375.
28. So famous was Calvé's portrayal that Arthur Rubinstein actually thought Calvé had created the role of Carmen.
29. *New York Times*, December 15, 1906.
30. Vincent Sheean, *Oscar Hammerstein 1*, 175.
31. Helen Sheehy, *Eleanora Duse*, 78.
32. *Musical America*, November 1907.
33. Interview, a clipping from an unidentified magazine, January 1907, found in the New York Library of Performing Arts.
34. Algernon St. John-Brenon, *The Morning Telegraph*, no date, quoted in Robert Tuggle, *The Golden Age of Opera*, 42.
35. Blanche Marchesi, *Singer's Pilgrimage*, 47.

Chapter 6

1. Anonymous critic from the *Extrablatt*, describing Gutheil-Schoder, quoted in De la Grange, Vol. 2, 253.
2. Anonymous critic for *Musical Courier*, of a performance of *Carmen* at the Opéra-Comique, November 5, 1902, with Charlotte Wyns and Albert Alvarez as Carmen and Don José respectively.
3. *New York World*, November 14, 1907.
4. Finck (no citation or first name, but, presumably, Henry T.), quoted in Lahee, *Grand Opera Singers of Today*, 230. Riding the wave of her Elektra, Mazarin was asked to sing an aria from *Carmen* from the stage of the Manhattan Opera House via the "radio telephone," as it was then called. It was the first time a singing voice was sent over the air-waves and when she learned that some sailors had actually heard it at sea, the soprano was only too happy to follow up with excerpts from *Elektra*. One can only imagine the reaction.
5. Van Vechten, *Interpreters*, 121.
6. *New York Times*, November 26, 1909.
7. *The Press* [Philadelphia], November

18, 1908, quoted in John F. Cone *The Manhattan Opera Company*, 183.

8. During World War I, the Italians arrested Labia as a German spy and incarcerated her for a year in Ancona.

9. *New York Times*, September 2, 1909.

10. Mrs. George B. Carpenter, *Chicago Daily Journal*, April 5, 1906. This review is from the Metropolitan on tour in Chicago. Soon after the company moved on to San Francisco, where Fremstad sang Carmen to Caruso's José only hours before the deadly earthquake struck in the early morning of April 18.

11. Olive Fremstad, quoted in Mary Watkins Cushing, "A Complexity of Gypsies," *Opera News*, February 6, 1960.

12. An eyewitness remembering the occasion for *Musical America*, December 19, 1911, quoted in the *Record Collector*, March 1997.

13. Geraldine Farrar, *Such Sweet Compulsion*, 126.

14. Sergei Levik, *The Levik Memoirs: An Opera Singer's Notes*, 102.

15. Levik, 103.

16. *Ibid.*, 102.

17. *Ibid.*, 107.

18. Listen, for example, to the contralto Eugenia Zbrueva in Carmen's final confrontation with José.

19. Levik, 407.

20. Allan Keiler, *Marian Anderson, A Singer's Journey*, 148.

21. Marian Anderson, *My Lord What a Morning*, 177.

22. Levik, 514, 515, 518.

23. *Ibid.*, 468, 469.

24. Olga Haldey, *Mamontov's Private Opera*, 5. Mamontov was an older cousin of Stanislavski and a clear inspiration.

25. Max Graf, *Legend of a Musical City*, 160.

26. *Times of London*, July 4, 1895.

27. Michael Aspinall, liner notes, *The Creators of Verismo, Volume 1*, Marston, 2010.

28. Michael Scott, *The Record of Singing*, 148.

29. Henry-Louis de La Grange, *Mahler*, 448. Renard, who had begun her career as a mezzo, was also a popular Mignon, Manon, and Charlotte in *Werther*.

30. De La Grange, *Mahler*, 478.

31. G. S. L., *Musical Courier*, October 31, 1901.

32. Max Kalbeck, *Neues Wiener Journal*, quoted in De la Grange, *Mahler, Vienna the Years of Challenge*, 254.

33. Gustav Mahler, quoted in de la Grange, *Mahler, Vienna the Years of Challenge*, 253.

34. Carl Van Vechten, *Interpreters*, 193.

35. Reginald de Koven, *New York Herald*, February 22, 1919.

36. Mary Garden with Louis Biancolli, *Mary Garden's Story*, 228

37. According to Jim McPherson in "A Mary Garden Scrapbook" (*Record Collector*, June 1996) she sang Carmen in 1935 at the Cleveland Municipal Stadium. It would have been her last operatic performance anywhere.

38. Mary Garden, quoted in "The Garden District," *Opera News*, August 2004.

Chapter 7

1. Colette, "Emma Calvé," *Opera*, April 1955. The Colette here is the famous French novelist Sidmie-Gabrielle Colette, who was a friend of Calvé.

2. *Geraldine Farrar: The Story of an American Singer by Herself*, 112.

3. Frederic Dean, "Carmens of Forty-Two Years," *New York Times*, October 31, 1920.

4. *Musical America*, quoted in Cardell Bishop, *The San Carlo Opera*, 28.

5. *Opera News*, April 21, 1958, obituary.

6. *Avisador Comercial Havana*, January 2, 1918, quoted in *Musical America*, February 2, 1918.

7. Ray C. B. Brown, critic from the *San Francisco Chronicle*, 1920, quoted in Cardell Bishop, *San Carlo Opera Company of America*, 41.

8. *The Observer*, quoted in *Two Centuries of Opera at Covent Garden*, 367.

9. Vitaphone #3336.

10. Geraldine Farrar, *Geraldine Farrar: The Story of an American Singer by Herself*, 27.

11. *New York Herald*, February 27, 1914, quoted in Elizabeth Nash, *Geraldine Farrar: Opera's Charismatic Innovator*, 82.

12. *New York Herald*, November 20, 1914, quoted in Nash, 86.

13. Richard Aldrich, *New York Times*, November 20, 1914, quoted in Nash, 87.
14. Nash, 91.
15. Lesley Mason, "Carmen," *Motion Picture News*, November 13, 1915, quoted in Nash, 97.
16. Geraldine Farrar, *Such Sweet Compulsion*, 169.
17. Farrar would return in future summers to film *Joan the Woman* and some fourteen other films.
18. *Musical America*, October 6, 1918.
19. In 1915 a full-length film directed by Raoul Walsh with Theda Bara as Carmen also appeared to considerable acclaim. The film has been lost, but Bara wrote an article about it for *the New York Mail*, entitled "My Wild, Free, Untrammeled Carmen."
20. Arthur E. Knight, Fifty Great Vocal Records, *The Record Collector*, Vol. IX, No. 8 January 1955, 182.
21. Farrar and Watkins, "Diva's Decades," *Saturday Evening Post*, January 16, 1932, quoted in Nash, 110.
22. Geraldine Farrar, *Such Sweet Compulsion*, 170.
23. Geraldine Farrar, quoted by Dean Frederic in *The Bookman*, Vol. XLII, No. 4, December 1915, 412.
24. Henry T. Parker, "Mme. Farrar as Carmen," *Boston Evening Transcript*, April 6, 1916, quoted in Nash, 111–112.
25. Geraldine Farrar from Frederick T. Martens, *The Art of the Prima Donna and Concert Singer*, quoted in Nash, 86.
26. *Ibid.*, 86.
27. Robert Baxter, liner notes, "Geraldine Farrar," Marston Records.
28. Geraldine Farrar, quoted in liner notes by Roland Vernon, "Farrar in French Opera," Prima Voce.
29. Roland Vernon, liner notes, "Geraldine Farrar, in French Opera," Nimbus Records, 1995.
30. Geraldine Farrar, *Such Sweet Compulsion*, 194.
31. Her principal teachers were Emma Thursby in New York and Lilli Lehmann in Germany.
32. Vernon, liner notes.

Chapter 8

1. Goffredo Petrassi, quoted in Harvey Sachs, *Music in Fascist Italy*, 144.
2. *New York Times*, March 3, 1923.
3. Farrar, *Such Sweet Compulsion*, 139. In her own memoirs, Jeritza insists that it was Puccini's wish to keep the infamous pose after she accidentally fell into it during a rehearsal.
4. W. H. Henderson, *The Art of Singing*, 478.
5. Henderson, *New York Post*, January 14, 1928, found in *The Art of Singing*, 347.
6. Olin Downes, *New York Times*, January 14, 1928.
7. W. H. Henderson, *The New York Sun* (January 1929, exact date not given), from the Metopera Database.
8. Formerly, the Court Opera; renamed after the Great War by the Ministry of Culture.
9. Ferderic Spotts, *Hitler and the Power of Aesthetics*, 230.
10. Susan McClary, *Carmen*, 125.
11. A movie, *The Girl of Your Dreams* (*La Niña de Tus Ojos*), starring Penelope Cruz, is based on the making of these films. In it, Goebbels replaces Hitler, who was rumored to have been in love with Argentina.
12. Lotte Lehmann, *My Many Lives*, 174.
13. Thomas Mann, *Magic Mountain*, 602.
14. Though not totally complete, Marston, who transferred it to CD, tells us that the 78s employed 36 sides (20 on ten-inch discs and 16 on 12-inch.)
15. Sidney Homer, *My Wife and I*, 191. Though Louise Homer once studied Carmen herself, she never performed it, illness preventing a single scheduled performance at the Met.
16. Homer, 191.
17. As recounted in the Supraphon documentary *Emmy Destinn, the Greatest Czech Soprano*.
18. Vaclav Holzknecht and Bohumil Trita, *Ema Destinnova*, 61.
19. Guy Dumazert, liner notes, *Les Grandes Carmen*.
20. Olin Downes, *New York Times*, January 25, 1926.
21. *New York Times*, July 10, 1923.

22. Downes, *New York Times*, January 25, 1926.
23. *New York Times*, September 29, 1936.
24. Nadezhda Obukhova, *Nadezhda Andreevna Obukhova*, Moscow, 1970, 105ff; trans. Ella Barova.
25. Kurt Malisch, liner notes, *Vocal Artistry Behind the Iron Curtain—Russian Singers of the Era* (Lebendige Vergangenheit).
26. Maria Maksakova, *Maria Petrovna Maksakova*, Moscow, 1985, 94ff; trans. Ella Barova.
27. John Rosselli, *Singers of Italian Opera*, 209.
28. Lina Pagliughi, quoted in *The Last Prima Donna*, Lanfranco Rasoni, 171.
29. Arthur Rubinstein, *My Many Years*, 20.
30. Vincent Sheean, *First and Last Love*, 83ff.
31. According to Stefan Zucker, Bel Canto Society.
32. Gina Cigna, quoted by Lanfranco Rasponi, *The Last Prima Donnas*, 209.
33. Florica Cristoforeanu was a Romanian soprano, who also sang Carmen in Italy, following Zinetti in the role at La Scala for 4 performances, after which the opera was not performed until 1936 when Pederzini assumed the role.
34. Gianna Pederzini, quoted by Lanfranco Rasponi, 301.
35. Conchita Supervia, quoted in an interview in *Musical Courier*, June 15, 1935.
36. Supervia created the title role of *Der Rosenkavalier* for Italy in Rome in 1911.
37. Edward Moore, *Forty Years of Opera in Chicago*, 151.
38. Louis Schneider, L Réouverture de l'Opéra-Comique, *Miroir du Monde*, November 19, 1932; translated by the author.
39. Harold Rosenthal, *Two Centuries of Opera at Covent Garden*, 500.
40. John Steane, "Carmen: not just hips and lipstick," *International Opera Collector*, Winter 1996.

Chapter 9

1. *Musical Courier*, April 5, 1943.
2. Adolf Hitler, monologue, as quoted in Frederic Spotts, *Hitler and the Power of Aesthetics*, 107.
3. *Musical Courier*, March 1, 1945.
4. "Happy Birthday, Carmen," *Opera News*, December 13, 1975.
5. Dorothy Kirsten with Lanfranco Rasponi, *A Time to Sing*, 37.
6. Edward Moore, *Chicago Daily Tribune*, from a promotional ad in *Musical America*, February 2, 1929.
7. *Times-Star*, Cincinnati, no date; from a brochure of her reviews.
8. Irving Kolodin, *New York Sun*, October 13, 1946, from publicity material for *Musical America*, February 1948.
9. Harold Rosenthal, *Two Centuries of Opera at Covent Garden*, 667.
10. A runner-up in the Metropolitan Auditions of the Air in 1939, Heidt had sung small roles with the company but was let go after one season after her first husband reportedly accused her of neglecting her family and blamed the Met in their divorce proceedings. Though the famous tenor had nothing to do with this "scandal," she would later marry Eugene Conley.
11. Quoted in "Edward Johnson Announces," *Musical Leader*, June 8, 1935.
12. Rosa Ponselle and James Drake, *Rosa Ponselle: A Singers Life*, 143.
13. Ponselle, quoted in James Drake, *Rosa Ponselle: A Centenary Biography*, 275.
14. Rosa Ponselle and James Drake, fn, 147.
15. *New York Times*, December 28, 1935.
16. *Time*, January 6, 1936.
17. Olin Downes, *New York Times*, January 17, 1936.
18. The Spring Season was an experiment; a short season after the regular season to bring in more revenue and give lesser-known singers a chance. It only lasted two years.
19. Pitts Sanborn, *New York World-Telegram*, May 12, 1936, from promotional material in *Musical America*.
20. Lawrence Gilmore, *New York Herald Tribune*, May 12, 1936.
21. *Time*, May 25, 1936.
22. Phillip Miller, *American Record Guide*, July 1969.
23. Marjorie M. Fisher, *Musical America*, November 25, 1936.
24. Herbert Peyser, *New York Times*, June 19, 1938.
25. *New York Times*, January 25, 1942.

26. *Opera News*, November 19, 1960.
27. One time in 1942 Swarthout actually cancelled a matinee performance of *Carmen* in Chicago because she was afraid she would not get back to New York in time for a broadcast. Coe Glade replaced her.
28. Robert Coleman, *New York Daily Mirror*, no date given, quoted in *Opera News*, January 2001.
29. Virgil Thomson, *New York Herald Tribune*, March 9, 1945.
30. Robert Lawrence, *New York Herald Tribune*, February 24, 1942.
31. Paul Hume, *Washington Post*, March 2, 1975.
32. Mary Jane Phillips-Matz, *Rosa Ponselle, American Diva*, 272.
33. Margaret Howard, "Muelle — Known to Every Singer" *New York Times*, August 25, 1915.
34. Marie Castagne of the Opéra-Comique, however, claimed to have introduced the full body shawl.
35. Valentina, "Designing for Opera," *Opera News*, March 10, 1941.
36. *Newsweek*, "Letters," February 25, 1952.
37. Victoria Etnier Villamil, *From Johnson's Kids to Lemonade Opera*, 95.
38. Jerome Bohm, *New York Herald Tribune*, December 29, 1945.
39. Arthur Berger, *New York Herald Tribune*, December 2, 1946.

Chapter 10

1. Rudolf Bing, *5000 Nights at the Opera*, 148.
2. Richard Wagner to Christian Stocks, *Selected Letters*, quoted in Evan Baker, *From the Score to the Stage*, 208.
3. *Musical Courier*, April 5, 1943.
4. Tyrone Guthrie, *A Life in the Theater*, 250.
5. Cecil Smith, *Musical America*, February 1952.
6. *Time*, February 11, 1952.
7. A. M. Nagler. *Misdirection, Opera Production in the Twentieth Century*, 95–99.
8. Helena Matheopoulos, *Diva*, 14.
9. Lotfi Mansouri, 56.
10. Walter Felsenstein, quoted in Peter Paul Fuchs, *The Music Theater of Walter Felsenstein*, 133.
11. Felsenstein, quoted in Fuchs, 92.
12. John Higgins, *London Times*, March 9, 1972.
13. Cecil Smith, *Opera Annual, 1954–5*, 52.
14. Smith, *Opera*, August 1955.
15. *New York Times*, December 16, 1967.
16. Steven Blier, *Opera News*, December 1998.
17. Callas was not the only singer to record but never perform the role of Carmen. Leontyne Price, Jesse Norman and Anna Moffo are other notable examples, and, of course, the examples of singers who recorded Carmen's arias but not the complete role are without number.
18. Carlo Marinelli, quoted in Simionato, *How Cinderella Became a Queen*, 115.
19. Fedora Barbieri, interview with Mary Jane Matz, *Opera News*, January 26, 1953.
20. Steven Blier, *Opera News*, December 1998.
21. *Time*, March 28, 1960.
22. Critic for *Bild-Telegraf* quoted by *New York Times*, December 25, 1955.
23. Sydney Gruson, *New York Times*, December 25, 1955.
24. *Time*, March 26, 1956.
25. Christa Ludwig, *In My Own Voice*, 76.
26. Ludwig, 76.
27. Jay S. Harrison, *New York Herald Tribune*, October 17, 1958.
28. *Paris Presse, L'Intransigeante*, February 3, 1964. The Triumph of Regina Resnik. An extraordinary, spell-binding, captivating, disquieting Carmen."
29. Robert Potterton, *The Record Collector*, Vol. XVII, No. 8, December 1967.
30. Ida Cook, *Opera*, "Regina Resnik," January 1963.
31. Verrett, 82.
32. *Musical America*, December 10, 1943.
33. Grace Bumbry, quoted in Rosalyn M. Storey, *And So I Sing*, 167.
34. Shirley Verrett, *I Never Walked Alone*, 117, 118.
35. Felsenstein, 86.
36. *Carmen* would not return to the Salle Favart until 1980 after which time it could finally be performed anywhere in Paris.

37. The Palais Garnier, which had been under construction since 1861, had had its inaugural performance just two months before the premiere of *Carmen* at the Salle Favart.

38. They included De Gaulle, who entered to *Aida*'s Triumphal March, Ingrid Bergman, Jean Cocteau, Coco Chanel, the Spanish Ambassador, and the Shah of Iran. The political ramifications inherent in the occasion were huge.

39. "Paris Opéra's Spectacular New Production of Carmen," *London Times*, November 16, 1959.

40. René Violier, *La Tribune de Geneve*, December 22, 1959. "Without doubt this Carmen deserves a place in the history of the Opéra next to the Violetta of Claudia Muzio and the Medea of Maria Callas." Translated by the author.

41. Richard RePass, *Opera*, February 1961.

42. *Opera*, February 1961.

43. Harold Schonberg, *New York Times*, November 16, 1960.

44. Robert L. A. Clark, "South of North: Carmen and French Nationalisms," included in *East of West, Cross-cultural Performance and the Staging of Difference*, 210, 211. The "white" Carmen is not identified.

Chapter 11

1. *Opera News*, "Happy Birthday, Carmen," December 13, 1975.

2. Donal Henahan, "Carmen—Opera's Liberated Woman," *New York Times*, March 7, 1975.

3. Gail Lavielle, from her title *Carmen: The Seduction of the Century*.

4. In addition to Crespin, Carmens attending: Rosalind Elias, Sandra Warfield, Joann Grillo, Joanna Simon, Winifred Heidt, Coe Glade, Irra Petina, Claramae Turner, Risë Stevens, Regina Resnik.

5. Shirley Verrett, *I Never Walked Alone*, 124.

6. The Metropolitan had not used the original dialogue since Lilli Lehmann made her debut in the role on November 25, 1885, and the opera was performed in German. Reviewing that performance, the critic for the *New York Times* observed that the use of dialogue contributed to the "lightness and briskness" of the opera.

7. Harold Schonberg, *New York Times*, September 20, 1972.

8. Most notable of these was Horne's leap to a high B on the last syllable of *la liberté* and subsequent more than two octave plunge to a chest-heavy A below middle C.

9. Régine Crespin, "Ma Carmen," *L'Avant-scène*, mars-avril, 1980. The composer Ned Rorem believed the same.

10. *New York Times*, "Crespin's Carmen Is in Love with Death," December 7, 1975.

11. Peter Davis, "Crespin acts Carmen at the Met," *London Times*, December 9, 1975.

12. *New York Times*, November 11, 1977.

13. Supervia and Gay were also from Barcelona.

14. Teresa Berganza, quoted in Helena Matheopoulos, *Diva*, 252.

15. Berganza, Matheopoulos, 253.

16. Berganza, from a letter to Peter Diamond, that appeared in the Edinburgh Festival program, August and September 1977, translated from the Spanish (no translator named).

17. Berganza, letter to Diamond.

18. Claudia Cassidy, *Chicago Daily Tribune*, November 17, 1954.

19. Julia Migenes-Johnson, quoted in Enrique Fernández, "Carmen Cojones," *The Village Voice*, September 1984.

20. Fernández, *The Village Voice*, September 1984.

21. Pauline Kael, *The New Yorker*, October 29, 1984.

22. Fernández, *The Village Voice*, September 1984.

23. Elina Garanča, quoted in "Gypsy in Her Soul," *Opera News*, January 2010.

24. Leslie Rubinstein, *Opera News*, October 1984.

25. Joseph Horowitz, *New York Times*, November 15, 1978.

26. Paul Griffiths, *London Times*, February 24, 1983.

27. Baltsa quoted in Helena Matheopoulos, *Diva*, 242.

28. Thor Eckert, Jr., *Christian Science Monitor*, March 19, 1987.

29. Donal Henahan, *New York Times*, February 14, 1987.

30. Baltsa, quoted in Matheopoulos, 243.

31. Paul Griffiths, *London Times*, May 22, 1985.
32. Donal Henahan, *New York Times*, March 12, 1986.
33. Andrew Porter, review from the *New Yorker*, April 7, 1986, as found in the author's *Musical Events, 1983–1986*, 463.
34. Joséph Volpe, *The Toughest Show on Earth, My Rise and Reign at the Metropolitan Opera*, 184.
35. Arthur Bloomfield, *San Francisco Opera*, 284.
36. Matthew Gurewitsch, *Opera News*, March 1997.
37. Bernard Holland, *New York Times*, November 2, 1996.
38. John von Rhein, *Chicago Tribune*, February 14, 2000.
39. Anne Midgette, *Washington Post*, November 10, 2008.
40. Anthony Tommasini, *New York Times*, December 2, 1996.

Chapter 12

1. "Conversation with Bruce Duffie," 1997. http://www.bruceduffie.com/kasarova.html.
2. Donald Henahan, "By the Way, the Singers Were Good Too," *New York Times*, August 23, 1987.
3. Elina Garanča; live backstage interview with René Fleming, HD broadcast, Metropolitan Opera, January 16, 2010.
4. Garanča, quoted in "Gypsy in her Soul," *Opera News*, January 2010.
5. A chat with Anita Rachvelishvilli, Maria Nockin, operatoday.com, February 4, 2015.
6. Martin Bernheimer, "Expo 86: Riotous, Avant-Garde 'Carmen' in Vancouver," *New York Times*, May 14, 1986.
7. *Ibid.*
8. *Ibid.*
9. Donald Henahan, "By the Way, the Singers Were Good Too," *New York Times*, August 23, 1987.
10. Roberto Herrscher, *Opera News*, January 2011.
11. Others leading the Bieito Carmen include Nora Gubisch, Jossie Pérez, Patricia Bardon, Ruxandra, Donose, Elena Maximova, Justina Gringyte, Ginger Costa-Jackson, Irene Roberts, Jennifer Johnson Cano.
12. Uria-Monzon can also be heard to somewhat better advantage in a 2011 pirate video of the Bieito production from Barcelona opposite Armiliato.
13. One can see Vergara as a traditional Carmen in *Placido Domingo: Hommage a Sevilla*, a documentary in which she and Domingo perform the final scene in an actual bullring.
14. Fiona Maddocks, Carmen review, *The Observer*, January 23, 2011.
15. From an interview with Viktoria Vizin in 2012, as part of a short documentary on the Vlamaase Opera production; published on YouTube February 19, 2013.
16. The filmed production can now either be rented on Amazon video or bought as a pirate.
17. Larry L. Lash, *Opera News Online*, June 2009.
18. "That 'Sweet' Word—Freedom," April 22, 2008, press release from the Bolshoi Press Office.
19. Allan Ulrich, *San Francisco Examiner*, October 23, 1996.
20. Helena Matheopoulos, interview with Olga Borodina, *Diva: The New Generation*, 269.
21. Fred Cohn, *Opera News Online*, September 21, 2004.
22. Simon Williams, *Opera News*, November 2006.
23. "In Conversation with Anne Sofie von Otter," Gramophone website, November 6, 2012.
24. Simon Williams, *Opera News*, November 2014.
25. Antonacci, "Garden of Earthly Delights," interview, Times Online, December 3, 2006.
26. Régine Crespin, "Conversation with Crespin," Carlo Faria, *Opera News*, December 13, 1975.
27. M. de Thémines, *La Patrie*, translated in liner notes to Solange Michel recording.
28. Dick Pels and Aya Crébas, "Carmen—Or the Invention of a New Feminine Myth"; *The Body, Social Process and Cultural Theory*, 363.

29. James Conlon, "The Carmen Myth," *Opera News*, March 22, 1997.
30. Pels and Crébas, 361.
31. Geraldine Farrar, quoted by Dean Frederic in *The Bookman*, Vol. XLII, No. 4, December 1915, 414.

Appendix B

1. Though the information for this chronology comes from many sources, including early writers such as Charles Pigot, much also comes from *L'Avant-scène, Carmen* (1980 and 2007); a chronology by OperaGlass (http://opera.stanford.edu/Bizet/Carmen/history.html); and The Bizet Catalog compiled by Hugh MacDonald (http://digital.wustl.edu/bizet/works/Carmen.html).

Bibliography

Anderson, Marian. *My Lord, What a Morning.* Viking Press, 1956; reprint, Madison: University of Wisconsin Press, 1984.
Arral, Blanche. *The Extraordinary Operatic Adventures of Blanche Arral.* Translated by Ira Glackens, edited by William R. Moran. Portland, OR: Amadeus Press, 2002.
Arruga, Lorenzo. *La Scala.* Translated by Raymond Rosenthal. New York: Praeger, 1976.
L'Avant-scène Opéra, No. 26, *Carmen.* Premiere edition, March 1980.
L'Avant-scène Opéra, No. 26, *Carmen.* Mise à jour, February 2007.
Baker, Evan. *From the Score to the Stage: An Illustrated History of Continental Opera Production and Staging.* Chicago: University of Chicago Press, 2013.
Bennahum, Ninotchka Devorah. *Carmen: A Gypsy Geography.* Middletown, CT: Wesleyan University Press, 2013.
Bing, Rudolf. *5000 Nights at the Opera.* Garden City, NY: Doubleday, 1972.
Bloomfield, Arthur. *50 Years of the San Francisco Opera.* San Francisco: San Francisco Book Company, 1972.
Blyth, Alan. *Opera on Record.* London: Harper Colophon, 1982.
Bolitho, Hector. *Marie Tempest.* Philadelphia: J. B. Lippincott, 1937.
Brener, Milton. *Opera Offstage: Passion and Politics Behind the Great Operas.* New York: Walker and Company, 1996.
Brockway, Wallace, and Herbert Weinstock. *The World of Opera: The Story of Its Origins and the Lore of Its Performance.* New York: Pantheon, 1962.
Buckler, Julie A. *The Literary Lorgnette: Attending Opera in Imperial Russia.* Stanford: Stanford University Press, 2000.
Calve, Emma. *My Life.* Translated by Rosamond Gilder. New York: D. Appleton and Company, 1922.
Carré, Albert. *Souvenirs de Théâtre.* Paris: Librairie Plon, 1950.
Carreras, José. *José Carreras: Singing from the Soul, an Autobiography.* Originally published in German, translated by a staff of specialists. Seattle: Y.C.P. Publications, 1991.
Chapin, Schuyler. *Musical Chairs: A Life in the Arts.* New York: G. P. Putnam's Sons, 1977.
Christiansen, Rupert. *Prima Donna: A History.* London: Pimlico, Random House, 1995.
Clark, Robert L. A. "South of North: Carmen and French Nationalisms," in *East of West*, edited by Claire Sponsler and Xiaomei Chen. New York: Palgrave, 2000.
Cone, John F. *Oscar Hammerstein's Manhattan Opera Company.* Norman: University of Oklahoma Press, 1966.

Conrad, Peter. *A Song of Love and Death: the Meaning of Opera.* New York: Poseidon Press, 1987.
Contrucci, Jean. *Emma Calvé la Diva du Siècle.* Paris: Éditions Albin Michel S. A., 1989.
Cowgill, Rachel, and Hilary Poriss, eds. *The Prima Donna in the Long Nineteenth Century.* New York: Oxford University Press, 2012.
Crespin, Régine. *On Stage, Off Stage: A Memoir.* Translated by G. S. Bourdain. Boston: Northeastern University Press, 1997.
Crichton, Kyle. *Subway to the Met: Risë Stevens' Story.* Garden City, NY: Doubleday and Company, Inc., 1959.
Croyden, Margaret. *Conversations with Peter Brook 1970–2000.* New York: Faber and Faber, 2003.
Culshaw, John. *Putting the Record Straight: The Autobiography of John Culshaw.* New York: Viking Press, 1981.
Curtiss, Mina. *Bizet and His World.* New York: Alfred A. Knopf, 1958.
Cushing, Mary Watkins. *The Rainbow Bridge.* New York: G. P. Putnam's Sons, 1954.
D'Alvarez, Marguerite. *All the Bright Dreams: An Autobiography.* New York: Harcourt, Brace and Company, 1956.
Davis, Ronald L., *Opera in Chicago.* New York: Appleton-Century, 1966.
De la Grange, Henry-Louis. *Gustav Mahler, Vol. 2: Vienna, The Years of Challenge, 1897–1904.* New York: Oxford University Press, 1995.
_____. *Mahler.* New York: Doubleday, 1973.
Dean, Winton. *Bizet.* London: J. M. Dent & Sons LTD, 1965.
Dibbern, Mary. *Carmen: A Performance Guide.* Hillsdale, NY: Pendragon Press, 2000.
DiGaetani, John L., and Josef P. Sirefman, eds. *Opera and the Golden West: The Past, Present and Future of Opera in the U.S.A.* London: Associated University Presses, 1994.
Dover Opera Guide and Libretto Series. *Carmen.* Translated and introduced by Ellen H. Bleiler. New York: Dover, 1970.
Drake, James A. *Rosa Ponselle: A Centenary Biography.* Portland, OR: Amadeus Press, 1997.
Eaton, Quaintance. *The Boston Opera Company.* New York: Appleton-Century, 1965.
_____. *The Miracle of the Met: An Informal History of the Metropolitan, 1883–1967.* New York: Meredith Press, 1968.
Eisler, Paul E. *The Metropolitan Opera: The First Twenty-five Years, 1883–1908.* Croton-on-Hudson, NY: North River Press, Inc., 1984.
English National Opera, John Nicholas, series ed. *Carmen.* London: ENO, 1982.
Farrar, Geraldine. *Such Sweet Compulsion: The Autobiography of Geraldine Farrar.* New York: The Greystone Press, 1938.
Fauser, Annegret, and Mark Everist, eds. *Music Theater and Cultural Transfer, Paris, 1830–1914.* Chicago: University of Chicago Press, 2009
Fawkes, Richard. *Opera on Film.* London: Duckworth, 2000.
Fiedler, Johanna. *Molto Agitato.* New York: Nan A. Talese, 2001.
Finck, Henry T. *My Adventures in the Golden Age of Music.* New York: Funk & Wagnalls Company, 1926.
_____. *Success in Music and How It Is Won.* New York: Charles Scribner's Sons, 1922.
Fitzgerald, Gerald, and Jean Seward Uppman, eds. *Annals of the Metropolitan Opera: The Complete Chronicle of Performances and Artists: Chronology 1883–1985,* 2 vols. Boston: G. K. Hall, 1989.
Fuchs, Peter Paul, ed. and trans. *The Music Theater of Walter Felsenstein: Collected Writings.* New York: W. W. Norton, 1975.

Garden, Mary, and Louis Biancolli. *Mary Garden's Story.* New York: Simon & Schuster, 1951.
Gaudier, Charles. *Carmen de Bizet: Étude Historique et Critique Analyse Musical.* Paris: Librarie Delaplane, 1922.
Gould, Evlyn. *The Fate of Carmen.* Baltimore: Johns Hopkins University Press, 1996.
Gourret, Jean. *Encyclopédie des Cantatrices de l'Opéra de Paris.* Éditions Mengès, 1981.
Greenfeld, Edward, Ivan March, and Robert Layton. *The Penguin Guide to Opera on Compact Discs.* London: Penguin, 1993.
Gross, Arthur, and Roger Parker, eds. *Reading Opera.* Princeton: Princeton University Press, 1988.
Gruber, Paul, ed. *Guide to Opera on Video,* The Metropolitan Opera Guild. New York: W. W. Norton, 1997.
____. *Guide to Recorded Opera,* The Metropolitan Opera Guild. New York: W.W. Norton, 1993.
Guthrie, Tyrone. *Tyrone Guthrie: A Life in the Theater.* New York: McGraw-Hill Book Company, 1959.
Haldey, Olga. *Momontov's Private Opera: The Search for Modernism in Russian Theater.* Bloomington: Indiana University Press, 2010.
Hauk, Minnie. *Memories of a Singer.* London: A. M. Philpot, LTD, 1925; reprint edition, New York: Arno Press, 1977.
Henderson, W. J. *The Art of Singing.* New York: The Dial Press, 1938.
Henson, Karen. *Opera Acts: Singers and Performance in the Late Nineteenth Century.* Cambridge: Cambridge University Press, 2015.
Homer, Sidney. *My Wife and I: The Story of Louise and Sidney Homer.* New York: Macmillan, 1939.
Horne, Marilyn, with Jane Scovell. *Marilyn Horne: The Song Continues.* Fort Worth: Baskerville Publishers, Inc., 2004.
Howard, Kathleen. *Confessions of an Opera Singer.* New York: Alfred A. Knopf, 1918.
Huneker, James. *Bedouins.* New York: Charles Scribner's Sons, 1920.
Hurst, P. G. *The Age of Jean De Reszke: Forty Years of Opera, 1974–1914.* London: Christopher Johnson, 1958.
Hurst, P. G. *The Golden Age Recorded: A Collector's Survey.* Published by the author, at Eaton Thorne, Henfield, Sussex, 1946.
Jackson, Paul. *Saturday Afternoons at the Old Met: The Metropolitan Opera Broadcasts, 1931–1950.* Portland, OR: Amadeus Press, 1992.
____. *Sign-Off for the Old Met: The Metropolitan Opera Broadcasts, 1950–1966.* Portland, OR: Amadeus Press, 2003.
____. *Start-Up at the New Met: The Metropolitan Opera Broadcast, 1966–1976.* Portland, OR: Amadeus Press, 2006.
Jampol, Joshua. *Living Opera.* New York: Oxford University Press, 2010.
Kater, Michael H. *Never Sang for Hitler: The Life and Times of Lotte Lehmann.* Cambridge: Cambridge University Press, 2008.
Keiler, Allan. *Marian Anderson: A Singer's Journey.* London: A Lisa Drew Book/Scribner's, 2000.
Kellogg, Clara Louise. *Memoirs of an American Prima Donna.* New York: G. P. Putnam's Sons, 1913.
Kertesz, Elizabeth, and Michael Christoforidis. "Confronting Carmen beyond the Pyranees: Bizet's Opera in Madrid, 1887–1888." *Cambridge Opera Journal,* 20, 2008.
Kisten, Dorothy. *A Time to Sing.* Garden City, NY: Doubleday & Company, 1982.
Klein, Herman. *The Golden Age of Opera.* New York: E. P. Dutton, 1933.

_____. *Great Women Singers of My Time.* New York: E. P. Dutton, 1931.

_____. *Herman Klein and the Gramophone,* a compilation of articles from *The Gramophone,* ed. and with a biographical sketch by William Moran. Portland, OR, Amadeus Press, 1990.

_____. *The Reign of Patti.* London: T. Fisher Unwin Ltd., 1920.

Klein, Richard. *Cigarettes Are Sublime.* Durham: Duke University Press, 1993.

Kolodin, Irving. *The Metropolitan Opera: 1883–1966.* New York: Alfred A. Knopf, 1966.

Krehbiel, Henry Edward. *Chapters of Opera.* New York: Henry Holt and Company, 1911.

Kutsch, K. J., and Leo Riemans. *Grosses Sängerlexicon,* 5 volumes, third edition. Munich: K. G. Saur, 1999.

Lacombe, Hervé. *Georges Bizet: Naissance d'une identité créatrice.* Librairie Arthéme Fayard, 2000.

_____. *The Keys to French Opera in the Nineteenth Century.* Translated from the French by Edward Schneider. Berkeley: University of California Press, 2001.

Lahee, Henry C. *Famous Singers of Today and Yesterday.* Boston: L. C. Page & Co., 1898.

Lavielle, Gail. *Carmen: The Seduction of the Century.* Seattle: Pst...Inc., 1997.

Leblanc, Georgette. *Souvenirs: My Life with Maeterlinck.* Translated from the French by Janet Flanner. New York: E. P. Dutton, 1932.

Lehmann, Lilli. *My Path Through Life.* Translated by Alice Benedict Seligman. New York: G. P. Putnam's Sons, 1914.

Lehmann, Lotte. *My Many Lives.* Translated by Frances Holden. New York: Boosey & Hawkes, 1948.

Levik, Sergei Yurevich. *The Levik Memoires: An Opera Singer's Notes.* Translated by Edward Morgan. London: Symposium Records, 1995.

Lewis, Arthur H. *La Belle Otero.* New York: Trident Press, 1967.

Litvinne, Félia. *Ma Vie et Mon Art.* Paris: Librairie Plon, 1933; reprint edition, New York: Arno Press, 1977.

Ludwig, Christa. *In My Own Voice: Memoirs.* Translated with reference material by Regina Domeraski. New York: Limelight Editions, 1999.

Malherbe, Henry. *Carmen.* Paris: Éditions Albin Michel, 1951.

Mansouri, Lotfi, with Donard Arthur. *Lotfi Mansouri: An Operatic Journey.* Boston: Northeastern University Press, 2010.

Marchesi, Blanche. *Singer's Pilgrimage.* Boston: Small, Maynard and Company, 1923.

Marchesi, Mathile. *Marchesi and Music: Passages from the Life of a Famous Singing Teacher.* New York: Harper & Brothers, 1898.

Marsh, Robert C., comp. and ed. Norman Pellegrini. *150 Years of Opera in Chicago.* DeKalb: Northern Illinois University Press, 2006.

Martens, Frederick H. *The Art of the Prima Donna and Concert Singer.* New York: D. Appleton & Co., 1923.

Matheopoulos, Helena. *Diva: Great Sopranos and Mezzos Discuss Their Art.* Boston: Northeastern University Press, 1991.

Matheopoulos, Helena. *Diva: The New Generation.* Boston: Northeastern University Press, 1998.

Mays, Desirée. *Opera Unveiled.* Santa Fe: Art Forms Inc., 2006.

McClary, Susan. *Carmen.* Cambridge: Cambridge University Press, 1992.

McCracken, James, and Sandra Warfield. *A Star in the Family.* New York: Coward McCann & Geoghegan, 1971.

McGovern, Dennis, and Deborah Grace Winer. *I Remember Too Much: 89 Opera Stars Speak Candidly of Their Work, Their Lives and Their Colleagues.* New York: William Morrow, 1990.
Mercer, Ruby. *The Tenor of His Time: Edward Johnson of the Met.* Toronto: Clarke, Irwin Company Limited, 1976.
Mérimée, Prosper. *Carmen.* Translated by Andrew Brown. London: Hesperus, 2004.
_____. *Carmen and Other Stories.* Translated by Nicholas Jotcham. Oxford: Oxford University Press, 1989.
_____. *Carmen et Autres Nouvelles.* Lausanne: Editions Rencontre, 1967.
Moran, William, ed. and introd. *Herman Klein and the Gramophone.* Portland, OR: Amadeus Press, 1990.
Mordden, Ethan. *Demented: The World of the Opera Diva.* New York: Simon & Schuster, 1984.
_____. *The Splendid Art of Opera: A Concise History.* New York: Methuen, 1980.
Nagler, A. M. *Misdirection: Opera Production in the Twentieth Century.* Translated by Johanna C. Sahlin. Hamden, CT: Archon, 1981.
Nash, Elizabeth. *Always First Class: The Career of Geraldine Farrar.* Washington, D.C.: University Press of America, 1981.
_____. *Geraldine Farrar: Opera's Charismatic Innovator.* Jefferson, NC: McFarland, 2012.
Necula, Maria-Cristina. *Life in Opera: Truth, Tempo, and Soul: Encounters with Stars, Innovators, and Leaders of Today's Opera World.* Milwaukee: Amadeus Press, 2009.
Newman, Ernest. *Seventeen Famous Operas.* New York: Alfred A. Knopf, 1954.
Nichols, Roger. *The Harlequin Years: Music in Paris 1917–1929.* Berkeley: University of California Press, 2002.
Opstad, Gillian. *Debussy's Melisande, The Lives of Georgette Leblanc, Mary Garden and Maggie Teyte.* Woodbridge: Boydell Press, 2009.
Overture Opera Guides in association with EN. *Carmen.* London: Alma Classic Ltd., 2013.
Pahlen, Kurt. *Great Singers, from the 17th Century to the Present Day.* Translated by Oliver Coburn. New York: Stein and Day, 1974.
Parker, D. C. *Bizet.* London: Routledge & Kegan Paul Limited, 1951.
Pennino, John. *Risë Stevens: A Life in Music.* Fort Worth: Baskerville Publishers, Inc., 2005.
Phillips, Harvey E., *The Carmen Chronicle.* New York: Stein and Day, 1973.
Pigot, Charles. *Georges Bizet et Son Oeuvre.* Paris: Librairie Ch. Delagrave, n. d.
Pleasants, Henry. *The Great Singers: From the Dawn of Opera to Our Own Time.* New York: Simon & Schuster, 1966.
_____. *Opera in Crisis: Tradition, Present, Future.* New York: Thames and Hudson, 1989.
Ponselle, Rosa, and James A. Drake. *Ponselle: A Singer's Life.* Garden City, NY: Doubleday & Company, 1982.
Porter, Andrew. *Musical Events: A Chronicle, 1983–1986.* New York: Summit Books, 1983, 1984, 1985, 1986, 1989.
Powrie, Phil, and Ann Davies. *Carmen on Screen: An Annotated Filmography and Bibliography.* Woodbridge: Tamesis, 2006.
Powrie, Phil, et al. *Carmen on Film: A Cultural History.* Bloomington: Indiana University Press, 2007.
Prawy, Marcel. *The Vienna Opera.* New York: Praeger, 1970.

Raitt, A. W. *Prosper Mérimée.* New York: Scribner's, 1970.
Rasponi, Lanfranco. *The Last Prima Donnas.* New York: Limelight Editions, 1990.
Rose, Michael. *The Birth of an Opera: Fifteen Masterpieces from Poppea to Wozzeck.* London: W.W. Norton, 2013.
Rosenthal, Harold. *Two Centuries of Opera at Covent Garden.* London: Putnam & Company Limited, 1958.
Rosselli, John. *Singers of Italian Opera: The History of a Profession.* New York: Cambridge University Press, 1992.
Roussel, Jean-Jacques Hanine. *Simionato: How Cinderella Became a Queen.* Translated by Samuel Chase with Teresa Bretegani, Albert and Adriana Miner. Dallas: Baskerville Publishers, Inc., 1997.
Roy, Jean. *Bizet.* Paris: Éditions du Seuil, 1983.
Rubin, Stephen E. *The New Met in Profile.* New York: Macmillan, 1974
Rutherford, Susan. *The Prima Donna and Opera, 1915–1930.* New York: Cambridge University Press, 2006.
Sachs, Harvey. *Music in Fascist Italy.* New York: W. W. Norton, 1987.
Sadie, Stanley, ed. *The New Grove Dictionary of Opera.* 4 volumes. New York: Macmillan Reference Limited, 1998.
Schoen-René, Anna Eugénie. *America's Musical Inheritance: Memoirs and Reminiscences.* New York: G. P. Putnam's Sons, 1941.
Schwandt, Christoph. *Georges Bizet: A Biography.* Translated by Cynthia Klohr. Lanham, MD: Scarecrow Press, 2013.
Schwarz, Boris. *Music and Musical Life in Soviet Russia 1917–1970.* New York: W. W. Norton, 1972.
Scott, Michael. *The Record of Singing to 1914.* New York: Charles Scribner's Sons, 1977.
_____. *The Record of Singing: Volume 2, 1914–1925.* Boston: Northeastern University Press, 1979.
Shaw, George Bernard. *Shaw's Music: The Complete Musical Criticism of Bernard Shaw,* 3 volumes; edited by Dan H. Laurence. London: The Bodley Head, Ltd., 1981.
Sheean, Vincent. *First and Last Love.* New York: Random House, 1956.
_____. *Oscar Hammerstein 1: The Life and Exploits of an Impresario.* New York: Simon & Schuster, 1956.
Sheehy, Helen. *Eleanora Duse, A Biography.* New York: Alfred A. Knopf, 2003.
Somerset-Ward, Richard. *Angels and Monsters: Male and Female Sopranos in the Story of Opera.* New Haven: Yale University Press, 2004.
Soper, Richard T. *Belgian Opera Houses and Singers.* Spartanburg, SC: The Reprint Company Publishers, 1999.
Soubies, Albert, and Charles Malherbe. *Histoire de l'Opéra Comique: La Seconde Salle Favart, 1840–1887.* Geneva, Switzerland: Minkoff Reprint, 1978
Spotts, Frederic. *Hitler and the Power of Aesthetics.* Woodstock, NY: The Overlook Press, 2002.
Stanislavski, Constantin, and Pavel Rumyantsev. *Stanislavski on Opera.* Translated and edited by Elizabeth Reynolds Hapgood. New York: Theatre Arts Books, 1975.
Steane, J. B. *The Grand Tradition: Seventy Years of Singing on Record 1900 to 1970,* second edition. Portland, OR: Amadeus Press, 1993.
Stinchelli, Enrico. *Greatest Stars of the Opera: The Lives and Voices of Two Hundred Golden Years.* Rome: Gremese International, 1992.
Story, Rosalyn M. *And So I Sing: African-American Divas of Opera and Concert.* New York: Warner Books Inc., 1990.
Stricker, Remy. *Georges Bizet.* Éditions Gallimard, 1999.

Swarthout, Gladys. *Come Soon, Tomorrow: The Story of a Young Singer.* New York: Dodd, Mead & Company, 1944.
Tuggle, Robert. *The Golden Age of Opera.* New York: Holt, Rinehart and Winston, 1983.
Turnbull, Michael T. R. B. *Mary Garden.* Portland, OR: Amadeus Press, 1997.
Van Vechten, Carl. *The Music of Spain.* New York: Alfred A. Knopf, 1918.
_____. *Interpreters.* New York: Alfred A. Knopf, 1917; reprint, New York: Arno Press, 1977.
Verrett, Shirley, with Christopher Brooks. *I Never Walked Alone: The Autobiography of an American Singer.* Hoboken, NJ: John Wiley & Sons, 2003.
Villamil, Victoria Etnier. *From Johnson's Kids to Lemonade Opera: The American Classical Singer Comes of Age,* Boston: Northeastern University Press, 2004.
Vishnevskaya, Galina. *Galina: A Russian Story.* Translated by Guy Daniels. San Diego: Harcourt Brace Jovanovich, 1984.
Volpe, Joseph, with Charles Michener. *The Toughest Show on Earth: My Rise and Reign at the Metropolitan Opera.* New York: Alfred A Knopf, 2006.
Walsh, T. J. *Monte Carlo Opera: 1879–1909.* Dublin: Gill and Macmillan Ltd., 1975.
Williams, Jeanne. *Jon Vickers: A Hero's Life.* Boston: Northeastern University Press, 1999.
Wisner, Arthur. *Emma Calvé: Her Artistic Life.* New York: R. H. Russell, 1902; reprint, Forgotten Books, 2012.
Wolff, Stéphan. *Un Demi-Siècle d'Opéra-Comique (1900–1950).* Éditions André Bonne, 1953.
Wright, Lesley A., ed. *Carmen: Dossier de Presse Parisienne (1875).* Weinsberg: Musik-Edition Lucie Galland, 2001.
_____. "Rewriting a Reception: Thoughts on Carmen in Paris, 1883," *Journal of Musicological Research*, 28, 2009.

Index

Numbers in ***bold italics*** indicate pages with photographs.

Academy of Music (New York) 23, 37
Accroche-coeur (spit curl) ***96***, 111
acting styles 57–62; in early 20th century 69–77; of Farrar 80, 82, 83–84; in films 81–82 (*see also* film versions); of first-generation Carmens 27–30, 54–55; increasing importance 72–77; innovations 69–77, 162–164 (*see also* avant-garde productions); of Opéra-Comique chorus members 10; of Russian singers 69–72; *see also* direction; staging of Calvé
African American singers 71–72, 128–130, 132, 145–147
Aida (Verdi) 128
Air des Cartes 66, 69–70, 76, 140
Alagna, Roberto 152
Alboni, Marietta 96
Alda, Frances 79
Aldrich, Kate 149, 158–159
Aldrich, Richard 80
"Alley Cat Carmen" 118, ***118***
Amato, Pasquale 80
American Opera Company 117
American productions: in early 20th century 78–86; Farrar in 79–86; Jeritza in 87–89; in mid-20th century 102–118, 120–132; in 19th century 37–40; of regional companies 102; *see also* Metropolitan Opera (New York)
American singers: in French productions 127–128; in Italian productions 125–130; in Viennese productions 126–128
L'Amico Fritz (Mascagni) 58, 59
Amparan, Belan 132
Andalusische Nachte (Andalusian Nights) (film) 90
Anderson, Marian 2, 71–72

Anitua, Fanny 99
Antonacci, Anna Caterina 149, 161–162
Arden, Fanny 122–123
Arditi, Luigi 26
La Argentina 106
Argentina, Imperio 90, 195*n*11
Arkhipova, Irina 140
L'Arlesianne Suite 21
Arnaud, Anna 49
Arnoldson, Sigrid 32, 44
Arral, Blanche 17, 19, 47
Aspinall, Michael 73
Asquith, Anthony 120
Australian productions: in 19th century 34–35
avant-garde productions 119, 120, 148–164; of Bieito 151–153; of Carsen 156; of Corsaro 153–154; critiques 150; of Dante 149–150; of Désiré 158; of Hartmann 155; of Kramer 154; of Kusej 155, 161; of Lawless 160; of McVicar 159, 160–161; of Pintilie 150; of Pountney 150, 156–157; "Produceritis" and 150–151; of Py 158; of Rudolfson 159–160; of Sivadier 160–161
L'Avant-Scène 135

Baclanova, Olga 93
Balfe, Michael 12
Baltsa, Agnes 140–142, ***141***
Bampton, Rose 2
Bara, Theda 195*n*19
Barbieri, Fedora 47–48, 123, 124
Barcelona 35–36
Bartoli, Cecilia 2
Basel 130
Baxter, Robert 85
Bayreuth 128, 130
Beecham, Thomas 101, 137

Index

Bel canto 23, 27, 28, 69, 73, 95, 134, 196
Belgian productions, in 19th century, 22–23, 24
Bellincioni, Gemma 59, 73, 96
Bellini, Vincenzo 95
Berg, Arnold 89
Berganza, Teresa 99, 137–138
Berger, Arthur 115
Berlin 23, 34, 118, 119
Berlioz, Hector 18
Bernard, Gabriel 49, 54, 55
Bernhardt, Sarah 58
Bernheimer, Martin 150
Bernstein, Leonard 134, 135
Besanzoni, Gabriella **96**, 96–97
Bieito *Carmen* 151–153
Bing, Rudolf 116–118, 121–122, 127, 134
Bizet, Geneviève (Geneviève Halévy) 14, 189n24
Bizet, Georges 13, 31; alleged affair with Galli-Marié 14; commissioned by Opéra-Comique 9–10; deviation from traditional opéra comique 11–12; illness and death of 19–20, 21; proposed changes for Vienna production 21–22, 190n2; pushes for casting of Galli-Marié 13–14; use of Mérimée's novella 9–10
Bizet, Jacques 20
black singers 71–72, 128–130, 132, 145–147
Bloomfield, Arthur 145
Blythe, Stephanie 2
The Bohemian Girl (Balfe) 12
Bohm, Jerome 115
Bolshoi Stone 34
Bolshoi Theater 93, 129, 140, 156
Bookman 83
Borodina, Olga 149, **157**, 157–158
Borrows, George 83
Boston 81, 84
Bouffar, Zulma 13
Bourskaya, Ina 87
Branzell, Karin 32
Bressler-Gianoli, Clotilde 47, 55, 62–65, **64**, 66, 85
Bréval, Lucienne 47, 55, 111
Brohly, Suzanne 51
Brook, Peter 138–139
Brunet, Sylvie 161
Brussels 22–23, 24, 45
Buades, Aurora 99, 136
Budapest 34
Bumbry, Grace 121–122, 129, 130, 132
Busch, Hans 117

Calixto, Bieito 151–153
Callas, Maria 122–123
Callas Forever (film) 122–123
Calvé, Emma 29, 37, 44, 52, 55, 57–62, **59**, 63, 79, 89, 110; in *Cavalleria Rusticana* 59, 61; costumes **59**, 61, 85, 111; dancing 61; declining performance 62; lasting impact 57–58, 62; performs for Queen Victoria 57; repertoire 58; reviews 59–60; stylistic approach 57–58, 59–62; voice and singing 58
Campanini, Italo 24, 26
Canadian productions 39
Caracalla Baths (Rome) 148
card scene 66, 69–70
Carl Rosa Opera Company 35, 37
Carmen: amorality 10, 12, 28, 38, 39, 50, 163; as anti-heroine 28; death 4–5, 162; many facets 2, 162–164; in Mérimée's novella 3–6, 9–10, 12, 15, 83; real-life inspirations for 6–7; sopranos vs. mezzo-sopranos as 8, 18–19, 95–99; vocal challenges 18–19, 26–27; vulgarity 38, 39, 63, 68, 118, 120
Carmen (film) 80–82, **81**
Carmen (Malherbe) 9–10, 14, 15
Carmen (Mérimée) 3–6, 9–10, 12, 15, 83, 93
Carmen Chronicle (Phillips) 134
Carmen, Dossier de Presse Parisienne (Wright) 11
Carmen Jones 129, 134
Carmen, la de Triana (film) 90
Carmencita and the Soldier 92–93, 119
Carré, Albert 45–47, 106
Carreras, José 142
Carsen, Robert 156
Caruso, Enrico 68, 79, 82
Carvahlo, Leon 41–45
Castagna, Bruna 107, 108, 110
Castagné, Marie 44, 55
Cavalieri, Lina 67
Cavalleria Rusticana (Mascagni) 27, 35, 59, 61, 73, 88
Cebotari, Maria 2
Cernay, Germaine 51, 52
Chaliapin, Feodor 72
Chanson Bohèmienne 10, 69, 89, 111, 125
Chapuy, Marguerite 20
Charpentier, Gustave 75, 79
Chenal, Marthe 47, 52
Chicago Opera 78, 103
Children's Chorus 74
The Chocolate Soldier (film) 114
The Christian Science Monitor 142
Christiana Theater (Sweden) 32
Christoforidis, Michael 35
Cigna, Gina 97
cinema *see* film versions
Clairin, George 19

Index

Cluytans, André 54
Columbia Opera 127
Come Soon Tomorrow (Swarthout) 111
Commettant, Oscar 12, 43–44
Conried, Heinrich 68
Contraltos 96
Cook, Ida 128
Coote, Alice 2
Corelli, Franco 97, 124
Corsaro, Frank 153–154
Cossotto, Fiorenza 123, 124–125, *125*, 161
costumes 85, 111–114, *121*; of Calvé *59*, 61, 85, 111; of Galli-Marié 19, *43*, 61; Lanvin-designed 101, 113; of Ponselle 111, *112*, 113; Spanish shawl *59*, 61, 85, 111–113; of Stevens 114; Valentina-designed 111, *112*, 113
Court Opera (Vienna) 87–88
Covent Garden (London) 24, 37, 101, 120
Crespin, Régine 133–134, 135, *136*, 137, 138, 162
Cristoforeanu, Florica 97, 196n33
Culshaw, John 52
Curtiss, Mina 15

Daily Telegraph 30
dancing: ballet 21; by Calvé 61; by Cossotto 125; by Galli-Marié 11, 17
Dandridge, Dorothy 134
Dante, Emma 149–150
Davidova, Maria 72
Davis, Peter 135
Davis, Ronald 75
Dean, Frederic 61, 78, 83
Dean, Winton 12, 35
de Banville, Théodore 15–16
de Belocca, Anna 38, 39–40
de Bury, Blaze 18
Debussy, Claude 75
De Gaulle, Charles 131
De Koven, Reginald 75
de Leuven, Alfred 9–10
de l'Isle, Jeanne Marié 12, 47, 50, 51, *51*, 192n32
del Monaco, Mario 124, 127, 140
Delna, Marie 47
de los Angeles, Victoria 99, 136–137, 138
del Puente, Giuseppe 24
de Lucia, Fernando 95, 97
de Lussan, Zélie 37, 47, *57*, 128; performs for Queen Victoria 56–57
de Reszke, Jean 44
DeMille, Cecil B. 81
Dérivis, Maria 22–23, 38
Désiré, Louis 158
Dessay, Natalie 48
Destinn, Emmy, *91*, 91–92

dialogue, spoken 11, 45, 48, 51, 67, 101, 120, 130–131, 134, 196n6
Diamond, Peter 138
direction: of avant-garde productions 119, 148–164 (*see also* avant-garde productions); increasing importance 72–77, 148–149, 150–151; Russian innovations and 69–72; by theatrical directors 117–118; *see also* acting styles; staging
"Directoritis" 151
Djamileh (Bizet) 9, 13
Djanel, Lily 108–110, *109*, 114
Dobbs, Mattiwilda 129
Dolaro, Selina 37
Domashenko, Marina 154–155
Domingo, Placido 139
Don Carlo (Verdi) 117
Donizetti, Gaetano 12, 22, 24, 27, 56, 95
D'Oustrac, Stéphanie 160–161
Downes, Olin 89, 92, 106, 107
Drury Lane 24
Dublin 37
Dugazon voice 18, 95, 190n50
du Locle, Camille 9, 13, 14, 18, 19, 22, 41
Duncan, Todd 129
Duse, Eleanora 58–59, 63
Dyarko 7

Earl's Court (London) 145
Easton, Florence 87
Eckert, Thor 142
Eddy, Nelson 114
Edinburgh Festival 138
Ehnn, Bertha 21–22, 23, 29, 34, 190n4
Elias, Rosalind 132
English productions, in 19th century 37
Enriquez, Franco 129
Espert, Nuria 145, 162
Ewing, Maria 142–145, *144*, 162
experimental productions *see* avant-garde productions
Expo 86 World Festival (Vancouver) 150
Eyre, Richard 149, 150, 158

Faggioni, Piero 138
Falstaff (Verdi) 36
Farrar, Geraldine 1, 69, 78, 79–86, *80*, 89, 97, 106, 110, 164; *Bookman* interview with 83–84; in film versions 80–82, *81*, 83; later career and retirement 86; Metropolitan Opera debut 79–80; recordings 85–86; stylistic approach 80, 83–84, 86; as transitional figure 86
Fassbaender, Brigitte 145
Faust (Gounod) *see* Marguerite (Gounod's *Faust*)
La Favorita (Donizetti) 22

212 Index

Felsenstein, Walter 119–120, 130, 131
Feminism 88, 139, 163
Fernández, Enrique 138, 139
Ferrabini, Ester 7878
Ferrier, Kathleen 2
Festival Castell de Perelada 152
Fétis, Felix 24
Figner, Nicolai 70
La Fille du Régiment (Donizetti) 12, 24, 56
films and videos: alphabetical listing 185–187; Bumbry in 130; Callas in 122–123; Farrar in 80–82, *81*; Migenes-Johnson in 139; Obraztsova in 140; Ponselle in 111; silent 80–82, *81*; Simionato in 124; sound 82–83
Finck, Henry 30, 60
Flower Song 70, 155
Flying Down to Rio (film) 79
Franco, Francisco 99–101, *100*, 139, 153–154
Fremstad, Olive 32, 49, 68, 194n10
French productions: American singers in 127–128 (*see also* Opéra-Comique); of Paris Opéra 131–132; *see also* Opéra-Comique
French singers 133–134, 135, 161; unique style 47–55
Friché, Claire 47
Fröding, Gustaf 31

Gades, Antonio 125
Gallet, Louis 22
Galli, Antonio 12
Galli-Marié, Célestine 9, 11–20, 22, 49–50, 92, 94, 95, 189n20, 189n42, 190n57; acting style 12, 15–18, 40; alleged affair with Bizet 14; appearance 15, *43*; Bizet's death and 19–20, 190n57; in *The Bohemian Girl* 12; casting 13–14; costumes 19, *43*, 61; dancing 11, 17; early career 12–13; in England 37; family 12; in *Faust* 18; final performances at Opéra-Comique 22, 43–44; in Italy 35; in *Mignon* 13, 18, 22; in Paris premiere 10–12; in Paris revival 41–42, 43–44; in *La Serva Padrona* 12–13; in Spain 35–36; voice and singing 8, 18–19
Galli-Marié voice 95
Gallic school of singing 48
Gallo, Fortune 78, 103
Garanča, Elina 139, 148–149, 158, 189n42
Garcia, Manuel 26
Garden, Mary 47, 55, 74–77, *76*, 78, 82, 86, 89, 103, 106, 110, 113
Gatti-Casazza, Giulio 68, 79, 87–89, 105
Gaudier, Charles 22
Gay, Maria 47, 55, 68–70, *69*, 84, 86, 94, 136

Gedda, Nicolai 124
Geneva 34
Genoa 35
Gentele, Gören 134–136
Gentle, Alice 78–79
Gergiev, Valery 158
German productions 161; of Felsenstein 119–120; in Nazi era 89–90; during Weimar Republic 89
German singers 74, 145–147
Germanno-Ferni 96
Gerville-Réache, Jeanne 49, 66–67
Gheorghiu, Angela 189n42
Gigli, Beniamino 99
Gilman, Lawrence 107
Glade, Coe 102–103, *103*
Gluck, Christophe 66
Glyndebourne Festival 117, 143, 145, 159, 160, 161
Godard, Jean-Luc 138
Goebbels, Joseph 90
Goetz, Hermann 22
Going My Way (film) 114
Gold Line Arena (Hamburg) 156
The Golden Age of Opera (Klein) 24
Gounod, Charles 18, 24, 27, 32, 48, 58, 129
Graf, Herbert 117
Graf, Max 73
Graham, Susan 2
Graves, Denyce 145, *146*, 147
Gregor, Hans 119
Gubisch, Nora 161
Guiraud, Ernest 22, 28, 130
Gurewitsch, Mathew 145
Gutheil-Schoder, Marie 74, *74*, 89, 126
Guthrie, Tyrone 117–118, 124, 126, 131
Gye, Frederick 24
Gypsy Blood (film) 82

Habanera 6, 28, 35, 67, 69, 70, 85, 91, 94, 111, 114, 119, 153, 161–162; in Galli-Marié's performances 6, 16, 17; at premiere 10
Halasz, Laszlo 108
Halévy, Fromental 14
Halévy, Geneviève (Geneviève Bizet) 14, 189n24
Halévy, Ludovic 9, 10, 11, 14, 20, 23
Hall, Peter 143
Hamlet (Thomas) 59
Hammerstein, Oscar 62–63, 66–67, 75, 78
Hammerstein, Oscar, II 129
"Hard" vs. "soft" *Carmens* 119–122
Harris, Augustus 56
Hartmann, Matthias 155
Hauk, Minnie 21, 23–26, *25*, 34, 37–38, 40, 42, 43, 57, 189n39

Index

Haymarket (London) 37
Heidt, Winifred 102, 103, **104**, 104–105, 196*n*10
Henahan, Donal 133, 137, 142, 143, 148, 151
Henderson, W.H. 60–61, 88, 89
Henson, Karen 16
Her Majesty's Opera (London) 24
Herrera, Nancy Fabiola 161
Hersee, Rose 34–35
Higgins, John 120
Hindemith, Kurt 89
Hispanic Carmens 160, 161
Hitler, Adolf 89, 93, 102, 108–109, 114
Hitler and the Power of Aesthetics (Spotts) 90
Homer, Louise 91, 195*n*15
Homer, Sidney 91
Horne, Marilyn 134–135
Horowitz, Joseph 140
Hunt-Lieberson, Lorraine 2, 7, 49

Ibsen, Henrik 63
Igez, Bodo 134
Indépendence Belge 24
Inghelbrecht, D. E. 52
Irons, Jeremy 122
Isaac, Adèle 42
Italian productions: American singers in 125–130; during Fascist era 95–99; in French 124; mezzo-sopranos in 8, 18–19, 95–99; in mid-20th century 122–125; in 19th century 35
Italian Royal (London) 24
Italian singers 161–162
L'Italiana in Algeri (Rossini) 107
Ivanovna, Medea (Medea Mei-Figner) 34, 70, **71**

Jarvi, Neeve 158
Jauner, Fritz 21
Jeritza, Maria 86, 87–89, 106
Jews, in Nazi Germany 89–90
Johnson, Edward 105–111, 114, 116
Joncières, Victorin 12
Julien (Charpentier) 79
Juyol, Suzanne 51–52

Kael, Pauline 139
Kasarova, Vesselina 148, 155–156, **156**
Kaufmann, Jonas 155, 161
Keiler, Allan 71
Kellogg, Clara Louise 38–39, **39**, 40
Kertesz, Elizabeth 35
Ketten, Cécile 50, 93–94
Kirsten, Dorothy 103
Kleiber, Carlos **140**
Klein, Herman 17, 19, 24, 26, 28, 30, 59–60
Klose, Margarethe 92

Kolodin, Irving 104–105
Komische Opera (Berlin) 119, 120
Korngold, Erich 88
Kramer, David 154
Krasteva, Nadia 155–156
Kroll Opera House (Berlin) 89
Kusej, Martin 155, 161

Labia, Maria 67
Lance, Albert 131
Lane, Gloria 126
languages of productions 37, 124
Lapitsky, Joseph 72
La Scala *see* Scala
Lasky, Jesse 81
Lassalle, Jean 44
Latvian National Opera 148
Lawless, Stephen 160
Lawrence, Marjorie 2
Leblanc, Georgette 45–47, **46**, 50, 51, 55
Lehmann, Lilli 37
Lehmann, Lotte 90
Levik, Sergei 34, 69, 70, 72
Levine, James 145
Lewisohn Stadium 107
Lhérie, Paul 9, 11, 14, 15
light opera *see* Opéra-comique
lighting 128; *see also* staging
Litvinne, Félia 15, 34
"Live from Lincoln Center 154
Lombard, Alain 133–134
London productions 101; Destinn in 92; in early 20th century 117–118; in mid-20th century 117, 120; in 19th century 24–26, 37; Queen Victoria at 56–57
London Symphony 82–83
London Times 131
Lucca, Pauline 29–30, 34, 38, 40, 59, 63, 65, 74, 126
Ludwig, Christa 126–127
Lunn, Louise Kirkby 92
Lyubatovich, Tatyana 72

MacDonald, Jeanette 114
Madama Butterfly (Puccini) 129
Madeira, Jean 126
Madrid 36–37
Maeterlinck, Maurice 45–47
The Magic Mountain (Mann) 91
Mahler, Gustav 73–74, 89, 116
Maksakova, Maria 93, **94**, 94–95
Malherbe, Henry 9–10, 14, 15
Malibran, Maria 96
Malreaux, André 131
Mamontov, Savva 71, 72
Manhattan Opera Company 62–63, 66–68, 78

214   Index

Mansouri, Lofti 119
Mapleson, James Henry 24, 28
Marchesi, Blanche 63–65
Marchesi, Mathilde 18
Margaine, Clémentine 161
Marguerite (Gounod's *Faust*) 18, 24, 27, 32
Marie (Queen of Romania) 56
Marié de l'Isle 12, 47, 50, 51, *51*, 192*n*32
Mariinsky Theater (Russia) 34, 69, 70
Marinelli, Carlo 124
Martinez, Ana Maria 160, 161
Mascagni, Pietro 27, 35, 59, 88
Massé, Victor 15
Massenet, Jules 58, 75, 95
Matz, Mary Jane 124
Matzenauer, Margarete 87
Mazarin, Mariette 67
McClary, Susan 90
McCracken, James 134
McFerrin, Robert 129
McVicar, David 159, 160–161
Mei-Figner, Medea 34, 70, *71*
Meier, Waltraud 145
Meilhac, Henri 9, 10, 13, 42
Melba, Nellie 44
Mémoires (Vénard) 6
Menotti, Gian Carlo 126, 128, 129
Merentié, Margueritte 47, 51
Mérimée, Prosper 3–6, 9–10, 15, 26, 83
Metropolitan Opera (New York) 37–38, 49, 61, 62, 78, 88–89, 97, 105, 129, 132; under Bing 116–118, 121–122, 127; under Conried 68; early 20th century productions 68–69; Farrar's engagement at 79–86; Gentele's production and 134–136; Guthrie's productions and 117–118, 124, 126, 131; under Johnson 105–111, 114; mid- to late-20th century productions 133–135, 140–147; Stevens's engagements at 114–115; telecasts from 142, 148, 149, 150
Meyer, Kerstin 32, 132, 134
Meyerbeer, Giacomo 95
Mezzo-sopranos: Italian 95–99; vs. sopranos 8, 18–19, 95–99
Michel, Solange 44, 51, 53–54, *54*
Midgette, Anne 147
Migenes-Johnson, Julia 139
Mignon (in Thomas's *Mignon*) 13, 18, 22, 32, 53, 78, 108, 114, 194*n*29
Miller, Phillip 107
Mintz, Ar 7
Misdirection: Opera Production in the Twentieth Century (Nagler) 119
Modern Art Theater 71
Mödl, Martha 51
Moe, Olfine 31–32

La Mogador (Céleste Vénard) 6
La Monnaie (Brussels) 22–24, 45
Moore, Edward 101, 103
Moscow Art Theater 92–93
movies *see* films and videos
Muelle, Marie 111
Müller, Georg 21
Muratore, Lucien 75–76
Musical America 78, 116
Musical Courier 102, 117
Mussolini, Benito 95, 97
Muzio, Claudia 95

Nadushka, Mintz 6–7
Nafe, Alicia 161
Nagler, A.M. 119
Namara, Marguerite 82–83
Naples 35, 124–125
naturalism *see* Verismo
La Navaraise (Massenet) 58
Nazi Germany 89–90
Nemirovich-Danchenko, Vladimir 93, 119, 120
Netrebko, Anna 158
Neues Deutsches Theater (Prague) 114
New Opera Company (New York)
New York City Opera 108, 126, 127, 129, 154
New York Herald 80
New York Mirror 106
New York Times 35, 38, 40, 44, 63, 67, 80, 93, 106, 147
New Yorker 143
Newsweek 114
Niehoff, Dina 32
nontraditional productions *see* avant-garde productions
Nordica, Lillian 2
Nozze di Figaro (Mozart) 58

Obraztsova, Elena 140
Obukhova, Nadezhda 93–94
Oeser, Fritz 130–131
Offenbach, Jacques 13
Old Vic (London) 117
Olszewska, Maria 103
Opéra Bastille 158
Opéra comique 41; *Carmen's* deviation from traditions 10, 11, 12; spoken dialogue 11, 67
Opera in Chicago (Davis) 75
Opera in Crisis (Pleasants) 150
Opera News 102, 124, 133, 145
Opera North (Leeds) 154
Opéra-Comique 7–8, 9, 12, 13, 22, 58, 66, 67, 101, 106, 108, 138, 161, 192*n*15; acting styles 27–30, 54–55, 119; *Carmen*

premiere and 10–12; under Carré 41–45, 45–47; under Carvahlo 41–45; under du Locle 41; French singing style and 47–55; loses *Carmen* to Paris Opéra 131; Paris revival and 41–55; *see also* Paris revival
Orfeo (Gluck) 66
Otero, Caroline 47

Pagliacci (Leoncavallo) 27, 35, 73, 74, 129
Pagliughi, Lina 96
Paladilhe, Émile 14
Palais Garnier 131, 198n37
Paris Opéra 131–132
Paris revival 41–55; Adèle Isaac in 42; Carvahlo's missteps in 42; Gallie-Marié in 41–42, 43–44; obstacles to producing 41–42; stylistic approaches in 41–44
Parker, H.T. 84
Pasqua, Giuseppina 36
Pathé recordings 51
Patti, Adelina 2, 28, *29*
Pavlovskaya, Emiliya 34
Pederzini, Gianna 97, *98*, 123
Pelléas et Mélisande (Debussy) 45, 52, 66
Pennino, John 118
Perelli, Lucy 44, 51, 52
Perrin, Émile 7, 12
Petina, Irra 114
Petrassi, Goffreso 87
Peyser, Herbert 108
Philadelphia 39, 67, 107
Philadelphia Opera House 67
Phillips, Harvey E. 134
Pintilie, Lucian 150
Pirandello, Luigi 63
Pleasants, Henry 150, 153
Podles, Ewa 2
Poleri, David 126
Pollak, Anna 118–119
Ponchard, Charles 10, 14
Ponnelle, Jean-Pierre 142
Ponselle, Rosa 105–107, 108, 110, 113
Porter, Andrew 143
Pougin, Arthur 62
Pountney, David 150, 156–157
Prague 92, 114
Prague National Opera 92
Prawy, Marcel 29
premiere(s) 10–12; audience reaction to 10–11, 12; chronology 172; critical response to 11–12
Prénom Carmen 138
Prêtre, Georges 122, 125
Private Opera 72
"Produceritis" 150–151
productions: "hard" vs. "soft" 119–122; languages of 37, 124; *see also* specific operas, venues, and directors
"The Psychology of Carmen" (Dean) 83
Py, Oliver 158

Queen Marie of Romania 56
Queen Victoria of England 56–57

Rachvelishvili, Anita 149–150
Radev, Marianne 120
Rankin, Nell 120, *121*, 132
Rasponi, Lanfranco 97
Raveau, Alice 47
realism *see* Verismo
recitatives 21, 130–131, 134, 190n3
recordings: alphabetical listing 177–184; of Destinn 91; of Farrar 85–86; first complete 91; in French 51–52; in Opéra-Comique tradition 51–52; Pathé 51; of Supervia 101
Regnault, H. 19
Reiner, Fritz 117
Renard, Marie 73, 194n29
Resnik, Regina *127*, 127–128, 130, 132
La Revue Théâtrale 49
Rey, Florien 90
Rhodes, Jane 131–132
Rigoletto (Verdi) 129
Rose Hersee Opera 34–35
Der Rosenkavalier (Strauss) 101
Rosenstock, Joseph 126
Rosenthal, Harold 105
Rosi, Francesco 139
Rosing, Vladimir 117
Rossini, Gioachino 95, 96, 99, 107
Rouleau, Raymond 131
Royal Opera (London) 56–57, 129, 145, 148–149, 161, 162
Royal Theater (Sweden) 32
Roze, Marie 8, 13–14, 38, 39, *39*
Rubinstein, Arthur 97
Rudolfson, Lars 159–160
Ruffo, Titta 103
Russian productions: avant-garde 119, 120, 149–150; contemporary 149–150, 154–159; in early 20th century 69–72; on international tours 92–93; in mid-20th century 140; in 19th century 32–33; in Stalinist Russia 93–95

Sadler's Wells (London) 117
St. John Brenon, Algernon 63
St. Margarthen Summer Festival 156
St. Petersburg 34
Saint-Saëns, Camille 2, 18, 66
Salle Favart (Paris) 9, 20, 41–44, 192n16, 197n36; *Carmen* revival at 41–55 (*see*

also Paris revival); fire at 45; number of peformances 44–45; *see also* Opéra-Comique
Salmaggi, Alfredo 107
San Carlo Opera 78, 103
San Francisco 107
Sante Fe Opera Festival 159, 160
Sardou, Victorien 15
Sargent, Malcolm 83
Sarkissyan, Emma 120
Saura, Carlos 138
La Scala (Milan) 36, 78, 96, 97, 107, 122, 124, 125, 149
Scharley, Denise 132
Schenk, Otto 126, 140
Schippers, Thomas 127
Schoenberg, Arnold 89
Schonberg, Harold 122, 132, 135
Schumann-Heink, Ernestine 2
Schwarz, Boris 32
score, new editions of 130–131
Scotto, Renata 2
Seguidilla 17, 35, 53, 83, 85, 91
La Serva Padrona (Pergolesi) 12–13
Shaham, Rinat 160
Shaw, George Bernard 29, 60, 61
Sheean, Vincent 52, 97
Shipp, Heather 154
Silja, Anja 2
Sills, Beverly 2
Simionato, Giulietta *123*, 123–124, 125
singing: bel canto 23, 27, 28, 69, 73, 95, 134, 196; French style 47–55; by sopranos vs. mezzo-sopranos 8, 18–19, 95–96; vs. acting 72–77; *see also* vocal styles
Sivadier, Jean-François 160–161
Slavina, Mariya *33*, 34
"Slice of life" operas 88; *see also* Verismo
Smith, Cecil 120
Smith, Muriel 129
"Soft" vs. "hard" *Carmens* 119–122
Soldene, Emily 37
sopranos, vs. mezzo-sopranos 8, 18–19, 95–99
Soviero, Diane 2
Spanish shawl *59*, 61, 85, 111–113; *see also* costumes
Spanish singers/productions: Bieito *Carmen* 151–153; Franco's Spain and 99–101, 153–154, 160; in 19th century 35–37; in 20th century 136–138
spit curls, *96*, 111
spoken dialogue 11, 45, 48, 51, 67, 101, 120, 130–131, 134, 196n6
Spoleto Festival 128, 129
Spontini, Gaspare 122
Spotts, Frederic 90

Staatsoper (Berlin) 89
Staging: of avant-garde productions 119, 148–164 (*see also* avant-garde productions); in Guthrie's Met production 117–118; "hard" vs. "soft" *Carmens* and 119–122; increasing importance 116–117, 148–149, 150–151; lighting and 128; in Menotti's Spoleto Festival production 128; new directions in 162–164; opera as total theater and 116–117, 119; of premiere 11, 16; *see also* direction
Stalin, Josef 93, 95, 140
Stanislavski, Konstantin 71, 72, 119, 120
Stevens, Risë 1, 2, 7, 114–115, 124; as "Alley Cat Carmen" 118, *118;* debut as Carmen 114–115; early career 114–115; in Guthrie's Met production 118, *118*, 124, 126; in Hollywood 114; stylistic approach 118; vocal problems 115
Stignani, Ebe 98–88
Stilwell, Jean 150
Stockholm 31–32
Strakosch, Max 38
Stratas, Teresa 2
Strauss, Richard 67, 87, 95
sung recitatives 21, 130–131, 134, 190n3
Supervia, Conchita 99–101, *100*, 108, 113, 136
Svoboda, Josef 134
Swarthout, Gladys 110–111, 113, 197n27
Swedish productions, in 19th century, 31–32
Sydney Harbor (Australia) 160
Sydney Morning Herald 31
Sylva, Margeurite 47, 67–68, 82
Symphony Hall (Boston) 81

Tagliana, Emilia 34
Taming of the Shrew (Goetz) 22
Tarquini, Tarquinia 79
Tarquini d'Or, Mathilde 54
Taylor, Gavin 145
Tchaikovsky, Peter 16, 18
Te Kanawa, Kiri 2
Teatro Bellini (Naples) 35
Teatro Lirico (Barcelona) 35–36
Teatro Real (Madrid) 36
Theater of Musical Drama 72
Théâtre de la Monnaie (Brussels) 22–24, 45
Théâtre-Lyrique 22–24
Thebom, Blanche 132
Theresienstadt 90
Thiecla 7
Thomas, Ambroise 13, 22
Thomson, Virgil 110
Thorborg, Kerstin 32

Time 106, 107, 118, 126
Times (London) 30, 56
Tommasini, Anthony 147
Toronto 39
Tosca (Puccini) 88
Toscanini, Arturo 68, 79, 80
Die Tote Stadt (Korngold) 88
Tourangeau, Huguette 130
Tourel, Jennie 108, 110, 114, 143
La Tragédie de Carmen 138–139
Trebelli, Zélia 28–29, 37
Troyanos, Tatiana 130

United States *see* American productions
Uria-Monzon, Béatrice 152–153, *153*, 199n12

Valentina (costumer) 111, *112*, 113
Valleria, Alwina 24, 26
Vallin, Ninon 47, 51, 52–53, *53*
Van Vechten, Carl 56, 67, 75–76
Vavrille, Annie 152
Venard, Céleste (La Mogador) 6
Verdi, Giuseppe 27, 36, 78, 95, 96, 105, 116, 117
Verga, Giovanni 59
Vergara, Victoria 154, 199n13
Verismo 27, 29, 56–65, 85, 86, 88, 95; Calvé and 57–62; Italy as birthplace 35; "slice of life" operas and 88; *see also* acting styles; direction
Verrett, Shirley 128–130
Veselovskaya, Maria 72
Viardot, Pauline 2, 18
Victoria, Queen of England 56–57
videos *see* films and videos
Vienna 87–88, 140, 145
Vienna Court Opera 21–22, 73–74, 190n2, 190n3
Viennese productions: American Carmens in 126–128; in 19th century 21–22, 29, 30

Village Voice 138
Villazón, Rolando 155
Visconti, Luchino 122
Visconti, Raymonde 51
Vix, Genevieve 47
Vlaamse Opera (Antwerp) 154
vocal range: contralto 96; of dugazon 18, 95, 190n50; soprano vs. mezzo-soprano 8, 18–19, 95–99
vocal styles *see* singing
Volpe, Joseph 145
von Karajan, Herbert 124, 130, 142
von Otter, Anne Sofie 32, *159*, 159–160

Wagner, Richard 11, 58, 90, 95, 116
Wagner, Wieland 128
Wakenvitch, George, *121*
Webster, Margaret 117
Weimar Republic 89
Welsh National Opera 150
Wertheimer, Gustav 30
Wettergren, Gertrud 32, 106–107, 110
Williams, Camilla 129
women's rights 88, 139, 163
Wright, Lesley 3, 11
Wyns, Charlotte 44

Yradier, Sebastián 6

Zagars, Andrejs 148
Zambello, Francesca 148–149, 161
Zeffirelli, Franco 122–123, 140, 145, 147, 148, 155, 158
Zenatello, Giovanni 68
Zinetti, Giuseppina 96, 97
Zuloaga, Ignacio 55
Zürich 142, 155
Zürich Opera 155

www.ingramcontent.com/pod-product-compliance
Lightning Source LLC
Chambersburg PA
CBHW032053300426
44116CB00007B/719